ROMANIAN
Cookbook

Traditional Romanian Recipes

ISBN (13): 978-0-9797618-6-7
ISBN (10): 0-9797618-6-7

Published by Reflection Publishing LLC
P.O.Box 2182, Citrus Heights, CA 95611-2182
Website: www.reflectionbooks.com
Email: info@reflectionbooks.com

INTRODUCTION

The paradox of cooking is that it is essentially the process of changing and appropriating ingredients, techniques and ideas, while at the same time representing the core of a nation's tastes, smells, and customs. The tradition of creating memorable dishes is a process of giving and taking throughout history. And as a nation changes and its people take shape, so too does that culture's relationship to food. Food becomes something that encompasses and reflects the essence of a culture and ties a country to its people.

The human relationship with food is the most primal, the most visceral and the most varied of any that we experience. Our pallet is a highly sensitive structure that allows us to experience smell and taste simultaneously. And with these senses we can also trigger memory. The memory of a time and place can be revisited as we bite into a fresh, warm piece of cheese pie. We think of the smells and tastes of our childhood and say, "Grandma made it best."

This nostalgic experience is part of our personal history, while the process of cooking maps the cultural history of a nation. Romanian cooking is therefore, at its core, the most eclectic, varied and complex cooking found it Eastern Europe because of its national history. Romanian cooking encompasses the taste of the Mediterranean because of the Ottoman occupation and the Slavic and Austro-Hungarian influences due to its geographical proximity to Russia and Hungary. With such culinary influences from South, East and West, the richness of the food does not come from the hearty ingredients, but from the history of occupation, integration and symbiosis with its surrounding regions.

Romanian cuisine is not simply the amalgamation or duplication of these nation's dishes, but has a flavor all its own. The richness and variety of tastes found in uniquely Romanian food satisfy not only the appetite but the soul as well. Romanian dishes are considered comfort foods because of their complex and savory character. The rich ingredients, local to the

Romanian heartland, come together to create the seductive flavors that warm the body and nourish the heart.

The warmth of the dishes reflects the warmth of the people and their willingness to share their bounty. A meal is not a meal unless you have friends and family to share it with you. The foundation of any Romanian meal begins with hearty portions accompanied by a sweet glass of Romanian wine and those you love all around you. The pleasure of a meal comes alive when you steal, change and appropriate ingredients, techniques and ideas while exploring the many tastes smells and customs of Romanian cuisine. We hope that this cookbook will be a treasure for you and your family as you explore all that the nation has to offer and share the recipes with your loved ones.

Iulia Bodeanu, Davis, CA

Thank you to our SPONSORS!

We thank our sponsors who made this book possible:

Reflection Publishing LLC   Address: P.O. Box 2182, Citrus Heights, CA 95611-2182, Tel: (916) 792-6272, Website: www.reflectionbooks.com; E-mail: info@reflectionbooks.com

Bonita Home Care   Contact: Liana Ciontos, Administrator, Address: 7189 Liverpool Lane, Roseville, CA 95747, Tel: (916) 523-1510; E-mail: bonitahomecarelc@yahoo.com

Diamond Oaks Residential Care   Contact: Abigaila Budac, Administrator, 501 Butler Ct, Roseville, CA 95678, Phone: 916-782-8177, Fax: 916-782-8177, E-mail: ca_budac@yahoo.com

G & E Painting   Contact: Ghedeon Onica, Tel: (916) 956-7067; E-mail: g.e_painting@yahoo.com

Centurion Mortgage: **Dina Hoffman**, Mortgage Consulatant; Address: 1223 High Street, Auburn, CA 95603; Tel: (877) 386-3498, Office: (530) 886-4089, Cell: (916) 847-986, email: dina_hoffman@yahoo.com, Website: www.CenturionHomeLoans.org: Offer: Pre Foreclosure and Short Sales, Loan Modifications, Refinances up to 125% (new program), First Time Buyer Programs, Down Payment Assistance, Commercial & Small Business Loans, Investment Properties with only 10% down payment.

We also thank to individual donations:

Bianca Tudosa, Austin TX
Rodica Popovici, DDS, El Sobrante, CA
Delia and Emanuel Petrisor, Orangevale CA
Gheorghe and Elisabeta Bledea, Folsom CA

Thank you to our CONTRIBUTORS!

Special thanks to all who sent their own recipes:

Dorel Andriuca, Roseville, CA
Alexandrina Antonescu-Watson, Santa Rosa, CA
Mihaela Ardelean, Sacramento, CA
Doina Brownell, West Sacramento, CA
Abigaila Budac, Roseville, CA
Liana Ciontoş, Roseville, CA
Nicolae Dic, Fair Oaks, CA
Eugen Georgescu, Orangevale, CA
Katica Goţ, Oliverhurst, CA
Gabriela Margareta Helvey, Sacramento, CA
Ioana Ene, Sacramento, CA
Olga Iancu, Sacramento, CA
Bianca Iosif, Sacramento, CA
Mihaela Iosif, Sacramento, CA
Ligia Lazar, Woodland, CA
Pia Lazar, Woodland, CA
Gabriela Lăzureanu, Roseville, CA
Monica Mois, Sacramento, CA
George Muntean Sr., Sacramento, CA
Anitta Pat Zalla, Sacramento, CA
Delia Petrisor, Orangevale, CA
Emilia Popescu, Citrus Height, CA
Veronica Solomon, Antelope, CA
Lucia Tudosa, Austin, TX
Nicoleta Tuns, Sacramento CA
Sonia Radu, Sacramento, CA
Ruxandra Vidu, Sacramento, CA
Nicolae Vidu, Citrus Heights, CA
Ramona Vilceanu, Marysville, CA

Thank you to those who contributed editing:
       Ruxandra Vidu, Sacramento, CA
       Margareta Amy Lelea, Davis, CA

APPETIZERS

TOMATOES AND PEPPERS STUFFED WITH CHEESE
(roşii şi ardei graşi umpluţi cu brânză)
Sent by Ruxandra Vidu, Sacramento, CA

1 lb cottage cheese, 1-2 tbsp feta cheese, 4 oz butter, 1 tbsp minced dill, a few big tomatoes and peppers

Wash, dry and core the peppers. Remove all seeds. Choose firm and round tomatoes, cut a slice on top and remove the inside with all the seeds. Dry with paper towel. Drain the cottage cheese well and mix with feta cheese and butter. Fill tomatoes and peppers with the cheese mixture, and then spread a little dill on top. Refrigerate for at least ½ hr before serving.

ROMANIAN EGGPLANT SPREAD
(salată de vinete)
Sent by Monica Mois, Sacramento, CA

2-3 eggplants, ½ small grated onion, ¼ cup mayonnaise (or as much as you want), salt and pepper

Wash eggplant, place in baking pan and bake at 375 ºF for about one hour, or until soft when pierced with a fork and the eggplant has sort of collapsed into itself. You can also grill the eggplant by putting them directly on the grate – whole- on your barbeque. Grill until skin is blackened and charred and eggplant is very soft and starting to deflate. If you use the grill method – leave out the liquid smoke.

Peel eggplant when cool enough for you to stand it and chop in small pieces. Mash it up a bit with a fork. Mix well with onion, mayonnaise, salt and pepper (to taste). Serve on bread. You may also serve it with sliced tomatoes or bell peppers.

TOMATOES STUFFED WITH VEGETABLES
(roşii umplute cu zarzavat)

3 boiled potatoes, 2 carrots, 1 parsnip, 1 celery root, 2-3 tbsp peas (optional), 1 chopped onion, mayo, tomatoes, salt, and lettuce

Boil all the vegetables except the onion, tomatoes and lettuce. Let cool then cube everything and mix with the chopped onion and salt. Mix the vegetables with mayo and then stuff the tomatoes from which the insides have been removed, with the mixture. Refrigerate. When serving, place them on a bed of chopped lettuce.

TOMATOES STUFFED WITH EGGPLANT
(roşii umplute cu vinete)

1 big eggplant, 2 onions, 3 tbsp oil, tomatoes, salt, pepper, parsley

Bake the eggplant, let it drain well, and chop with a wooden or glass chopper. Set in a bowl and mix with the oil poured little by little. Add finely chopped onion, salt and pepper. Choose small and firm tomatoes and remove the inside with all the seeds. Fill with the eggplant mixture, then place all stuffed tomatoes on a platter and decorate them with a sprig of parsley for each tomato. You can also use stuffing peppers instead of tomatoes.

STUFFED MUSHROOMS
(ciuperci umplute)

1 lb chicken livers, 1 onion, small, chopped, 1 small bunch parsley, chopped, 1 egg, salt and pepper to taste, 8 mushrooms, large, 1 stick of butter.

Boil livers in dry wine. Grind liver; add onion, parsley, egg, salt and pepper. Mix well. Clean and stem mushrooms. Stuff mushrooms with the liver mixture. Place in baking dish with pat of butter on each. Bake at 300 ºF for 30 min to 1 hr depending on size of mushrooms. Serve hot.

MUSHROOMS WITH WHITE SAUCE
(ciuperci cu sos alb)

2 cans of white, chopped mushrooms, homemade mayonnaise (half a cup), sour cream to the mayonnaise (half a cup), salt, pepper, a tea tbsp chopped fresh or pickled tarragon (if fresh, add vinegar to taste)

Homemade mayonnaise: one yolk of an egg, half a teaspoon of regular mustard. Mix together with an electric mixer. Start pouring in vegetable oil while mixing in small quantities. 250 ml oil should be used per egg. If the mayonnaise seems too thick add a few drops of water till it receives oil again and has a thinner consistency.

Add the sour cream to the mixture, together with the mushrooms and mix. Chop the tarragon and add to mixture. Add salt and pepper to taste. Serve with bread and fresh veggies such as bell peppers, tomatoes, and cucumbers. If you like, you can add small pieces of smoked mozzarella and ham.

BUTTER WITH BLUE CHEESE
(unt cu brânză Rockford)

7 oz butter, 2 oz blue cheese

Sieve the cheese, place it in a bowl, add the butter and mix with a wooden tablespoon until creamy. Refrigerate until serving.

BUTTER WITH CRAYFISH
(unt cu raci)

7 oz butter, 25 crayfish, 1 tsp tomato paste, salt

Boil the crayfish in salt water. When they are boiled and cooled, get the meaty parts, grind or chop them finely and then mix with butter, salt and a teaspoon tomato paste. Mix until creamy. Refrigerate until serving.

BUTTER WITH MUSTARD
(unt cu muştar)

7 oz butter, 1 oz mustard, salt

Beat the butter with a wooden tablespoon until creamy. Add mustard and salt. Mix well. Refrigerate until serving.

BUTTER WITH SARDINES
(unt cu sardele)

7 oz butter, 1 tin sardines, salt

Squeeze excess oil from sardines. Sieve or finely chop. Mix them with butter and a little salt, if needed.

HERRING BUTTER
(unt cu heringi)

7 oz butter, 1 herring

Split the herring lengthwise on the belly line. Remove the roe and then keep the herring in water for 5-6 hours. Then drain, remove the skin, backbone and all bones. Finely chop the herring fillet and mix with butter.

COLORED BUTTER SPREAD
(pastă de unt)

Butter, black: 7 oz butter, 7 oz olives

Pit the olives and then keep them in warm water for 5-6 hours. Drain well, sieve and then mix with butter.

Butter, green: 7 oz butter, 1 tbsp spinach puree, salt

Scald the spinach leaves, drain, sieve, then mix with butter. Add salt to taste.

Butter, pink: 7 oz butter, 1 tsp roasted beet puree, salt

Sieve the roasted beet. Mix a teaspoon of beet puree with the butter. Add salt to taste.

Butter, yellow: 7 oz butter, 3 hard-boiled yolks, salt

Sieve the yolks and mix with the butter. Add salt to taste.

DEVILED EGGS
(ouă umplute)
Sent by Katica Goţ, Oliverhurst, CA

12 eggs, hard-boiled = 24 deviled eggs, 3 tbsp liver pâté pork or chicken, 1 tbsp butter, 1 tbsp sour cream, 1 tbsp mayonnaise, salt, black pepper, chopped parsley

Boil and remove shells from eggs. Slice in half and remove yolks into a bowl. Smooth the yolks with a fork, add liver pâté, butter, mayo, salt, black pepper and parsley. Smooth well until you have a fine filling. Fill eggs and serve with sour cream stirred with mayo on the top.

STUFFED EGGS WITH SOUR CREAM SAUCE
(ouă umplute cu sos de smântână)

6 eggs, 1 raw yolk, 1 crustless slice of white bread soaked in milk, 1 tsp butter, 1 finely chopped and sautéed in butter onion, finely minced parsley and dill, salt, pepper, 1 tbsp breadcrumbs, lettuce. For sauce: 1 cup sour cream, 1 tsp flour.

Hard boil the eggs, let cool, shell and then cut in two lengthwise. Remove the yolks. Place the yolks in a bowl and mix with the butter, raw yolk, bread, parsley and dill. At the end, add the onion, salt and pepper. Fill the egg halves with this mixture so as to resemble one whole egg. Toss with breadcrumbs and fry in butter. Once they are ready, place in a pan and pour the sour cream well mixed with the flour on top. Let boil at slow heat. Serve warm, on a plate decorated with lettuce.

STUFFED EGGS
(ouă umplute)

6 eggs, 2 oz butter, 1 tsp finely minced parsley, salt, pepper, lettuce

Hard boil the eggs, shell and cut them in two lengthwise after they are cool. Carefully remove the yolks and place them in a bowl. Mix them with the butter. Add parsley, salt and pepper and then use the paste to fill the egg whites. Spread some chopped parsley on top. Arrange the stuffed eggs on a bed of lettuce on a plate.

STUFFED EGGS WITH CHEESE
(ouă umplute cu brânză)

6 eggs, 1 raw yolk, 2 tbsp butter, 2 tbsp grated sheep cheese, 1 tsp minced dill, salt, dill

Hard boil the eggs and let cool. Shell and cut them in two lengthwise. Remove the yolks and place in a bowl. Mix with butter, adding a raw yolk, the cheese and salt. Fill the whites with this paste. Spread some chopped dill on top. Arrange the stuffed eggs on a platter and decorate with dill sprigs around the eggs.

STUFFED EGGS WITH FISH PASTE
(ouă umplute cu pastă de pește)

6 eggs, 1 tsp mustard, 1 tbsp oil, fish paste to taste, 6 olives and lettuce

Hard boil the eggs and let cool. Shell and cut them in two lengthwise. Remove the yolks and place in a bowl. Mix with the oil poured drop by drop. Add the fish paste and mix. Then add the mustard. Fill the whites and arrange on a plate. On each egg half place half an olive cut to make a flower. Decorate the plate with some lettuce leaves.

STUFFED EGGS WITH MUSTARD
(ouă umplute cu muştar)

6 eggs, 2 tbsp oil, 1 tbsp mustard, 1 tbsp minced dill, 1 tbsp sugar, salt, 6 olives

Hard boil the eggs, shell and let cool. Cut in two lengthwise. Remove the yolks and mix them with the oil poured drop by drop. Add the salt, sugar, mustard and the chopped dill. Fill each white half with this paste and garnish each with half an olive.

STUFFED EGGS WITH MAYO
(ouă umplute cu maioneză)

6 eggs, 1 tbsp butter, 1 tbsp sour cream, salt, pepper, mayo, pickled peppers (olives), lettuce

Hard boil the eggs, shell and let cool. Cut in half crosswise, remove the yolks and place them in a bowl. Mix the yolks with the butter and sour cream. Add salt and pepper. Fill each egg half and arrange filled side down on a plate on which you previously put mayo. On top of each egg, place a piece of pickled pepper or olive, cut to make a flower. Decorate around the eggs with chopped lettuce.

STUFFED EGGS WITH SOUR CREAM SAUCE
(ouă umplute cu sos de smântână)

12 slices french baguette, a little lard, 6 eggs, 2 tbsp sour cream, 1 tbsp butter, 1 small onion, salt, pepper. For sauce: 1 tbsp flour, 1 tbsp butter, 1 cup chicken stock, 2 egg yolks, 1 tbsp minced dill, 2 tbsp milk, salt

Hard boil the eggs, let cool, shell and cut in two lengthwise. Remove the yolks, put them in a bowl, crush them and mix with the onion which was previously sautéed in a tbsp of butter. Let cool, add the sour cream, salt and pepper. Fill the egg halves with this paste. Fry each baguette slice in lard, and then remove the soft bread, leaving the crusts intact. Replace the bread taken out with the stuffed egg half. Place on a platter and pour the hot sauce on top. Sauce: Fry the flour with the butter for a short time, add the stock and let boil for 5 minutes. Remove from heat and add the yolks, mixing with a spoon, then add the milk, dill and salt.

FISH ROE SALAD
(salată de icre)

200gr (~7oz) fish roe, 1 slice of bread, 150ml oil (~5 floz), salt, lemon juice.

200gr of fish roe are mixed with one slice of bread in a mixer bowl. Add the oil continuously in small amounts, mixing everything with the mixer as is usually done for mayonnaise. Be careful not to pour too much oil at once because you can spoil everything. As you get towards the finish, the roe should become whiter and triple their volume. Afterwards it needs seasoning with salt and lemon juice, according to your own taste. The roe taste better if some onion is added (cut in small pieces). It is served spread on slices of bread (as one usually does with the butter) and goes well with olives as an appetizer.

TARAMA OF SALT HERRING ROE
(salată de icre din scrumbii sărate)
Sent by Alexandrina Antonescu-Watson, Santa Rosa, CA

Roe from one herring, 1 tsp grated onion, juice from 1/2 lemon, one crustless slice of moistened bread, 1/2 cup oil, 2 tbsp club soda

Crush the roe with a fork in a small bowl. Remove the membranes and mix with the moistened and then squeezed bread. Mix in the same direction, adding the oil drop by drop. After all the oil is used up, add the grated onions, lemon juice, mix, adding the club soda last. Garnish with pitted olives cut to resemble flowers.

BOLOGNA BASKETS FILLED WITH VEGETABLES
(cupe de parizer umplute cu legume)

7 oz bologna (6 slices), 1/2 tbsp lard, 1 tbsp butter, ½ lb peas, 1 hard-boiled egg, salt

Leave the casings on the bologna slices and fry them in lard just on one side. The edges will turn up forming a basket. Each such basket is filled with one tbsp of boiled and buttered peas. Place one slice of egg on top. The baskets can also be filled with sliced boiled carrots or very thin boiled potato slices.

BOLOGNA PASTE
(pastă de parizer)

½ lb bologna, 2 hard-boiled eggs, mustard to taste, salt, pepper, lettuce, radishes

Grind the bologna together with the eggs. Mix the resulting paste with mustard, add salt and pepper. Place the paste on a plate, garnish with chopped lettuce and radishes carved as flowers. You can use this to fill sandwiches too.

BOLOGNA CORNUCOPIAS
(cornete de parizer)

6 bologna slices (not very thin), 12 olives, 2 boiled potatoes, 2-3 tbsp mayo, salt, pepper, lettuce

Roll the bologna slices to form cornucopias. Anchor each with a toothpick and attach an olive to each end of the toothpick. Fill each cornucopia with small cubes of potato which have been mixed with the mayo, salt and pepper. Cut the lettuce noodle fashion and place on a round platter. Place the cornucopias on the platter with the tips in the center.

BREAD STICKS FILLED WITH CHEESE
(cornuri cu brânză)

½ lb butter or margarine, ½ lb feta cheese, 1/2 tsp caraway, 12 thick bread sticks

Mix the butter well with the cheese, add caraway. Cut off the sticks' heels and take the soft bread inside out. Fill with the cheese mixture and place on a buttered baking sheet. On top of each stick place a little piece of butter. Bake for 10-15 minutes. Serve hot.

BREAD STICKS FILLED WITH HOT DOGS
(cornuri cu crenvurşti)

4 oz butter, 6 hot dogs, 6 thick breadsticks

Cut each breadstick and each hot dog lengthwise. Hollow out the breadstick halves, butter them and then place one hot dog half inside with the cut part on the inside. Place the filled breadsticks on a buttered baking sheet and bake for 10-15 minutes. Serve hot.

PEPPERS IN OIL
(ardei cu untdelemn)

6 medium-sized bell peppers, green or red, ½ cup olive oil, ½ cup white wine vinegar, ½ cup cold water, 2 tsp imported paprika, 1 tbsp salt, Freshly ground black pepper, 12 ripe black olives, preferably Mediterranean type, feta cheese, or substitute feta cheese, cut into 1-inch cubes, 8 to 12 scallions, trimmed and washed.

Roast the peppers in the following fashion: Impale them, one at a time, on the tines of a long-handled fork and turn them over a gas flame until the skin blisters and darkens. Or place the peppers on a baking sheet and broil them 3 inches from the heat for about 15 minutes, turning them so that they color on all sides. As the peppers are roasted, wrap them in a damp towel and let them rest for 5 minutes. Rub them with the towel until the burned skins slip off, but leave the stems intact. In a deep bowl combine the olive oil, vinegar, water, paprika, salt and a few grindings of pepper. Beat vigorously with a whisk or a fork until the ingredients are combined, then taste for seasoning. Add the peppers and turn them about with a tablespoon until they are coated on all sides. Marinate at room temperature for 3 or 4 hours, turning the peppers over occasionally. Then cover the bowl tightly with foil or plastic wrap and refrigerate for at least 24 hours before serving. Peppers in oil are traditionally served on a platter, moistened with some of their marinade and garnished with black olives, cheese and scallions. Serve as a salad course or as an accompaniment to *mititei*.

FILLED BUNS
(chifle umplute)

6 buns, 4 oz butter, 5 oz cheese, 1 egg, ½ cup sour cream, 1 ½ cup milk, salt, 1 tsp minced dill

Cut the buns in half and soak in milk so that even the crust is moistened. Mix the cheese with the egg, salt and dill. On each bun half, put a tbsp of the cheese mixture and cover with the other half. Divide the butter in 12 parts. Set one piece of butter on the baking sheet, the filled bun on top and another piece of butter to cover the bun. Then pour 1 teaspoon of sour cream on top of each bun. Bake until golden brown. Serve hot.

WHITE GOAT - CHEESE - AND - HERB SPREAD
(brânză de Brăila frecată)

½ pound goat cheese, or substitute feta cheese, ½ pound unsalted butter, softened, 2 tbsp finely cut fresh chives, 2 tbsp finely cut fresh fennel leaves or ½ tsp powdered fennel, 2 tbsp finely chopped fresh parsley plus 8 fresh parsley sprigs, 1 tsp imported paprika, 1 tsp caraway seeds, 2 medium-sized tomatoes, sliced, 16 ripe black olives, preferably Mediterranean type, 16 whole red radishes, trimmed, washed and dried, 8 scallions, trimmed and cut into 3-inch lengths.

Rub the cheese through a medium-meshed sieve into a bowl with the back of a spoon, or force the cheese through a food mill set over a bowl. Add the butter and beat vigorously with a wooden spoon, mashing the cheese and butter together against the sides of the bowl until the mixture is light and fluffy. Beat in the chives, fennel, chopped parsley, paprika and caraway seeds, and taste for seasoning. Mound the cheese-and-herb mixture in the center of a platter and arrange the tomatoes, olives, parsley sprigs, radishes and scallions attractively around it. Serve at room temperature with rye or pumpernickel bread as a first course or as an accompaniment to cocktails.

FRIED CORNMEAL MUSH
(mămăligă prăjită)

cold *mămăligă* (leftover cooked *mămăligă* is perfect for this), 1 egg, cheese, sour cream (or yogurt).

Cool mămăligă and cut it into ¼-inch-thick slices. Dip each slice in beaten egg. Sprinkle generously on each side with grated yellow cheese. Using a nonstick skillet, fry in hot butter on both sides until golden. Serve with sour cream or yogurt.

VEGETABLE SPREAD
(zacuscă)
Sent by Abigaila Budac, Roseville, CA

12 -14 jars (change servings and units), 8 lbs fresh eggplants, 6 lbs red peppers, 2 lbs onions, 2 lbs carrots, 2 tsp salt (to taste), 1/2 tsp black pepper, 2 cups tomato paste, 2 cups olive oil, 4 Daphne (laurel) leaves

Over an open flame (gas stove or grill) completely blacken the skins of the eggplants and peppers. Peel skins off immediately. The easiest way to get the last bits off is to do it under a slow running faucet. Puree each of the three vegetables separately in a food processor. And place each in a separate bowl when you are finished. Peel and grate (small pieces) the carrots and place in a separate bowl. Place oil and onion in a large pot. Sauté the onions for about 4 minutes to medium-low heat. Add grated carrots and sauté stirring continuously for another 4 minutes. Add eggplant, peppers, tomato paste, Daphne leaves, salt and pepper. Cook until a thin layer of oil remains on top and when a spoonful of zacuscă is removed, only the oil should run off the spoon, not the zacuscă. Taste and adjust salt and pepper to meet your tastes. Tablespoon mixtures into sterilized jars as you choose. It is easiest if they are all the same size. Wipe rims clean and place clean lids and rings on jars. Place into a single layer in large pot (water bath canner if you have one). Fill pot with water up to the necks of the jars. Bring to a boil and boil for 20 minutes. Remove from heat and allow them to cool in water bath. When cool, remove them from water and then you are ready to go. If oil separates just mix it back in when ready to serve.

A traditional vegetable spread found in Romania (probably in other neighboring countries as well). It is delicious on crust bread or even as a topping on rice for a quickie vegetarian meal. It is also excellent as a sandwich spread. This recipe is for a large batch intended for canning. You can cut it back if you want a smaller batch for immediate consumption.

COTTAGE CHEESE WITH DILL
(urdă cu mărar)

½ lb cottage cheese, 2 oz butter, 1 tbsp minced dill, salt

Mix the cheese with the butter and salt until it becomes a paste. Add the minced dill and mix well. Use this to fill sandwiches. You can also serve with green onions.

SALADS

CELERIAC SALAD
(salată de țelină)

**2-3 celeriacs, juice of one lemon, 1-2 carrots, 1 big apple, 100 g
mayonnaise, salt, black pepper**

Cut each celeriac in half and peel away the skin using a large knife. The
skin is very fibrous so it is important to cut about 3 mm deep under the
skin. Peel away the skin from carrot(s) too. Coarsely grate the celeriac,
apple and carrots, and put in a bowl. Season them with salt and paper
and toss in the lemon juice. Cover with a plastic wrap and set aside for 20-
30 minutes. Squeeze out the excess liquid and mix in the mayonnaise.
Season everything with salt and black pepper, if necessary. Serve the
salad in small bowls, decorated with green onion.

Variations: Replace mayonnaise with French or Italian dressing.

BOEUF SALAD OR ROMANIAN POTATO SALAD
(salată de boeuf)
Sent by Ruxandra Vidu, Citrus Heights, CA

**3 medium carrots, 5 red potatoes, 1 piece of chicken breast, 2 tbsp
mustard, 2-3 pickled cucumbers, 1-2 eggs for dressing, salt and
pepper to taste, mayonnaise**

Wash the potatoes and boil them in their skin. Take out the skin and cut
the potatoes in small cubes. Boil the carrots and then take them out to cool.
Then boil the meat in the same bowl. Cut the carrots and the meat in small
cubes. Cut the pickles in small cubes and then drain them well by pressing
out the liquid using your hands. You can keep some slices of each item for
decorating. Place all in a bowl and add salt, pepper, mustard and

mayonnaise. The mayonnaise should be real mayonnaise. You get the best results by mixing mayonnaise with mustard and seasonings first, before you mix with vegetables and meet. Keep some mayonnaise for "dressing" the salad. Mix well the salad, taste it for seasoning, add more condiments if necessary. Arrange the salad on a serving platter. Smooth with a knife and then cover with the rest of the mayo mixture. Garnish with a few olives, hard-boiled egg white, or egg slices, pickled red peppers, parsley, etc. Try to shape flowers, or other designs.

POACHED BRAINS
(creier fiert)

1 beef or 2 veal brains, 1/2 lemon, 1 tbsp melted butter, salt, pepper, green lettuce

Keep the brains in cold water for an hour. Remove the membranes and set to boil with warm water and salt for 15-20 minutes. Drain the water and slice the brains. Arrange on a platter and pour lemon juice mixed with melted butter over it. Add some pepper and decorate with green lettuce. You may also serve cold. In this case, replace the butter with olive oil.

BRAINS SALAD
(salată de creier)

1 beef or veal brain, juice from ½ lemon, 4 oz oil, salt, pepper, a few olives, parsley

Keep the brain in cold water for an hour. Remove the membrane and set to boil in warm salt water. Boil for 15-20 minutes. Let cool and then mix with oil, adding it a little at a time. Use a wooden spoon. Add lemon juice, salt, pepper, and then garnish with pitted olives and some parsley sprigs.

CABBAGE SALAD
(salată de varză albă)

1 medium cabbage, 2 tbsp oil, 2-3 tbsp vinegar, salt

Cut Julienne the washed cabbage. Rub it with salt until soft. Squeeze excess liquid. Mix with oil, vinegar and salt (if needed). Serve with roasts. Optional: you can sprinkle with fresh garlic sauce.

CAULIFLOWER SALAD
(salată de conopidă)

1 head (medium) cauliflower, 2 tbsp oil, 2 tbsp vinegar, salt

Wash the cauliflower, divide in flowerets and boil in salt water. Drain and place in salad bowl. Pour a dressing made of oil, vinegar and salt on top.

CELERY AND APPLE SALAD
(salată de țelină cu mere)

2-3 celery roots, 2-3 apples, 2 tbsp oil, vinegar to taste, salt

Julienne the peeled and washed celery and mix with the peeled and thinly sliced apples. Add oil, vinegar and salt.

DRIED BEANS SALAD
(salată de fasole boabe)

½ lb dried beans, 2 tbsp oil, 2-3 tbsp vinegar, 1 big onion, salt, pepper

Boil and cool the beans. Drain and then mix with chopped onion. Add oil, salt, vinegar and some pepper.

DRIED BEANS SPREAD
(iahnie de fasole)
Sent by Nicoleta Tuns, Sacramento CA

500 g dried beans, 2 onions, 1 carrot, 1 green pepper, 1 small turnip, 1 tbsp Vegeta (soup seasoning mix), 1-2 tbsp paprika, 60 ml olive oil, salt to taste

Soak in water the beans at least 12 hours before cooking. Then wash them thoroughly, remove the skin and boil them for at least 1 hour. You can change the water 2-3 times. When the beans are boiled, drain the water. Separately, chop the carrot, the green pepper, the turnip and one onion. Add water enough to cover them and then boil for about 15-20 minutes. When the vegetable are boiled, drain the water but keep a cut of that soup aside. Mash the beans with a mixer or blender and add a cup of soup and mix well. Heat up 30 ml olive oil and add the beans mixture, seasonings

(Vegeta, salt and pepper) and leave it on the stove at low heat for 10-15 minutes. Separately, julienne the onion and fry it in 30 ml olive oil in which 1 tbsp of paprika was added. When the onion becomes yellow, pour the mixture over the beans and serve.

EGGPLANT AND BELL PEPPER SALAD
(salată de vinete cu gogoşari)

2 big eggplants, 4 onions, 3 tbsp oil, 1 lb tomatoes, 4 peppers, 4 bell peppers

Prepare as for fried eggplant salad.

FRIED EGGPLANT SALAD
(salată de vinete prăjite)
Sent by Alexandrina Antonescu-Watson, Santa Rosa, CA

2 big eggplants, 5-6 onions, 5 tbsp oil, 1 ½ lb tomatoes, 5 roasted peppers (peeled and sliced), cheese, salt to taste

Roast the eggplants, peel while still hot and then leave on a slanted cutting board to drain. During this time, boil the tomatoes and strain, roast the peppers, peel them and cut into very thin strips. Finely chop the onions and then fry in hot oil until soft. Add the chopped eggplants, pepper strips, tomato paste and salt. Continue frying, stirring continuously, until most of the liquid is absorbed. Arrange on a plate, sprinkle some cheese and serve cold.

ONLY GREEN VEGETABLES
(vegetale verzi)
Sent by Dorel Andriuca, Roseville, CA

1/4 pound French string beans, ends removed, salt, 1/4 pound sugar snap peas, ends and strings removed, 1/4 pound asparagus, ends removed, 1/4 pound broccoli, ends removed, 3 shallots, 2 tbsp unsalted butter, 1 tbsp good olive oil, 1/2 tsp freshly ground black pepper

Blanch the string beans in a large pot of boiling salted water for 1 minute only. Lift the beans from the water with a slotted tablespoon or sieve and immerse them in a bowl of ice water. Add the snap peas to the same boiling water and cook for 1 minute, until al dente, adding them to the ice water and the beans. Cut the asparagus into 2-inch lengths diagonally and cook in the boiling water for 2 minutes, and add to the ice water. Cut the broccoli in floret, boil for 1 minute, and add to the ice water. When all the vegetables in the water are cold, drain them well.

When ready to serve, heat the butter and oil in a very large sauté pan or large pot. Sauté the shallots over medium heat for 5 minutes, tossing occasionally, until lightly browned. Add the drained vegetables to the shallots with 1/2 teaspoon salt and the pepper and toss

FRIED PEPPERS SALAD
(salată de ardei prajiţi)

12 peppers, 5 onions, 1 lb tomatoes, 3 tbsp oil, salt to taste

Wash the peppers, take the cores out and cut into very narrow strips. Chop the onions and fry in hot oil until soft. Add the peppers and tomato paste made from 1 lb tomatoes. Adjust the salt and let fry at slow heat until most of the liquid is absorbed. Serve cold.

GREEN BEANS SALAD
(salată de fasole verde)
Sent by Ruxandra Vidu, Citrus Heights, CA

1 ½ lb green beans, 2 tbsp oil, 2 tbsp vinegar, salt, 2 minced garlic cloves (to taste), parsley

Clean, wash and boil the beans. Drain, place in salad bowl and mix with oil, vinegar, salt and garlic to which 2-3 from the beans boiling liquid has been added. Garnish with a few sprigs of parsley.

HEALTH SALAD
(salată sănătatea)

2 cucumbers, 2 big apples, 2 medium carrots, 2 tomatoes, one heart of a big lettuce, juice from 1/2 lemon, 2 tbsp oil, salt

Peel and thinly slice the cucumbers and apples. Wash, clean and grate the carrots. Wash and tear the lettuce into small pieces. Mix all these with salt, lemon juice and oil. Place in the salad bowl and decorate with tomato slices. Cook just until the vegetables are heated through. Serve hot.

LEEK SALAD
(salată de praz)

3-4 leeks, salt, 1 tbsp oil, 1 tbsp vinegar

Wash the leeks and cut into thin rounds. Salt and add oil and vinegar.

POTATO SALAD I
(salată de cartofi) I

1 lb potatoes, 2 onions, 1 pickle, 1 hard-boiled egg, 2-3 tbsp oil, vinegar to taste, salt

Wash, boil, peel and let cool the potatoes. Then slice very thinly and mix with salt, thinly sliced onions, pickle rounds, oil and vinegar. Place in salad bowl and garnish with rounds of hard-boiled egg. You can also add some tomato slices.

POTATO SALAD II
(salată de cartofi) II

14 oz potatoes, 2 onions, 1 herring, 2 oz olives, 2 tbsp oil, 1 tbsp vinegar, salt (if needed)

Wash, boil, peel and let cool the potatoes. Then slice and mix with the boned, desalted and thinly sliced herring, with the olives, chopped onions, oil and vinegar.

BASKETS FILLED WITH BEEF SALAD
(coşuleţe umplute cu salată de boeuf)

1 lb flour, 1/2 lb butter or lard, 1 egg, salt, beef salad

Mix the egg with the butter or lard and the salt. Beat well. Add the flour and make dough. From this dough, roll out small circles, about 1/2 inch thick. Place each circle in small tart molds. Take care to cover the bottom and sides of the mold well. Prick the dough with a fork and bake. When ready, carefully take the tarts out of the molds. Leave them to cool completely. You can make these up to two days in advance. Then fill them with beef salad. Cover with mayo and garnish with sliced black olives, roasted or pickled red peppers and slices of hard-boiled egg whites. Take some parsley and leaving only two or three leaves on the sprigs, arrange the sprigs so as to resemble handles for the basket. Arrange the baskets next to each other on a long platter.

RADISH SALAD
(salată de ridichi de lună)

3-4 bunches of radishes, 1 hardboiled egg, 2-3 tbsp sour cream, salt

Wash and thinly slice the radishes. Sieve the yolk and mix with sour cream; pour onto the radishes. Add thinly sliced egg white, salt and mix well.

RED CABBAGE SALAD
(salată de varză roşie)

1 medium red cabbage, 2 tbsp oil, 2-3 tbsp vinegar, 1/2 tsp sugar, salt to taste

Wash Julienne the cabbage. Mix with salt and rub with your hands until soft. Add oil, vinegar and sugar. Mix well. Another way: scald the chopped cabbage with boiling water and then let sit for 10-15 minutes. Drain and mix the cabbage with the oil, vinegar salt and sugar. Serve with roasts.

SPRING SALAD
(salată primăvară)

5-6 small Boston lettuce, 2 bunches radishes, 1 bunch carrots, 4 big potatoes, 3 hardboiled eggs, 2 bunches green onions, 1 cup sour cream, 1/2 tsp confectioner's sugar, 1 tbsp lemon juice or vinegar, salt

Wash the lettuce, cut it in pieces, arrange in a salad bowl, and add carrots, radishes and the boiled potatoes, slicing everything very thinly. Then add the sliced onions and sliced hard-boiled eggs. Mix the sour cream with the lemon juice, sugar and salt. 5 minutes before serving, mix the vegetables with this dressing. You can also prepare this salad with mayo instead of sour cream. In this case, add just two sliced hard-boiled eggs and prepare a mayo from the other two eggs.

ROASTED PEPPERS SALAD I
(salată de ardei copţi) I

12 nice peppers, 2-3 tbsp oil, 1 tbsp vinegar, salt, a few tomatoes

Roast the peppers, turning on all sides. Place in a pan, cover with a clean cloth and then a lid and let sit for 20 minutes. Peel, arrange in salad bowl, add salt, oil and vinegar and garnish with tomato slices.

BROILED PEPPERS WITH VINAIGRETTE
(ardei copţi)

Any color bell peppers (as many as you wish)
Sauce: 1 cup water, 3 tbsp of sugar, ½ tsp of salt, White vinegar (by taste)

Broil the bell pepper until skin is dark and easy to peel. Let them cool and peel their skin off. Lay them in a pot and salt them to taste. Make the sauce by adding the sugar, salt and vinegar to the water. Serve cold.

ROASTED PEPPERS SALAD II
(salată de ardei copţi) II

Any color bell peppers (as many as you wish)

Sauce: 1 cup water, 3 tbsp of sugar, ½ tsp of salt, White vinegar (by taste)

After the peppers are roasted and have sat covered, peel and remove core and all seeds. Cut into 1 inch thick strips, place in salad bowl, and add oil, vinegar and salt. Decorate with seedless tomato slices.

SALAD OF ROASTED BELL PEPPERS
(salată de gogoşari copţi)

6 big bell peppers, 2-3 tbsp oil, 1 tbsp vinegar, salt

Prepare exactly as the roasted pepper salad I.

SALT HERRING AND ONION SALAD
(salată de scrumbii sărate cu ceapă)

2 medium herrings, 3 big onions, 4 oz olives, 2-3 tbsp oil, 2-3 tbsp vinegar

Split the herrings lengthwise on their belly, remove roe and keep in tepid water for 5-6 hours. Then wash in cold water, skin them starting from the head to the tail, remove all of the big bones that make up the backbone with, cut in pieces about two fingers thick and then arrange them side by side on a long platter, so that it resembles the whole fish. Peel the onions, keep them in cold water and then slice very thinly. Arrange the onion slices around the fish and place pitted olives on top. Pour the oil and vinegar dressing.

VINAIGRETTE I
(vinegretă) I

1 small beet, 3-4 big potatoes, 1 carrot, a handful of green peas or dry beans, 1 pickle, 2 hard-boiled eggs, 1 onion, 3 tbsp oil, vinegar to taste, salt

Boil the beet, potatoes, carrot and peas or beans separately. Let cool. Thinly slice the potatoes, carrot and beet and then mix with the peas or beans, chopped onion, and rounds of hard-boiled eggs and pickle. Add salt, oil and vinegar. Mix well and let stand at least an hour to mix the flavors. Arrange in salad bowl.

VINAIGRETTE II
(vinegretă) II

1 small beet, 3-4 big potatoes, 1 carrot, a handful of green peas or dry beans, 1 pickle, 1 onion, 1 herring, 4 oz olives, 1 tbsp oil, vinegar to taste, salt if needed

Prepare as vinaigrette I. Keep the herring in warm water for 5-6 hours, with the belly split open. Remove all bones, cut into finger thick strips and add to the salad. Arrange everything in the salad bowl and garnish with olives.

VITAMIN SALAD
(salată vitamina)

1 carrot, 1 medium celery root, 2 small cucumbers, 1 big apple, 3 nice tomatoes, 5-6 ripe plums (or 2-3 tbsp of pitted sour cherries), 1/2 cup sour cream, juice from 1/2 lemon, 1 tsp confectioner's sugar, salt

Clean the carrot and celery root, julienne, and place in a salad bowl. Add thinly sliced cucumbers, peeled and seeded apple, sliced tomatoes, and sliced plums (or pitted sour cherries). Mix everything with the sour cream to which you added lemon juice, sugar and salt, just before serving.

ZUCCHINI SALAD I
(salată de dovlecei) I
Sent by Ioana Ene, Sacramento, CA

3 zucchini, 1 onion (to taste), 3 tbsp oil, vinegar (to taste), salt, pepper, tomatoes, dill

Wash and clean the zucchini, cut into pieces and set to boil in salt water. After they soften, let drain and cool. Then squeeze dry and chop with a wooden chopper. Then place in a bowl and beat with oil just like the eggplant salad. Add finely chopped onion, pepper, salt and a little vinegar. Arrange on a plate and garnish with tomato slices and some chopped dill. It makes a great dip, too.

COLD GRILLED EGGPLANT
(vinete la grătar)
Sent by Eugen Georgescu, Orangevale, CA

2 eggplants, 1 red pepper, feta cheese (by taste), 3 tbsp olive oil, 1 tbsp wine vinegar, 1 tsp balsamic vinegar, 2 tbsp fresh basil, salt

Cut the eggplant into 1/2" slices and grill each side. Salt the eggplant and let drain for 30 minutes. Rinse well, then brush with olive oil. Grill the eggplant on a hot grill pan until brown and cooked through. Grill the whole pepper, and put it in a brown bag to sweat. When it is cool, remove the skin, core, and slice. Place eggplant and peppers in layers on your serving dish. Coat with the mixed oil and vinegars and put in the refrigerator for 2-3 hours. Top with feta cheese (by taste), a little more olive oil, and the basil.

ZUCCHINI SALAD II
(salată de dovlecei) II
Sent by Ioana Ene, Sacramento, CA

3-4 zucchini, 1 tbsp oil, 1 tbsp vinegar, 2 minced garlic cloves (to taste), salt, some parsley and dill

Clean and wash the zucchini, then cut in medium sized pieces. Boil in salt water. When ready, drain, place in the salad bowl, pour oil, vinegar, garlic and 2-3 tbsp from the boiling liquid. Garnish with some chopped parsley and dill.

BAKED LIVER PATE
(pastă de ficat copt)

1 lb beef or veal liver, 2 onions (to taste), 3 tbsp oil, pepper, salt, a little vinegar (to taste), 1 egg, lettuce

Wash and dry the liver, then put it in the oven to bake. When it's ready, let it cool, and then grate it on the vegetable grater. Arrange it nicely in a bowl. Add the very finely chopped onions then the oil, salt, pepper and vinegar. Mix everything well and then arrange it on a plate and use lettuce and hard-boiled egg slices as garnish around the liver.

BRAINS IN JELLY
(creier în gelatină)

1 beef brain, 1 carrot, 1 onion, 1 parsnip, 1 bay leaf, 2-3 juniper berries, 1 hard-boiled egg, 1 ½ qt water, juice from ½ lemon, a few sprigs of parsley, gelatin, salt

Boil the thinly sliced carrot, parsnip and onion together with the bay leaf, juniper berries and some salt. Boil at slow temperature, covered. After the vegetables are ready, add the brain and let it boil. When ready, take the brain out carefully with a slotted spoon. Sift the liquid through a sieve and measure it. For each cup of liquid, add 3 tbsp of gelatin. Mix until the gelatin is melted and let it boil for a minute or two. Take it off the heat, add lemon juice, salt and pour on a large plate to form a ¼ inch layer.

Keep the rest of the gelatin warm. Clean the cooled brain of membranes. Slice it in 1 inch slices and then place on top of the chilled gelatin layer, 2-3 inches apart. On top of each slice, place a circle of egg, with one sprig of parsley in each yolk. Pour the rest of gelatin on top. Leave it in a cool place to gel. Before serving, cut with a glass to make rounds that would include brain, egg and parsley. Place on a platter and garnish the space among rounds with chopped gelatin and lemon slices.

CELERY ROOT WITH MAYO
(țelină cu maioneză)
Sent by Nicolae Vidu, Citrus Heights, CA

3 big celery roots, 150 g bologna, salt, mayo, pepper, tomatoes (or pickled peppers)

Peel and wash the celery roots and then grate them. Salt them and let them sit in a sieve for a half an hour. Then mix them with the mayo, the peeled and julienned bologna, pepper, salt. Place on a plate and garnish with tomatoes or red pickled peppers.

CHEESE WITH CARAWAY
(brânză cu chimen)

½ lb sheep cheese, 4 oz butter, 1 tsp caraway (ground very fine), 1 tsp paprika, salt, radishes

Sieve or grind the cheese. Mix with butter, add caraway and paprika, salt if needed. Mix well. Place on a plate and garnish with radishes cut in flower shapes. This paste can be used for sandwiches too.

CHICKEN LIVER PATE
(pateu din ficat de pasăre)

1 goose liver or 2-3 chicken livers, 2 onions or to taste, 5 oz butter, pickled peppers and cucumbers, 1 hard-boiled egg

Cut the onions in quarters. Place into a small saucepan with one tbsp of butter, the liver and a few tbsp of water. Cover and let boil until all liquid evaporates. Let cool and then grind the liver and onions. Mix this paste with the rest of the butter until creamy. Add salt, and then place on a plate, smoothing the top. Garnish with the pickled peppers and cucumbers and slices of the egg.

JELLIED CHICKEN
(piftie de pasăre)

3 lbs poultry, 1 onion, 1 carrot, 1 celery root, 1 parsnip, 2 bay leaves, 3-4 juniper berries, gelatin as needed, juice from one lemon, salt

Poultry jellies are prepared the same way as pork ones with the exception that you add only as much water as to cover the poultry pieces because they take less to boil. If, after boiling, the liquid is not sticky and gluey, add some gelatin. Divide the meat and place in a few deep plates. Garnish with some thin lemon slices. Strain the liquid and add on top of the meat. Place the plates in a cool place to gel. This recipe can be made with hen, rooster or goose. The tastiest one, though, is that made from turkey meat.

DRIED BEANS WITH MAYO
(fasole boabe cu maioneză)

14 oz dried beans, 1 big onion, salt, pepper, mayo, beets (pickled peppers, cucumbers)

Choose large beans for this recipe. Presoak the night before. The following day, drain and boil. After the first boil, change the water. This time start with warm water. Repeat this three times. The last time add salt. When ready, let cool in the water, then drain completely. Place in a bowl; add a little pepper, a finely chopped onion, salt. Mix with mayo and set in the serving bowl. Garnish with pickled beets, peppers or cucumbers.

HERRING OR MACKEREL PANCAKES
(chifteluțe din heringi sau scrumbii sărate)

2 herrings, 1 egg, 2 crustless slices of white bread, 1 onion, 1 tbsp parsley and dill, 2 tbsp oil, bread crumbs

Wash the fish well, slit lengthwise and keep them in tepid water for 5-6 hours. Take out of the water, remove all skin and bones. Then grind together with the raw onion and the bread soaked in milk or water and squeezed of excess liquid. Mix this with the egg, parsley and dill and make pancakes. Cover in bread crumbs and fry in hot oil. Serve hot.

HERRING PASTE WITH APPLES
(pastă de heringi cu mere)

1 big herring, 2 tbsp butter, 1 big apple, 1 hard-boiled egg, lettuce

Slit the fish lengthwise and keep in warm water for 5-6 hours. Then wash skin and debone the fish. Remove the head and tail but keep them. Chop or grind the fish very finely. Sieve the hard-boiled yolk and then mix with butter. Add the ground fish and make a paste. Then add the grated apple and mix some more. Place the paste on a long serving plate and shape it like a fish. Put the head and tail where they belong. Sprinkle the finely chopped egg white on top. Decorate with lettuce leaves placed around the fish paste. You can also use this paste for sandwiches.

HERRING PASTE WITH WALNUTS
(pastă de heringi cu nuci)

1 herring, 12 ground walnuts, 2 crustless slices of white bread soaked in water with a little vinegar, 1/2 grated onion, 1 tsp vinegar, 3 tbsp oil

Wash the fish, skin and debone it. Then grind or chop very finely. Place the fish paste in a bowl and mix with the soaked and squeezed bread, gradually adding the oil. After the oil is used up, add the onion, vinegar, walnuts and mix well. Place the mixture on a long serving plate, shaping like a fish. Put the head and tail where they belong. Keep cold until serving.

LIVER PATE WITH MUSHROOMS
(pateu de ficat cu ciuperci)

1 lb veal liver, 1 lb mushrooms, 2 onions, 10 oz butter, salt, pepper, 1 hard-boiled egg, olives (pickled peppers), parsley

Clean, wash and cut the mushrooms in big pieces. On the bottom of a pot, place 2 teaspoons of butter, the quartered onions, the mushrooms, the liver cut in big pieces and two tbsp of water. Cover and boil over slow heat, shaking the pot from time to time. When there is no liquid left, take off the heat, cool, and then grind everything. Place the butter in a bowl and add the ground mixture. Mix until creamy, add salt, pepper and place on a serving plate, smoothing the top. Garnish with slices of egg. On the yolk, place an olive or piece of pickled pepper and a parsley leaf.

MOSAIC BREAD
(pâine mozaic)

5 oz butter, 5 oz canned sardines, 5 oz lean ham, 4 oz Swiss cheese, 10 olives, ½ pickled pepper, 1 small french baguette, ½ cup milk

Grind the sardines, 1/3 of the ham and an egg-sized piece of crustless bread, soaked in milk and squeezed dry. Mix everything with the butter until creamy and homogeneous. Cut the rest of the ham, Swiss cheese, olives and pickled pepper in small cubes and mix with the prepared paste. Refrigerate it. Meanwhile, cut the heels of the baguette and take the soft bread inside out, leaving about half an inch of bread below the crust. Then fill with the refrigerated paste. Refrigerate. Cut with a very sharp knife in thin slices about half an inch thick. It is better prepared one day in advance.

MUSHROOMS FILLED WITH BRAINS
(ciuperci umplute cu creier)

12 stuffing mushrooms, ½ veal brain, 2 tbsp butter, 1 tsp minced parsley, 1 egg, salt, pepper, 1 tbsp breadcrumbs

Wash and salt the mushrooms. Chop the stems not too fine and fry in 1 1/2 tbsp of butter until soft. Boil the brain in salted water, remove the membranes, crush with a fork and mix well with the egg. Add the fried mushrooms, parsley, pepper, a little salt to the paste obtained and mix well. Fill the stuffing mushrooms with this mixture. Spread some breadcrumbs and then melted butter on each of them and then place in a buttered dish. Bake for 20-25 minutes. Serve hot or cold.

MUSHROOMS ON FRENCH TOAST
(ciuperci pe frigănele)

2 lbs mushrooms, 1 egg, 1 tbsp minced dill, 2 tbsp butter, salt

French toast: 1French baguette, 1 cup milk, 1 egg, salt, 1/2 tsp sugar

Wash and chop the mushrooms. Melt some butter in a pan and then fry them with the dill and salt. When ready, take off the heat and add a beaten egg. Mix well. Prepare the French toast and place a thick layer of mushrooms on top of them, smoothing with a knife. Then bake the pancakes for 10 minutes. Serve hot.

MUSHROOMS, JELLIED, WITH MAYO
(ciuperci cu gelatină şi maioneză)

2 lbs mushrooms, 1 onion, 1 tsp butter, gelatin, salt, mayo

Wash and cut julienne the mushrooms. Place in a pot with a whole onion, one teaspoon of butter and salt. Cover with water and let boil until the mushrooms are soft. Remove the onion and strain. Leave the mushrooms aside and strain again through cheesecloth. Add gelatin to this liquid (one tbsp of gelatin for each cup). Heat until the gelatin is melted. Place the mushrooms on the bottom of a deep plate (or several smaller molds). Pour the gelatin liquid on top. Strain when pouring. Refrigerate so that it gels. Serve with mayo.

JELLIED PORK
(piftie de porc)

3 lbs pork feet and/or head, 1 onion, 2 carrots, 1 parsnip, 1 parsley root, 1 celery root, 2 bay leaves, 3-4 juniper berries, 3-4 garlic cloves, salt

Wash and clean the feet and/or head. If hairy, singe. Split the feet in two lengthwise and break the head with the mallet. Place in a large pot and cover with water so that there are 3-4 inches of water above the pork pieces. Boil over slow to medium heat. Remove the foam as it forms. Then add salt, vegetables, bay leaves and juniper berries. Cover the pot almost completely. Boil until the meat falls off the bones. Remove the bones and place the meat on the bottom of one or several deep plates. Chop the garlic, add some salt and mix with the meat broth. Strain and then pour on top of the meat in plates. Refrigerate so that it gels. To obtain a nice, clear jelly you have to boil slowly, with the pot almost covered. The tastiest pork jelly is made out of pork feet and ears. You can use beef feet or a mixture of pork and beef feet.

PUDDINGS

ROMANIAN NOODLE
(tăiţei în stil româneasc)

8 ounces fine egg noodles, cooked, thoroughly drained and still
warm, 2 tbsp unsalted butter or margarine, melted, 2 eggs, lightly
beaten, ¼ tsp salt, 1 small apple, peeled and finely diced, ½ cup
golden raisin, plumped in apple juice, oil (for frying), ½ cup sugar,
½ tsp ground cinnamon

Toss the noodles with the butter. Cool, slightly, and then blend in the
eggs, salt, apple and raisins. In a large, heavy skillet heat 1/4-inch oil over
medium heat. Drop noodle mixture by tbsp into hot oil, flattening each
spoonful with back of tablespoon to form thin latke. Fry on both sides
until golden brown and crisp, about 3 minutes on each side. Do not turn
latkes until first side is golden and top is set. Drain on paper towels.
Combine sugar and cinnamon in shallow bowl and dip latkes in sugar
mixture on both sides.

BRAIN PUDDING
(budincă de creier)

1 large beef brain, 5 egg whites, 2-3 tbsp breadcrumbs, 1 tsp
minced dill, 1 onion, 1 tbsp butter, salt, pepper, a little flour. For
sauce: 1 cup sour cream, 1/2 cup milk, 1 tbsp flour, 1 tbsp butter, a
little minced dill, salt

Boil the brain, sieve it and then mix with the chopped and fried in butter
onion, dill, salt, pepper, bread crumbs and the whipped egg whites at the
end. Pour this mixture in a lidded mold which was previously buttered
and floured. The mold must be only 3/4 full. Place to boil in a larger pan

full of water. The sauce: Lightly fry the flour in butter and then add the milk. Add sour cream, dill and salt. Let come to a boil and then serve warm.

CHEESE PANCAKE PUDDING
(budincă de clatite cu brânză)

1 qt milk, 3 eggs, 3-4 tbsp club soda, ¼ tsp salt, 4 oz butter or lard, ½ lb sour cream, 5 oz grated cheese, flour as needed

Beat the eggs, mix with club soda, salt, flour, and then add the milk a little at a time, as for pancakes. Fry the pancakes, placing them, as they are made, in a pan. Lightly butter each pancake and then put some grated cheese on top. The last pancake is only buttered. No cheese is added to it. Cover the pan and place in a larger pan with boiling water in it. Let boil at slow heat, until the pancakes are hot. Before serving, turn onto a plate and cut in sections, as layer cakes. Serve with sour cream.

FISH PUDDING
(budincă de peşte)

3 lbs fish (pike or perch, preferably a mixture of the two), 2 tbsp butter, 5 eggs, 1 big onion, 2 crustless slices of white bread moistened in milk (or water), salt, pepper, 1 tbsp chopped parsley, butter and yolk sauce

Clean, wash and cut the fish in pieces. Remove all bones and grind together with the crustless bread which was moistened in milk or water and then squeezed. Beat the butter until creamy, adding the yolks one by one, then the finely chopped onion, parsley, salt, pepper, the fish mixture and the whipped egg whites at the end, mixing everything well. Butter a clean cloth, place the mixture within, tie the ends, not very tightly, and place in a pot with salt water. Boil for 30 minutes, covered. When ready, take out of the cloth, slice and serve warm with butter and egg sauce

HAM PUDDING
(budincă de şuncă)

3 tbsp butter, 1 cup milk, 3 tbsp flour, 5 eggs, 7 oz ham, salt, bread crumbs

Beat the flour with the milk, add the butter and set to boil stirring continuously. Let boil until the mixture comes off the pot walls. Let cool, add the yolks one by one, mix, add the chopped ham, then the whipped egg whites. Pour the mixture in a buttered and bread crumbed pan and let bake. Serve warm.

CAULIFLOWER GRATIN
(conopidă gratinată)
Sent by Dorel Andriuca, Roseville, CA

2 medium heads cauliflower (about 3 lb), trimmed and cut into florets, 1 tsp salt, 2 tsp butter, 1 cup breadcrumbs (optional), 3/4 cup shredded Gruyère cheese, 1cup grated parmesan, 1 cup grate Monterey Jack, 3 tbsp all-purpose flour, 2 cups 2% reduced-fat milk, 3 tbsp chopped fresh flat-leaf parsley, 1 tsp freshly ground black pepper

Boil cauliflower in salted water for about 5 minutes. Drain the water.

Preheat oven to 375°F. Melt butter in a saucepan over medium heat. Remove from heat. Stir in milk and flower until thickens up. Add salt, pepper and Gruyere, Parmesan and Monterey cheese.

Place cauliflower in a 2-quart broiler-safe baking dish lightly coated with 1/3 of the sauce. Add the cauliflower and pour over the sauce. You can finish it up with Gruyere cheese sprinkled on top or you can prepare a mixture of 1 tbsp of butter, ¼ cup Gruyere cheese, breadcrumbs, salt and pepper, and sprinkle on top Bake at 375oFfor 30 minutes. Let it cool for 5 minutes before e serving.

MACARONI AND CHEESE PUDDING
(budincă de macaroane cu brânză)

½ lb macaroni, 3 tbsp sheep cheese, 2 tbsp butter, 3 eggs, some bread crumbs

Boil the macaroni in salt water, drain, rinse with cold water and let drain again. Beat the eggs, add the cheese, and mix with the macaroni and the melted butter. Butter a baking sheet, put some breadcrumbs all over, place the macaroni and then bake. Turn onto a platter, cut into squares and serve hot.

MACARONI AND HAM PUDDING
(budincă de macaroane cu şuncă)

½ lb macaroni, 2 tbsp lard, 1 cup sour cream, 7 oz smoked ham, salt, pepper, 2 eggs, some butter and bread crumbs

Boil the macaroni, rinse with cold water and let drain. Beat the eggs, mix with the macaroni, and add salt, pepper, heated lard, cubed ham and sour cream. Mix everything well and set into a buttered and bread crumbed baking sheet. Bake until it starts to turn brownish. Serve hot, cut into squares.

MACARONI AND MEAT PUDDING
(budincă de macaroane cu carne)

½ lb macaroni, 10 oz beef sirloin, 3 big onions, 2 tbsp lard or butter, salt, pepper, 3 eggs, some bread crumbs

Boil the macaroni in salt water, drain, rinse with cold water and drain again. Finely chop the onions, fry in lard or butter until it turns yellowish, add the ground meat, salt, pepper and fry a little more. Mix the macaroni with the beaten eggs, then the fried meat and set in a buttered and bread crumbed baking sheet. Bake until brownish. Serve hot cut into squares.

MEAT PUDDING
(budincă de carne)

1 lb sirloin beef or veal, 2 slices white bread, 1 ½ tbsp butter, 5 eggs, salt, pepper, mushroom sauce

Cut the meat in pieces and fry in 1/2 tbsp of butter. Then grind twice, with the crustless bread previously moistened in milk and squeezed. Separately, beat a tbsp of butter and then add the yolks one by one, the ground meat, salt and pepper. Add the whipped egg whites at the end. Butter a pudding mold and place the mixture within. Cover tightly and then place the mold into a larger pan with boiling water. Let boil a half an hour from the moment it comes to a boil. Turn onto a plate and serve hot with mushroom sauce.

POTATO AND CHEESE PUDDING
(budincă de cartofi cu brânză)

For the potato paste use the same quantities as for the potato and meat pudding. Filling: 5 oz grated sheep cheese

Prepare the potato paste as for the potato and meat pudding. Add the cheese to the potato paste, mix well, place in a mold and bake until brownish. Serve warm.

POTATO AND MEAT PUDDING
(budincă de cartofi cu carne)

1 3/4 lbs potatoes, 1 tbsp flour, 3 eggs, 1 tbsp butter, 1 cup milk, 1 tsp sugar, salt, meat filling prepared like for meat ştrudel

Peel the potatoes, boil them, and crush with the potato press (or sieve or grind). Place in a bowl. Add warm butter, salt, sugar, milk, mix well, and then add flour and the yolks and the whipped egg whites at the end. Place half of this mixture in a buttered and bread crumbed pudding mold, then place the meat filling and finally the other half of the mixture. Dot with butter, bread crumbs and bake until brownish. Serve warm.

SPINACH PANCAKE PUDDING
(budincă de clătite cu spanac)

Same quantities as for cheese pancake pudding, replacing the cheese with spinach puree

Prepare the same as for cheese pancake pudding. Replace the cheese with mashed spinach. Serve with sour cream.

LAMB LIVER
(drob de miel)

2 lb lamb liver and lamb meat, 2 eggs, 1 slice of bread, 1 tbsp of sour cream, 1 spoonful of chopped parsley, 2 spring onions, salt and pepper.

Boil the meat and the liver and then mince them with the meat grinder. Add the eggs and the slice of bread and the rest of the ingredients, place them in a baking dish and put them in the oven at a medium high temperature. The dish can be baked wrapped in dough made of 1egg, 5 oz flour and 1 tbsp of oil. Lamb Liver is a traditional Easter dish.

WARM CHICKEN SALAD WITH WALNUT SHERRY VINAIGRETTE
(salată caldă de pui cu vinegretă)
Sent by Anitta Zat Palla, Sacramento, CA

4 chicken breasts, skinless, poached, 3 tbsp canola oil, 4 ounces walnuts, 2 scallions, sliced, 1 clove garlic, minced, ½ cup sherry, ¼ cup white wine vinegar, salt and pepper, salad greens, chives, chopped for garnish

To poach the chicken breasts, bring a pot of salted water, enough to cover the chicken, to a boil. Add the chicken. Return to a boil, then reduce the heat to a simmer and cook 10 minutes, or until the meat is white in the center. Remove chicken from the water. Salt and pepper the meat and keep warm.

In a sauté pan, heat 1 tbsp of the oil and add the walnuts. Sauté for 1-2 minutes, giving the nuts a touch of toasting. Remove from the pan. Add the scallions and garlic. Sauté for 1 minute. Add the sherry and simmer until reduced. Meanwhile, slice the chicken crosswise in strips. Add the vinegar and 2 remaining tbsp of canola oil to the sauté pan. Heat through. Add the chicken and walnuts to the pan. Toss with the vinaigrette. Serve the chicken over a bed of salad greens. Use all the vinaigrette in the pan to drizzle over the chicken. Sprinkle with chives to garnish.

ROMANIAN SOUFFLÉ
(suflé românesc)
Sent by Anitta Zat Palla, Sacramento, CA

4 sheets fillo pastry, 3 tbsp butter (melted, for brushing fillo), ¾ cup shredded gruyere or Swiss cheese, 3 eggs, 1 cup milk, 1/2 tsp salt, 1/8 tsp white pepper

Stack the Fillo horizontally on your work surface, brushing each sheet lightly with melted butter as you stack. Sprinkle the cheese over the bottom third of the Fillo. Roll up the Fillo very loosely, jelly-roll style. Coil the roll loosely in a greased 1-quart soufflé dish. Brush the coil with butter. If desired, cover and chill the dish up to 8 hours. Preheat the oven to 350ºF. In a bowl, beat the eggs lightly. Stir in the milk, salt and pepper. Pour the mixture over the Fillo and into the center of the dish. Bake the soufflé, uncovered for 30 to 35 minutes or until the top of the Fillo is golden, and a knife inserted in the center comes out clean. Serve the soufflé warm.

SOUPS & BORSCHES

ROMANIAN CABBAGE SOUP WITH BACON
(ciorbă ţărănească)
Sent by Abigaila Budac, Roseville, CA

2 onions, 2 green peppers, 1 cabbage, salt and pepper, several sprigs of dill and savory, 1½ qt water, 2 egg yolks, 2-3 tbsp heavy cream (sour cream), 1 tbsp vinegar

Chop up one slice of bacon, and fry it in a heavy stew pan until the fat melts. Cut into small pieces onions, green pepper and cabbage. Fry the onions in the pan until they are golden. Add the peppers and fry them, too. Remove the stew pan from the heat. Layer the cabbage and the rest of the bacon into the soup pot. Add spices between the layers with salt, pepper, and the herbs. Pour the water over it all and bring to a boil. Turn the heat down and simmer the soup for 40 to 50 minutes, until the vegetables are tender. Remove the soup from the heat. Beat the egg yolks with the cream and the vinegar in a little bowl. Stir in a ladleful of the hot soup. Whisk well and pour the mixture back into the soup to thicken and enrich it. Serve in deep bowls accompanied with fresh bread. This soup is a meal in itself, and wants only a piece of cheese and fresh fruit to make it complete.

SOUR CHICKEN SOUP
(ciorbă de pui)

1 frying chicken, 1 tbsp salt, 1 whole onion, 2 stalks celery, 2 black peppercorns, 2 pkg frozen mixed veggies, 1 tbsp tarragon, chopped, 1 tbsp chopped parsley, 3 tbsp sour cream, 1 lemon, 3 egg yolks

Cover chicken with cold water in a large pot; add salt and bring to a boil. When foam starts to form; remove as much as possible; lower the heat and boil gently for 15 to 20 minutes. Add whole onion; celery and pepper. Let boil another half hour or until the meat is cooked. Meanwhile, prepare veggies according to package directions. Add to the soup from which you have removed the celery and onion. Add tarragon and parsley and let boil 10 minutes more. In a large bowl beat together the egg yolks, sour cream and lemon juice. Add the soup to this mixture very slowly, just a little at a time. Stir constantly until it is all blended. Do not boil again.

ROMANIAN CIORBA
(ciorbă românească)

6 quarts water, 8 large potatoes, 1 can green beans, 2 large carrots, 8 tomatoes, 1 head cabbage, 3 onions, 4 large dill pickles, 1 6 oz. can tomato paste, 4 green peppers, 2 stalks celery, basil, oregano and thyme to taste

Bring water to a boil. Add potatoes, carrots, and celery. Add green beans. Blanch, peel and chop tomatoes. Add to soup. In a bowl, mix tomato paste with 1 cup of hot soup stock from pot until smooth. Add all back to pot and stir. Add cabbage. In a wok or skillet, brown onions and green peppers lightly, and then add to pot. Cook until cabbage is tender - about 5 minutes. Turn off heat. Add parsley, dill pickles and herbs. Add salt and pepper to taste.

CREAM OF BEAN SOUP
(supă cremă de fasole boabe)

3 qts water, ½ lb dried beans, 1 carrot, 1 parsley root, 1 onion, 1 tbsp butter or oil, chopped parsley, salt, cubed toasted bread

Pick over and wash the beans and pre-soak in tepid water the preceding night. Then drain this water and set to boil in fresh tepid water. After boiling for a minute or two, change the water. Repeat this procedure three times. The last time, add, in addition to the beans, the onion, carrot, and parsley root. Let it boil, covered, at low temperature. When the beans are tender, remove the carrot and parsley root, strain, then sieve the beans with the onion. Thin it with a little of the strained liquid. Set the soup to boil again, with a tbsp of butter or oil and salt. After coming to a boil, add the chopped parsley. Serve with croutons.

BEET SOUP
(supă de sfeclă roşie)

3 qts water, 2 lbs red beets, 1 tbsp flour, 1 tbsp sugar, 1 cup sour cream, 2 tbsp vinegar, salt, 1 tsp butter, boiled noodles or toasted bread

Clean the beets wash and grate. Set to boil with the water for 30-40 minutes (uncovered). Strain and then add to the liquid the salt, sugar and vinegar. After it comes to another boil, add the butter mixed with the flour and sour cream, mix well and let it boil for a little while. Serve with boiled noodles or toast.

CAULIFLOWER SOUP
(supă de conopidă)

2 qts water, 1 medium cauliflower, 1 parsley root, 1 carrot, 1 onion, 1 tbsp butter, 1 tsp flour, 1 tsp chopped dill, ½ cup sour cream, salt

Grate the parsley root, carrot and onion and boil in water until tender. Strain; add salt and a mixture of fried flour and butter, liquefied with some of the boiling liquid. Add the cauliflower in small bunches and boil at slow heat until the cauliflower is tender. Pour in the serving bowl on top of the dill mixed with the sour cream.

CARAWAY SOUP
(supă de chimen)

3 qts water, 1 big onion, 2 big carrots, 1 big parsley root, 1 celery root, 1 tbsp butter, 1 tbsp flour, 1 tbsp caraway, salt, pepper, cubed toasted bread

Boil the julienned vegetables with a tbsp of caraway. When ready, strain, set the liquid to boil again and add a mixture of fried flour and butter and the salt. Let boil for a little while more. Serve with croutons fried in butter.

GREEN CORN SOUP
(supă de porumb verde)

6 ears of corn, 6 qts water, 1 carrot, 1 parsley root, 1 onion, 2 cups milk, 1 tbsp butter, 1 tbsp flour, 1 egg, salt, ½ tsp chopped dill

With a very sharp knife, remove all kernels of corn. Set to boil the ears of corn with the chopped onion and vegetables. After boiling for one hour, strain and then set the clear liquid to boil again, with the corn kernels, at slow temperature, for half an hour. Strain again, sieve the kernels, mix with the strained liquid and set to boil again. When it comes to a boil, add the flour mixed with butter and milk. After coming to another boil or two, remove from heat and serve with a beaten egg, salt and chopped dill.

LENTIL SOUP
(supă de linte)

3 qts water, ½ lb lentils, 1 onion, 2 garlic cloves, 2 tbsp oil, 1 tsp flour, ½ tsp dry thyme, salt

Pick the lentils over, wash and pre-soak in tepid water the night before cooking. In the morning, throw away the water and set to boil with 3 qts/3 l cold water, finely chopped onion and the garlic cloves. When the lentils are almost done, add salt and let boil until done. Add flour fried in oil and mixed with a half teaspoon of thyme and then pour some lentil liquid on this fried flour. Let boil for a little while longer.

TOMATO SOUP I
(supă de roşii) I

1,5 l water, 2 lbs tomatoes, 1 big carrot, 1 big parsley root, 1 onion, 2 green peppers, 1 tbsp chopped dill, parsley and lovage (mixed), 1 tsp sugar, 1 tsp flour, 2 tbsp oil, 2 tbsp rice, salt

Wash the tomatoes and set to boil with 1 pint/500 ml water. When the tomatoes have softened, strain. Grate the carrot, parsley root and onion and set to boil with 1 l water, until all vegetables are tender. Then strain and add the tomato liquid to the vegetable liquid. Also add rice, quartered green peppers, salt and sugar, letting everything boil, covered, until the rice is half done. Add the flour fried in oil and let boil until the rice is done. Add chopped dill, parsley and lovage. This soup is also delicious served cold.

TOMATO SOUP II
(supă de roşii) II

1,5 l water, 2 lbs tomatoes, 1 carrot, 1 parsley root, 1 onion, 1 tsp sugar, 2 green peppers, 1 tbsp rice, 1 tsp flour, 1 tbsp butter, 1/2 cup sour cream, 1 tsp chopped dill, salt

Boil the tomatoes and vegetables as for tomato soup I. Mix the tomato liquid with the vegetable liquid, add salt, sugar, rice and sliced peppers, as well as a mixture obtained by frying the flour with butter and adding some soup. Let boil until the rice is done, then add the chopped dill. Before serving, beat some sour cream in. Serve hot.

CREAM OF CARROT SOUP
(supă cremă de morcovi)

3 qts water, 1 lb carrots, 1 onion, ½ tsp sugar, 1 tbsp butter, ½ cup sour cream, salt, cubed toasted bread

Julienne the carrots and onion and set to boil until the carrots are tender. Strain, and then sieve the carrots and onion. Add the puree obtained this way to the strained liquid and set to boil again, with the sugar, salt and butter. Let boil for a few minutes and then add sour cream when serving. Serve with croutons.

SOUR CREAM AND PEA SOUP
(supă cremă de mazăre uscată şi smântână)

7 oz dried peas, 2 potatoes, 1 onion, 1 tsp butter, 1 hard-boiled yolk, 1/2 cup sour cream, 1 tsp flour, salt, chopped dill, cubed toasted bread

Boil the peas with the vegetables. Strain and sieve only the peas and potatoes. Thin with some of the boiling liquid and set to boil with the hard-boiled yolk which you have previously mixed with butter, flour and sour cream and thinned with a little boiling liquid. Mix well, add salt and chopped dill and let boil for a minute or two. Serve with croutons.

CREAM OF PEAS SOUP
(supă cremă de mazăre uscată)

3 l water, 1/2 lb dried peas, 1 parsley root, 1 carrot, 1 onion, 1 tsp sugar, 1 tbsp butter or oil, 1 tsp chopped dill, salt, cubed toasted bread

Prepare the same way as cream of bean soup. Do not change the water. Serve with croutons.

CREAM OF POTATO SOUP
(supă cremă de cartofi)

2 l water, 1 lb potatoes, 1 onion, 1 cup sour cream, 1 tsp flour, 1 tbsp chopped parsley, 1 tsp butter, salt, toasted bread

Boil the cubed potatoes with the finely chopped onion. When they are done, strain. Sieve the potatoes and thin with some of the boiling liquid. Add salt and set to boil. When the soup starts to boil, add the sour cream well mixed with the flour. Let boil for a minute or two, add the chopped parsley and butter. Serve with toast.

CREAM OF SPINACH SOUP
(supă cremă de spanac)

3 l water, 500 g spinach, 1 lemon slice (with peel), 1 tbsp butter, 1 tsp flour, 1/2 cup sour cream, salt, French toast

Wash and pick over the spinach. Set to boil with the water. After boiling for a little while, remove from heat and sieve everything. Set to boil again, adding the lemon, salt and butter. Let it boil for another minute or two, and then add the sour cream mixed with flour. Serve with French toast.

LENTIL SOUP IN MINUTES
(supă de linte)
Sent by Anitta Pat Zala, Sacramento, CA

1/4 cup yellow lentils, 1/4 cup pink lentils, 1 tbsp olive oil or butter, 1/2 onion chopped, 2 garlic cloves, finely chopped, 1/4 cup fresh chopped cilantro, 1 tsp salt, 1/2 tbsp black pepper, 1 tsp

turmeric powder, 1 tsp garam masala, 1/2 tsp crushed red pepper flakes

In a pressure cooker add well-washed lentils with 2 cups water. Place on high heat until you hear the first sounds of hissing from the cooker. Immediately turn the stove off and leave cooker untouched additional 15 minutes. In a skillet add oil, garlic, onions, and ginger. Sauté for 3-4 minutes on medium-high heat. Add all spices; continue to sauté additional 2-3 minutes. Add mixture to lentils in pressure cooker along with cilantro. Cook lentil soup uncovered until desired thickness.

Toasted bread is a great accompaniment. A small pat of additional butter on each serving makes it creamier. Yogurt is also delicious and will cut the intensity of the spices. Quantity of spices can be adjusted or omitted to your liking. Salt and Pepper are most important, and the turmeric powder gives a nice yellow color to soup.

SPINACH SOUP
(supă de spanac)
Sent by Anitta Pat Zala, Sacramento, CA

1 stick butter, 8 oz cream cheese, 1 cup shredded Asiago cheese, 1 can condensed cream of celery soup, 1 ½ cup heavy whipping cream, 1 lb fresh spinach, chopped, 1 lb raw frozen and de-veined shrimp, 1 tsp white pepper (or to taste), 1 tsp garlic salt (or to taste), Salt to taste

In a large pot melt butter, cream cheese, and Asiago cheese over low heat. When completely melted, add cream of celery soup & heavy cream; whisk until creamy and smooth. Wash and drain fresh spinach. Add spinach to pot and simmer for 5-10 minutes. Next add shrimp, white pepper, garlic salt and continue simmering for 5-10 minutes, until shrimp are done. Finally add salt to taste.

POTATO SOUP
(supă de cartofi)
Sent by Anitta Pat Zala, Sacramento, CA

2 big potatoes, cubed, 1 (5.5 ounce) package au gratin instant potato mix, 1 (10.5 ounce) can condensed chicken broth, 1 1/2 cups water, 1 cup heavy cream

In a large saucepan or pot, combine potatoes, au gratin potato mix, chicken broth and water. Add more water to cover if necessary. Cook over medium heat, stirring occasionally, until potatoes are tender, about 40 minutes. Stir in cream and heat through. Serve.

VEGETABLE SOUP I
(supă de zarzavat) I

2 l water, 2 big carrots, 1 celery root, 2 potatoes, 2 green peppers, 1 piece of cabbage, 1 onion, 1 parsley root

Boil the vegetables as for vegetable soup with sour cream in a covered pot, for two hours. Strain and add salt.

VEGETABLE SOUP II
(supă de zarzavat) II

3 l water, 1 onion, 2 carrots, 1 celery root, 1 parsley root, 2 potatoes, 2 green peppers, 1 piece cabbage, 1 big tomato, 1 tsp chopped parsley, 1 tbsp butter, 1 tsp flour, salt

Boil the vegetables in salt water, at low heat, for one and a half hours. Sieve. Fry the butter with the flour in a pan and pour the sieved soup on top, stirring continuously. Let boil for a minute or two longer and then add the chopped parsley.

VEGETABLE SOUP WITH SOUR CREAM
(supă de zarzavat cu smântână)

3 l water, 1 onion, 1 small carrot, 1 small parsley root, a handful of green beans, 2 potatoes, 3-4 tomatoes, 1 tsp flour, 1 tbsp butter, 1 tsp chopped parsley and dill, 1/2 cup sour cream, salt

Set to boil the julienne carrot, parsley root and onion, the green beans cut in pieces, cubed potatoes. After boiling for a little while, add the peeled, seeded, and cut tomatoes and the salt. Fry the flour in butter and add to the soup, stirring continuously. Add the chopped parsley and dill and let boil, covered, at low temperature, for a few minutes. When serving, mix soup with one tbsp of sour cream per individual soup bowl.

BEEF SOUP
(supă din carne de vacă)

2 lbs beef, 3 l water, 2 carrots, 1 parsley root, 1 celery root, 1 green pepper, 1 onion and a few yellow peelings from the onion, 5 juniper berries (optional), 1 bay leaf (optional), salt, vermicelli

Set to boil the beef with the cold water. Let the pot uncovered until the liquid starts foaming. Remove this foam periodically with the slotted tablespoon until foaming stops. Add the vegetables, juniper berries, bay leaf and a little salt. Cover the pot almost but not completely and let boil, at low temperature, for 3 hours. When it is ready, strain it into another pot. The soup has to boil slowly to be really tasty. Serve with the desired accompaniment (noodles, vermicelli).

BROTH WITH MEAT PIES
(bulion cu pateuri de carne)

3 lbs beef, 3 l water, 1 carrot, 1 parsley root, 1 celery root, 1 onion, 1 bay leaf, 2-3 juniper berries, salt

Set the beef to boil with the cold water. Remove foam; add the cleaned and quartered vegetables, juniper berries and bay leaf. Boil covered, at low temperature, for an hour. Add salt and let boil for another two hours. Remove the vegetables, remove the meat which will be used as filling for the pies and strain and degrease the soup. Serve in cups with meat pies.

CHEESE SOUP
(supă cu brânză)

Beef or poultry soup, 3 tbsp grated sheep's cheese

Grate the cheese in the soup bowl and pour the hot, strained soup on top. Serve with croutons.

CHICKEN SOUP
(supă de pasăre)

2 lbs poultry parts, 3 l water, 2 carrots, 1 parsley root, 1 celery root, 1 green pepper, 1 onion, 1 bay leaf (optional), salt

Prepare the same way as beef soup. Serve with the accompaniment that you wish.

SOUP WITH CREAM OF WHEAT DUMPLINGS
(supă cu găluşte de griş)

Beef or poultry soup, dumplings: 2 eggs, 1/2 tsp butter, 5-6 tbsp cream of wheat, salt

Beat the butter with the eggs. Add the cream of wheat a little at a time (like rain), stirring continuously. The paste obtained should be the thickness of sour cream. Add salt. After the soup was strained into a clean pot, set to boil. When it comes to the first boil, take teaspoon full of the cream of wheat paste and drop them into the soup. Grease the teaspoon first to make it easier. The soup must boil slowly. After all the paste has been used up, cover the pot and let boil slowly for 10 minutes. Remove the lid and gently turn the dumplings. Cover again and let boil for another 10 minutes. Remove from the soup with the slotted spoon, gently place in the serving bowl (so they do not break) and pour the soup on top of them.

SOUP WITH "RAGS"
(supă cu zdrenţe)

Beef or poultry soup, rags: 2 eggs, 2-3 tbsp flour, salt

Beat the eggs with a fork; add the flour a little at a time and the salt. Mix with a tablespoon until you get a sour-creamlike paste. Set to boil the soup strained into a clean pot and when it comes to the first boil, pour the paste a little at a time, with the help of a fork. Cover the pot and let boil for a couple of minutes.

ROASTED CHICKEN WITH CARAMELIZED ONIONS SOUP
(supă de pui fript cu ceapă)
Sent by Anitta Pat Zala, Sacramento, CA

2 cups shredded roasted chicken, 2 tsp. vegetable oil, 2 medium onions, halved and thinly sliced, 8 cups chicken broth, 1/8 tsp. ground black pepper, 2 medium carrots, sliced, 2 stalks celery, sliced, ¾ cup uncooked trumpet-shaped pasta

Heat the oil in 10" skillet over medium-high heat. Add onions and cook until they begin to brown, stirring occasionally. Reduce heat to medium. Cook until onions are tender and caramelized, stirring occasionally. Remove skillet from heat. Heat the broth, black pepper, carrots and celery in 4-qt. saucepan over medium-high heat to a boil. Stir pasta and chicken in saucepan. Reduce heat to medium. Cook 10 min or until pasta is tender. Stir in onions and serve immediately.

SOUP WITH EGG
(supă cu ou)

Beef or poultry soup, 1 tbsp lemon juice, 1 egg

Beat the egg and lemon juice in the soup bowl and pour the soup on top a little at a time, stirring continuously. Serve with boiled rice.

SOUP WITH HOME MADE NOODLES
(supă cu tăiţei de casă)

Beef or poultry soup, noodles: 1 egg, 1 tbsp water, flour, salt

Prepare the noodles by mixing the egg, water, flour and salt and then form into noodle shapes such as with a grater or other tool. They may be boiled in the soup or separately in salt water. Strain, rinse with cold water and serve separately at the table.

VEGETARIAN SOUP
(ciorbă fără carne)

3 l water, 1 small carrot, 1 small parsley root, 1 big onion, 1 handful green beans, 1 small red beet, ¼ small cabbage, 2 green peppers, 1 tbsp butter or lard, 1 tbsp mixed chopped parsley and dill, 1/2 tsp flour, salt, 1 cup sour cream

Cut the carrot Julienne, parsley root and onion. Set to boil. After a few boils, add the beans cut into pieces and the julienned beet. Let boil for a half hour, and then add the cabbage and julienned peppers, salt and peeled, seeded and chopped tomatoes. Fry the flour in the oil, add vegetable liquid and then mix all this with the soup. When the vegetables are tender, add chopped parsley and dill. When serving, add a tbsp of sour cream in each person's bowl.

SOUP WITH OMELET
(supă cu omletă)

Beef or poultry soup, omlette: 4 eggs, 1 tbsp sour cream, 1 tbsp milk, 1 tsp butter, salt

Prepare the omelet by mixing the eggs, sour cream, milk, butter and salt and then cooking in a frying pan over a small flame gently turning the liquid mixture at the edges until it is cooked through evenly. Turn onto a cutting board and cut into thin strips. Place in the soup bowl and pour the strained soup on top.

SOUP WITH RICE
(supă de orez)

Beef or poultry soup, 1/2 tbsp rice for each person

Pick over the rice, rinse in cold water and put in the soup to boil slowly until done, stirring from time to time. The rice may be also boiled separately in water, and then added to the soup after having been rinsed with cold water.

SOUP WITH RICE AND SOUR CREAM
(supă cu orez şi smântână)

Beef or poultry soup, 4 tbsp rice, 6 tbsp sour cream, 6 lemon slices, salt

Boil the rice in salt water. When done, strain, rinse in cold water and let drain. Put the rice and lemon slices into the bowl and pour the hot, strained soup on top. Add the sour cream, mixing well.

ROMANIAN BORŞ
(borş românesc)
Sent by Monica Mois, Sacramento, CA

1-1/2 lb beef stew meat, 2-3 carrots, 1 onion, 1 cabbage head, 1-2 beets, 1 lb potatoes, 1 celery root, 1 14 ¾-can diced tomatoes, 1 tbsp. Fresh lovage (can be replaced with tarragon), 1 tbsp fresh parsley, 1-2 green bell pepper, ¼ cup oil, ¾ cup sour cream or yogurt, 1 oz. salt, lemon juice or citric acid, depends how sour you like the soup, (or 1 liter of store bought borş).

Boil the meat in cold water and salt. Dice the carrots, the celery root, the onion, and the green bell peppers. Shred the cabbage. Cook the vegetables in a skillet with oil and some water. Cut the potatoes in cubes. When the meat is half boiled, add the vegetables and potatoes. After the potatoes are boiled add the tomatoes, beet and the lemon juice (citric acid) and continue to boil for 10 more minutes. At the end, add the lovage, parsley, sour cream (yogurt) and salt. Serve it hot, topped with parsley. Make 10 serving.

BORS SOUP WITH MEATBALLS
(ciorbă de perişoare)

1-2 carrots, 1 parsley root, ¼ celery root, and 1 onion or a few green onions. Meatballs: 2 lb ground pork (or ground pork and ground beef mix), 1 onion, 0.5 cup of rice, 1 egg, dill, parsley, salt, and pepper.

Mix well by hand 1kg ground pork (or ground pork and ground beef mix), 1 onion finely chopped, 1 larger fistful of rice, 1 egg, finely chopped dill and parsley, salt, and pepper. Make meatballs of the size of small walnuts, roll them in flour, and set them aside (this recipe makes about 100 meatballs).

Fill about half of a 3l pot with cold water. Add to the water the following vegetables, cut very small or shredded 1-2 carrots, 1 parsley root, 1/4 celery root, and 1 onion or a few green onions. When the vegetables are softened, throw in a fistful of rice. After the rice is cooked, add the meatballs one by one. The meatballs cook pretty fast. After they are done, add 1 chopped tomato, 1 chopped green pepper, parsley, and celery leaves. To make it sour use fresh lemon juice. Taste for salt, and add a bit more pepper. Let boil a few times.

This makes a substantial quantity of soup, as you can very well imagine. These soups are meant to be reheated; they actually taste better the next few days after they are cooked. For just 4 portions, I use 300g meat and 2 tbsp of rice for the meatballs, add no rice in the soup, and put only half of the tomato and green pepper. The herb used to give sour soups is called leuştean (lovage), but it's hard to find in North America. Celery leaves are a reasonable substitute.

The sour soups are usually soured with borş, a liquid made out of wheat bran mixed with water and left to ferment. They are fairly sour, so you can use the juice of 2 lemons. They are also sometimes soured with sauerkraut juice or with green (unripe) fruits such as apricots. The soups are traditionally thickened with a mixture of sour cream and egg yolk, for taste.

BEAN SOUP WITH BORS AND SOUR CREAM
(borş de fasole boabe)

3 l water, ½ lb dry beans, 1 onion, 1 carrot, 1 parsley root, 1/2 tsp flour, 2 tbsp oil, borş (to taste), chopped parsley and dill, salt

Pick over, wash and presoak (in tepid water) the beans, the night before. Set to boil and after the initial first boil, change the water and set to boil again in tepid water. Repeat this procedure three times. To the last water, besides the beans, adds onion, carrot, parsley root and salt. Cover the pot and let boil until the beans are tender. Remove the vegetables and add a mixture made by fried flour in oil, boiled borş (to taste) and chopped parsley and dill. Let boil for a couple of minutes more.

GREEN BEAN SOUP WITH BORS
(borş de fasole verde)

2 l water, 0,5 l borş, 10 oz green beans, 1 small carrot, 1 onion, 1 small parsley root, 4 tomatoes, 1 green pepper, 1 tbsp oil, 1/2 tsp flour, chopped parsley and dill, salt

Set to boil in salt water, the finely chopped carrot, parsley root and onion. Add the beans, cut into pieces. When it starts to boil, let it for a few minutes, and then add the pepper and peeled and seeded tomatoes (sliced). Fry the flour in the oil, add some vegetable liquid to it and then add this mixture to the soup, stirring as you do it. Let boil until the beans are tender. Add the borsch and chopped parsley and dill and let boil for a few more minutes. You may serve this soup cold as well.

SOUP WITH GREEN BEANS AND SOUR CREAM II
(borş de fasole verde)

2 l water, 300 g green beans, 1 onion, 1 carrot, 1 parsley root, 1 lb tomatoes, 1 tbsp butter, 1 tsp flour, ½ cup sour cream, chopped parsley and dill, salt

Fry the finely chopped vegetables in butter, with the flour. Add the water, add the cut beans, salt and let boil at low temperature until the beans are tender. Add the boiled and drained tomatoes and let boil until completely done. Add chopped parsley and dill. Mix some sour cream in it when serving.

SOUP WITH LETTUCE AND BACON
(ciorbă de salată)

2 qts water, 2 heads of Boston lettuce with firm cores, 1 carrot, 1 parsley root, 1 big onion, 1 garlic clove (optional), 1 tbsp flour, 2 yolks, 2 tbsp sour cream, 2-3 tbsp vinegar, chopped parsley, salt; omelet from: 5 oz smoked bacon, 4 eggs, 2 tbsp milk, salt

Finely chop the carrot, parsley root, onion and garlic and set to boil in water for 1/2 hour. Strain, remove the vegetables. In the meantime, beat the yolks with the flour, sour cream; salt and vinegar, then add the strained liquid a little at a time, stirring continuously until it is all added. Set to boil and add the lettuce, cut into pieces. Let come to just one boil. For the omelet, cut the bacon into pieces, fry and then add to the eggs beaten with milk and some salt. Cut this omelet into thin strips, place into the serving bowl and pour the hot soup over it. Add chopped parsley.

ZUCCHINI SOUP WITH BORS AND SOUR CREAM
(borş de dovlecei)
Sent by Nicolae Vidu, Citrus Heights, CA

1,5 l water, 0,5 l borş, 1 onion, 1 small carrot, 1 parsley root, 2 big zucchini, 3-4 tomatoes, 1 tsp butter, ½ tsp flour, sour cream, salt, parsley, 1 tsp dill

Set to boil in water, the finely chopped onion with the thinly sliced carrot and parsley root. After the vegetables are tender, add the boiled borş; washed and cut zucchini; salt; chopped parsley and dill and the separately boiled and strained tomatoes. Let boil at low temperature. When the zucchini are almost done, add the flour fried in oil and let boil for a few more minutes. Serve with sour cream.

GIBLET SOUP
(ciorbă de potroace)

2 l water, 1 l sauerkraut juice, giblets and wings from one hen, turkey or goose (or mixed), 1 carrot, 1 parsley root, 1 big onion, 1/2 celery root, chopped parsley and dill, salt

Boil the giblets and wings with the finely chopped vegetables. Remove foam and add salt. When the meat is tender, add the sauerkraut juice that was boiled separately, the chopped parsley and dill and let boil for a few more minutes.

CABBAGE SOUP WITH MEAT
(ciorbă de varză cu carne)

3 l water, 1 lb fatty beef, 1 lb tomatoes, 1 small carrot, 1 small parsley root, 1 green pepper, 10 beans, 1 onion, 1 large red beet, 1 section cabbage, chopped parsley and dill, salt, sour cream

Set to boil, at low temperature, the meat cut in pieces. Keep removing the foam until there is no more. Add salt and let boil, slowly, covered, until the meat is almost done. Add the beet, onion, carrot and parsley, everything Julienned. After a few boils, add the thinly sliced pepper, cubed beans, and chopped cabbage. Let boil for a couple of minutes, and then add the peeled, seeded and chopped tomatoes. Let it boil, covered, until everything is tender. Add the chopped parsley and dill. When serving, add a tbsp of sour cream into each person's bowl.

LAMB SOUP WITH BORS
(borş de miel)

1 3/4 lbs lamb, 1 l water, 0,5 l borş, 1 onion, 1 carrot, 1 parsley root, 1 green pepper, 5-6 tomatoes, 2 tbsp rice, lovage, salt

Prepare the same as soup (sour) with veal. Add a beaten egg or a few tbsp of sour cream at the end.

CHICKEN SOUP WITH BORS
(borş de pui)

1 chicken, 2 l water, borş (to taste), 1 parsley root, 1 carrot, 1 onion, 2 tomatoes, 2 tbsp rice, 1/2 tbsp mixed chopped parsley and dill, 1 egg, salt to taste

Set to boil the julienned carrot, parsley root and onion. When the vegetables are half done, add the chicken pieces and its gizzards, salt, rice, peeled, seeded and chopped tomatoes. Remove foam; add the separately boiled and strained borş (quantity to taste). When the chicken pieces are almost done, add the chopped parsley and dill. At the end, beat one egg in.

MEAT BALL SOUP WITH BORS I
(borş de perişoare) I

2 l water, 0,5 l borş, 1 lb tomatoes, 1 small carrot, 1 small parsley root, 1 onion, salt, chopped parsley, dill, lovage; for Meatballs: 1 lb beef, 1 tbsp rice, 1 egg, 1 chopped onion fried in 1/2 tbsp lard, salt, pepper

Set to boil, finely chopped onion, carrot, and parsley root together with the beef bones. Let boil well, and then add the separately boiled borş, salt, chopped greens and the separately boiled and strained tomatoes. Let boil for a few minutes and then add the meat balls prepared by mixing the ground meat with the salt, pepper, egg, fried onion and rice. Let the meat balls boil. You may serve with a tbsp of sour cream in each bowl.

MEAT BALL SOUP WITH BORS II
(borş de perişoare) II

500 g beef preferably with bone (used for stew - cheapest you find - you will discard it!), 1 onion, 2 carrots, 1 parsnip, 1 celery root, 4 tomatoes, 2 red peppers, borş or the juice of 2 lemons, salt.

Meatballs: 300 g minced pork, 300 g minced beef, 1 tsp tomato, paste, 1/2 onion diced, 1 tbsp rice, salt and pepper.

Mix of herbs: 1 tbsp diced lovage (harder to find, adds lots of flavor - you can skip it if you do not have it, however it does make a difference), 1 tbsp diced parsley.

Serve it with sour cream

Make the meatballs first and mix all the ingredients. Set it on the side.

Take all the root vegetables, including the onion and cut it very small (I shred it). Cut the meat in large cubes. Add all in a large pot and cove with 3 l of cold water. Bring it to boil. Let it boil gently at low heat.

Add the tomatoes skinned and cut, the red peppers cut into thin and short strips and let it boil another 5 minutes.

Separately, boil the borş. If you do not use borş, add the lemon juice.

Form small balls from the meatballs mix and drop them gently in the low boiling water. Boil on low heat for 10 min max.

Add lemon juice (or borş) and boil another 5 min. Add the herbs. Serve with a tablespoon or 2 of sour cream.

MUTTON SOUP WITH BORS
(borş de berbec)

1 3/4 lbs mutton, 1 l water, 0,5 l borş, 1 onion, 1 carrot, 1 parsley root, 1 green pepper, 5-6 tomatoes, 2 tbsp rice, lovage, salt

Cut the meat in pieces and set to boil. Remove foam as it forms. Add salt and the quartered onion, carrot and parsley root and let boil, covered, at low temperature until the vegetables and the meat are tender. Remove the vegetables with the slotted spoon. Add to the soup julienned green pepper, peeled, seeded and chopped tomatoes, rice and boiled borş. When the rice is done, add chopped lovage.

FISH SOUP WITH GARLIC SAUCE
(ciorbă de pește)

Stock: 1 pound fish trimmings (the heads, tails and bones of any firm white-fleshed fish), 1½ cups coarsely chopped onions, 1 medium-sized bay leaf, 1 tsp salt, 6 cups cold water
Fish soup: ½ pound boned skinless halibut or other firm white-fleshed fish, coarsely chopped, 1 tsp salt, ¼ tsp freshly ground black pepper, 2 pounds halibut or other firm white-fleshed fish steaks, each cut 1 inch thick, 1 tbsp finely chopped garlic mashed to a smooth paste with ½ tsp salt, 1 medium-sized cucumber, peeled, seeded and cut into ¼-inch dice, 2 tbsp distilled white vinegar

Combine the fish trimmings, chopped onions, bay leaf, 1 teaspoon of salt and the 6 cups of water in a heavy 3- to 4-quart enameled or stainless-steel casserole. Bring to a boil over high heat; reduce the heat to low, and simmer partially covered for 30 minutes. Strain the entire contents of the casserole through a fine sieve into a deep bowl, pressing down hard on the fish trimmings and onions with the back of a tablespoon to extract all their juices before discarding them. Pour the stock back into the casserole and add the chopped fish. Stirring occasionally, bring to a boil over high heat. Reduce the heat to its lowest point and simmer uncovered for about 15 minutes, or until the fish can be easily mashed with the back of a spoon. Puree the contents of the casserole in a food mill, or rub them through a coarse sieve, and return to the casserole. Stir in the 1 teaspoon of salt and ¼ teaspoon of pepper, and immerse the fish steaks in the soup. Bring to a simmer over moderate heat and poach partially covered for 5 to 8 minutes or until the fish flakes easily when prodded gently with a fork. Do not overcook. With a slotted spatula, transfer the steaks to a large heated tureen or individual soup plates. With a whisk, beat 1 cup of the soup into the garlic paste and pour the mixture into a sauceboat. Add the cucumber and vinegar to the remaining soup, taste for seasoning, and ladle over the fish steaks. Serve at once, accompanied by the garlic sauce.

STUFFED ZUCCHINI SOUP WITH BEEF AND BORS
(borş de dovlecei umpluţi)

500 g beef, 2 l water, 1 tbsp rice, 1 carrot, 1 parsley root, 2 onions, 1 tbsp lard, 3 young zucchini, 1 celery root, 1 tbsp mixed chopped parsley and dill, salt, pepper, 0,5 l borş to taste, 1/2 cup sour cream

Set to boil, together with the beef bones, finely chopped parsley root, carrot, celery root and 1 onion. In the meantime, remove the peel off the zucchini, cut lengthwise, scoop out the insides and fill them with the ground beef mixed with an onion slightly fried in lard, rice, salt, pepper and some chopped greens. After the vegetables and the bones are well boiled, strain and set the liquid to boil again with the stuffed zucchini and the separately boiled and strained borş. Add the salt and let boil until the zucchini are tender. Add the chopped greens and serve with some sour cream mixed in at the end.

BORS STYLE VEAL SOUP WITH SAUERKRAUT
(borş de viţel)

1¼ pounds veal shank, sawed into 1-inch pieces, 2 quarts water, 2 tsp salt and freshly ground black pepper to taste, ¼ pound (1 stick) butter, 3 medium yellow onions, peeled and chopped, 1½ cup diced carrots (½-inch dice), 1 cup diced potatoes (½-inch dice), 1 cup chopped celery, 2 shallots, peeled and finely chopped,

½ cup chopped parsley, 1¼ cups sauerkraut juice (canned is fine.), additional salt and pepper to taste, if necessary, juice of ½ lemons, ½ cup chopped fresh dill, garnish: ½ pint sour cream

In a 6- to 8-quart stove-top covered casserole or soup pot, place the veal shank, water, and salt and pepper, cover and simmer for 2 hours. Remove the shank pieces and allow them to cool for a moment. De-bone the shank pieces and chop the meat coarsely and return it to the pot. Heat a large frying pan and add the butter, onion, carrots, potatoes, celery, shallots, and parsley. Sauté until the onions are clear and tender. Add the vegetables to the soup pot along with the sauerkraut juice. Simmer for 25 more minutes or so, and taste for salt and pepper. Add the lemon juice and dill. Simmer for a few more minutes and place in a soup tureen. Garnish with the sour cream and serve.

VEAL SOUP WITH BORS
(borş de viţel)

1 ¾ lbs veal, 2 l water, 1 l borş, 1 onion, 1 carrot, 1 parsley root, 1 celery root, 1 tbsp rice, 1 tsp chopped lovage, 1 egg, salt

Cut the veal in pieces, set to boil and remove foam periodically. Add salt and the quartered carrot, celery root, onion and parsley root. Let boil slowly, covered, until the meat is tender. Remove the veal pieces, move them into a clean pot, remove the vegetables and strain the liquid. Add this liquid to the veal pieces. Add the rice, the borş and let boil until the rice is done. Add the chopped lovage and before serving, beat one egg in.

CHICKEN SOUP WITH SOUR CREAM
(ciorbă de burtă cu pui)

2 large carrots, 1 medium onion, 1 parsley head, 5 medium cloves of garlic, 2 chicken breasts, ½ cup sour cream (for a lighter version, add fat free yogurt instead), 3 eggs, salt, pepper, ½ cup chopped dill

Boil the veggies (carrots, onion, and parsley head) and turn them into a paste with a food processor. Keep the water! Boil the chicken breast and cut it in very thin, long strips. Keep this water as well. Separately, in a soup pot combine the sour cream, eggs and mashed garlic cloves. Add the chicken strips and the water from veggies and chicken after they cool. Add salt and pepper. Serve with chopped dill on top. If you like it more sour, add vinegar to your plate, but not the whole soup.

LETTUCE SOUP WITH BACON
(ciorbă de salată)
Sent by Katica Goţ, Oliverhurst, CA

2 heads of lettuce, 250 g smoked bacon, 1 cup rice, 5 tbsp sour cream, 5 tbsp milk, 2 egg yolk, lemon juice or vinegar, salt

Heat 2 tbsp of lard or oil in a pot, add chopped smoked bacon. Stir and cook bacon then set it aside for 2-3 minutes.

Add 3 liters of water and chopped lettuce; boil for 10 minutes. Add rice, salt to the soup and boil until rice cooked too.

Separate in a deep ceramic bowl whisk 2 egg yolks with sour cream and milk. Add slowly about 1 liter of soup to the cream. Add this cream to the 2liter soup and boil for another 5 min stirring it slowly. Add lemon juice or vinegar. This soup is good hot or almost cold in summer.

TRIPE SOUP
(ciorbă de burtă)

4l water, a big piece of trip, a small fatty piece of beef for flavor, salt and 10 peppercorns, 2 carrots, 1 leafstalk of celery, 1 onion, 1 bay leaf, 2 yolks, vinegar and garlic.

Cut the meat and the trip in small pieces and boil it water together with the bay leaf and the salt and pepper. Add the carrots, celery and one whole onion and boil them with the meat. Scramble the yolks with 2 spoons of vinegar and then add them to the soup which is not boiling anymore. Crushed garlic and vinegar may be added in extra amounts as desired.

TURKEY SOUP
(ciorbă de potroace)

2 l water, turkey wings and necks, salt, pepper, the juice of 2 lemons, 2 carrots, 1 leafstalk of celery, 1 onion and 3 spoons of rice.

Boil the turkey wings and necks for approximately 1 hour. Then add the vegetables previously cut in small pieces and the rice and boil until they become tender. Add the salt and pepper. Sour it with the juice of the lemons. Sprinkle some parsley and dill and serve hot.

MEATBALL SOUP
(ciorbă de perişoare)
Sent by Nicoleta Tuns, Sacramento, CA

2 lb ground pork, 1 onion,1 carrots, 1 green pepper, ½ turnip, ½ celery root, 3 eggs, 1 cup of rice, 100 g tomato paste, 200 ml tomato sauce, 2 tbsp Vegeta (soup mix), 1 cup lovage

Chop the vegetables and boil them in 2-3 l water with Vegeta. When the vegetable are boiled, add tomato sauce and let them boil for another 10 minutes. Meatballs are made by mixing the meat with rice, tomato paste, 2 eggs and salt and pepper. Boil the meatballs in soup for about 50-60 min. When the meatballs are done, beat an egg and add to the soup. After a few minutes, add the chopped lovage.

ROMANIAN BEEF SOUP
(supă de văcuţă)

2 lbs beef (cut into thin strips), 2 large onions (chopped), 3 tbsp olive oil, 6 cups beef stock, 6 large potatoes (cubed), salt and pepper (to taste), 3 medium bay leaves, 6 tbsp flour, 2 tbsp vinegar, 2 tbsp cream (optional), 1 tbsp parsley (chopped),

Sauté onion in oil for 10 minutes. Add meat and sauté for 5 minutes. Add broth and simmer for 1 hour. Add potatoes, salt, pepper and bay leaves. Simmer for 20 minutes. Remove Bay Leaves. Remove ½ cup broth from the soup and slowly stir in the flour, add the flour mixture to the soup. Simmer for 3 minutes. Add vinegar, cream and parsley. Stir, remove from heat and serve.

BUCHAREST SOUP
(supă de fasole boabe de Bucureşti)

2 cans beans (any kind), 1/2 pound smoked pork – cubed, 1 tbsp olive oil, 1 tbsp flour, 1 small onion – chopped, 1 tsp paprika, 3 tbsp vinegar, salt and pepper to taste, 6 cups chicken soup

Sauté oil and flour together until become light brown. Add onion and paprika, sauté for 10 minutes. Add pork, sauté for 5 minutes. Add bean and stock and simmer for 10 minutes. Season them with vinegar, salt and pepper.

POTATO SOUP
(supă de cartofi)

1 medium onion, 1 medium carrot, 1 medium parsley root, 5 big potatoes, 5 cups chicken soup, 1/2 pound bacon, cooked, parsley, salt and pepper

Add onion, carrots, parsley root and potatoes to the stock. Simmer for 20 minutes. Add bacon, parsley, salt and pepper. Serve.

CREAMED POTATO SOUP
(cremă de cartofi)

2 large leeks, 1 tbsp olive oil, 1 pound potatoes, 1 can tomato paste, salt and pepper, 4 tbsp sour cream, 4 tbsp parmesan cheese, 4 cups chicken soup

Sauté the leeks in oil for 5 minutes. Add potatoes and stock. Simmer for 20 minutes. While still in the pan, mash coarsely. Mix in tomato paste, salt and pepper. Simmer for 5 minutes. Stir in sour cream and cheese. Serve.

FISH SOUP WITH SAUERKRAUT
(ciorbă de peşte)

2 pounds fish fillet, 2 cups sauerkraut juice, 2 tbsp rice, 1 large onion – chopped, 2 large carrots – chopped, 1 medium parsley root – chopped, 1 small celeriac – chopped, 2 quarts chicken stock, 2 cans tomatoes – chopped, 2 medium jalapeno – chopped, 1/4 cup parsley - chopped

Place fish in sauerkraut juice for 20 minutes. Meanwhile, bring rice, onions, carrots, parsley root, celeriac, tomatoes and jalapenos to a boil in the stock. Simmer for 20 minutes. Add fish and juice. Simmer until fish is done, 5 minutes for white fish or 10 for a meaty fish. Sprinkle with parsley and serve.

BROEDLAEWEND (BEEF SOUP)
(supă de văcuţă)

2 pounds beef - in thin strips, 2 large onion - chopped, 3 tbsp olive oil, 6 cups beef stock, 6 large potato - cubed, salt and pepper - to taste, 3 medium bay leaf, 6 tbsp flour, 2 tbsp vinegar, 2 tbsp cream - optional, 1 tbsp parsley - chopped

Sauté onion in oil for 10 minutes. Add meat and sauté for 5 minutes. Add broth and simmer for 1 hour. Add potatoes, salt, pepper and bay leaves. Simmer for 20 minutes. Remove 1/2 cup broth from the soup and slowly stir in the flour, add the flour mixture to the soup. Simmer for 3 minutes. Add vinegar, cream and parsley. Stir, remove from heat and serve.

POTATO CHEESE SOUP
(supă de cartofi cu brânză)

8 cups potatoes (peeled and cubed), 2 cups chopped onion, 4 cups chopped celery, 2 tsp salt, 6 cups water, 2 cups sour cream, 6 tbsp butter, 1 cup shredded sharp cheddar cheese

Place potatoes, onions, celery, and salt in the 6 cups of water in a large pot. Simmer about 15 minutes until vegetables are tender. Put in blender and puree until chunky. Add sour cream and blend. Return soup to pot and add butter and cheese. Simmer until hot. Do not boil.

CHICKPEA SOUP
(supă de năut)

2 tbsp olive oil, 1 large onion, 2 medium bell pepper, 1 stalk celery, 1 tsp ginger, 2 cloves garlic, 1 medium bay leaf, 1 tbsp paprika, 1/4 tsp cinnamon, 1 pinch saffron, 1 pinch cayenne, 1/4 tsp nutmeg, 6 cups chicken stock, 4 small sweet potato, 2 tsp basil, 2 tsp savory, 1 can tomatoes, 2 tsp honey, 2 cups chickpeas, 8 ounces turnip greens, 1 tsp soy sauce, salt and pepper to taste

Sauté onion in oil for 3 minutes. Add bell peppers and celery. Sauté for 3 minutes. Add ginger, garlic, bay leaf, paprika, cinnamon, saffron, cayenne and nutmeg. Sauté for 1 minute. Add stock, sweet potatoes, basil and savory. Bing to a boil, add tomatoes and honey. Simmer for 10 minutes.

Stir in chickpeas and simmer for 1 minute. Add greens, cover and simmer for 10 minutes. Season with soy sauce, salt and pepper and serve.

**BEEF, PORK, LAMB
POULTRY and FISH**

STUFFED CABBAGE ROLLS I
(sarmale) I
Sent by Ruxandra Vidu, Citrus Heights, CA

1 large soured cabbage or one large cabbage and sour kraut*, 1¾ lb ground meat (mixture of pork and beef is recommended), 4 large onions, 2 tbsp rice, 3 tbsp lard, ½ lb bacon, 5-6 tomatoes or 1 tbsp tomato sauce, salt, pepper, 1 l sour cream

Grind the meat with a raw onion. Place in a bowl and mix with rice, pepper, salt and finely chopped onion slightly fried in two tbsp of lard (or ¼ lb chopped bacon). Mix everything well. Core the cabbage with a sharp thin knife. Place the cabbage in hot water for a couple of minutes. Take it out and carefully remove the cabbage leaves, one by one, so that they do not tear. Cut larger leaves in 2 or 3 and then place a little meat mixture in each cabbage piece and roll in. The smaller the rolls are, the tastier they are. Place a layer of rolls in the pan (take a deep one), then cover with a layer of chopped (julienned) cabbage and bacon, then a layer of thinly sliced tomatoes. Do this layering until all the rolls are made. The last layer must be tomato slices or add tomato sauce. Add a heaping tbsp of lard, pour the borș and let simmer on top of the range for 30 minutes. Then place it in the oven so that the liquid is reduced. Serve with sour cream.

Note: When soured cabbage is not available, sour kraut instead of chopped (julienned) cabbage. Instead of borș, use some of the sauerkraut liquid.

ROMANIAN STYLE MĂMĂLIGĂ
(mămăligă)

2 ½ cups of water, 2 cups corn meal, salt

Bring the water and salt to a boil. Add the cornmeal in small quantities at a time, stirring continuously until you get a pasty, soft paste. Stop pouring the cornmeal (even if you did not use all of it), let it boil, stir every once in a while, up to 10 minutes. Let it cool for a few minutes and serve hot with your favorite dish.

Note: It can also be served cold or it can be put in the oven with cheese for additional taste.

STUFFED CABBAGE ROLLS II
(sarmale) II

500gr ground beef, 500gr ground pork (do not use the lean kind - it will enhance the flavor if you use the regular one), 1 tbsp tomato paste, salt and pepper, 2 tbsp rice uncooked, 1 large or 2 small cabbage, heads, 1 large onion, 250g smoked bacon cut in small pieces, 500 g (1 can) wine sauerkraut, 1 tbsp whole peppers, salt and pepper, 3 tbsp tomato paste, 1 laurel leaf, 1 small smoked pork hock - just for taste, water

Filling: Mix the ground beef, ground pork, tomato paste, salt and pepper (after taste - if you use the cabbage pickled in brine, remember that it can be quite salty!) and rice. Set it on the side at room temperature while you prepare the leaves of the cabbage.

If you use the pickled cabbage, taste it and if it is too salty wash it gently without breaking the leaves. If you use fresh cabbage, you have to add it whole in salted boiling water for 5 -10 minutes (depending how thick the leaves are). Once boiled take each leaf carefully and wrap about 1 - 2spoons of meat. The size of the rolls are really personal preference, in Southern Romania they are usually really small and going North towards Moldavia they get really big in size.

Separately, in a pan fry the bacon together with the onion until translucent (about 2-3min) and add the sauerkraut, salt (again taste the sauerkraut and see how salty it is), pepper, whole pepper and the tomato paste- cook another 3 minutes. Set it aside.

Use a deep crock/pan and spread evenly at the bottom about 1/3 of the sauerkraut mix. On top of it add one layer of rolls. Add another layer of sauerkraut and another layer of rolls. Finish with a layer of sauerkraut. On top add the small pork hock and the laurel and add water in order to barely cover the rolls.

Boil on stove top at med- slow heat approx. 2 hours - 2 ½ hours. We usually take out one roll after 2 hours and try to see if it is cooked thoroughly. Once cooked, take out the laurel and the pork hock and discard. Bake at 375°°F for another 30 minutes until you see a nice crust formed on top of it.

STUFFED CABBAGE LEAVES WITH SAUERKRAUT III
(sarmale) III

1 pound fresh sauerkraut, a 2½-to 3-pound white cabbage, ¼ cup long-grain unconverted white rice, 1½ pounds lean ground pork, 3 cups finely chopped onions, 1 tsp crumbled dried thyme, 1½ tsp salt, 8 tbsp unsalted butter (1 quarter-pound stick), cut into small bits, 1 cup tomato puree, mixed with 1½ cups water, ¼ tsp ground hot red pepper (cayenne), 1 cup finely chopped green pepper, 6 lean bacon slices, 4 tomatoes, cut lengthwise into quarters.

Drain the sauerkraut, wash it under cold running water, and let it soak in cold water for 10 to 20 minutes, depending upon its acidity. A handful at a time, squeeze the sauerkraut until it is dry. Set aside in a bowl. Remove the bruised and tough outer leaves of the cabbage and wash the head under cold running water. Drop it into a large pot of boiling water and cook briskly for about 10 minutes. Remove the cabbage with tongs, but let the water continue to boil. Carefully peel off as many of the outer leaves as you can without tearing them. Then return the cabbage to the boiling water and cook for a few minutes longer. Again peel off the softened outer leaves. Repeat the process until you have detached 12 perfect leaves. Pat them dry with paper towels and set them aside. Bring 1 quart of water to a boil over high heat and stir in the rice. Boil briskly, uncovered, for 10 minutes, or until partially cooked. Drain the rice in a sieve or colander, run cold water over it and set aside. Grind the pork together with ½ cup of the onions through the finest blade of a meat grinder into a deep bowl. Add the rice, thyme and salt, knead vigorously with both hands, then beat with a wooden tbsp until the mixture is smooth and fluffy. Lay the cabbage leaves side by side and, with a small knife, trim the base of each leaf of its tough rib end. Place about ½ cup of the pork filling in the center of each leaf (smaller leaves will take less), and roll up each leaf tightly, tucking in the ends to make a neat oblong package. Preheat the oven to 350. Melt the butter over moderate heat in a heavy 3- to 4-quart casserole. When the foam begins to subside, add the 2½ cups of onions and, stirring frequently, cook for about 5 minutes, or until they are soft and translucent but not brown. Add the puree-and-water mixture and ground red pepper and bring to a boil. Then with a fork stir the contents of the pan into the sauerkraut. Spread about one third of the mixture on the bottom of the casserole. Arrange 6 of the cabbage rolls side by side on top, and then sprinkle them with 1/3 cup of the green pepper. Cover the rolls with half of the remaining sauerkraut mixture, arrange the rest of the cabbage rolls on top and again sprinkle them with another 1/3 cup of the green pepper. Add the rest of the sauerkraut mixture and pour in any liquid remaining in the bowl. Sprinkle with the final 1/3 cup of green pepper and arrange the bacon strips on top. Bring to a boil on top of the stove, cover the casserole tightly, and bake in the middle of the oven for 1 hour. Then arrange the tomato quarters in one layer across the top of the bacon, recover, and bake ½ hour longer. Serve at once, directly from the casserole. Pork *sarmale* is traditionally accompanied by *mămăligă*.

Note: *Sarmale* is characterized in Romania by the acidulated flavor of fermented cabbage leaves. To ferment a cabbage, place it in an 8- to 10-quart casserole and cover with 6 quarts of cold water. Add 1½ cups of salt and bring to a boil. Lower the heat and simmer, partially covered, for 10 minutes. Place a heatproof plate on top of the cabbage to keep it sub-and set it aside for 3 days. Separate the large leaves, drain, and use in place of the fresh cabbage leaves described above.

LAYERED MEAT AND VEGETABLE DISH
(musaca)
Sent by Ruxandra Vidu, Citrus Heights, CA

3 pounds potatoes, 3 tbsp olive oil, 3 medium onion, 1 can tomatoes, 1 pound ground pork, 1 cup beef broth, salt and pepper to taste

Make a potato purée. Separately, sauté potatoes in oil for 10 minutes. Add onions and sauté for 10 more minutes. Transfer half of the potato purée to an ovenproof casserole dish. Layer the meat and tomatoes. Sprinkle with salt and pepper. Add the other half of the tomato purée. Add broth and place in the oven at 350°F for 1 hour.

EGGPLANT MOUSSAKA
(musaca de vinete)
Sent by Ruxandra Vidu, Citrus Heights, CA

5 medium eggplants, 1 ¾ lb ground sirloin, 3 big onions, 3-4 tbsp lard, 3-4 tomatoes, 1 egg, 1 cup sour cream, 1 tbsp flour, 2-3 tbsp broth or water, pepper, salt, chopped parsley, bread crumbs

Cut the eggplants into finger thick slices, salt and let sit for at least 30 minutes to drain their excess liquid. Finely chop an onion, fry slightly with a tbsp of lard, add the ground meat, pepper and salt and let fry lightly. Do not over fry. Squeeze each eggplant slice, dry with a cloth and then fry in lard on both sides. On the bottom of a pan greased with lard and covered with bread crumbs, arrange a layer of thinly sliced tomatoes, then a layer of eggplant, then a layer of ground meat mixture. Do this until all eggplants and all meat are used up. The last layer must be eggplant. Top with thin slices of tomatoes. Bake for half an hour. Then pour sour cream mixed with flour, a tbsp of meat broth and a beaten egg over the moussaka. Spread some chopped parsley over this and bake a little longer until it starts to brown. Serve immediately, cut into pieces.

MOUSSAKA FROM DORNA BUCOVINA
(musaca Dorna Bucovina)

1 large onion diced small, 2 carrots diced small, 200 g butter, 1 cup oil, 1 kilo ground veal, 1/3 cup Tzuica - which is a type of Shlibovitz or you can use Plum Brandy, 1 glass white dry wine (Pinot Grigio or Pinot Griş preferably), salt, pepper, dill - 4 tbsp diced, thyme - 2 tbsp diced, 1.5 kg potatoes peeled and cut in thin slices, 1 cup sour cream, 2 eggs, 250 g cheese (use Cashcaval, similar to Italian Cacciocavallo – or semidry cheese, like a Gouda or Edam) shredded

Sauce: 1 cup sour cream, 1 cup tomato juice, 1 tbsp honey, pepper, salt, 1 tbsp thyme, 1 glass of same wine you used above

Heat ½ cup oil and 100 g butter and fry gently the onion and carrots until translucent. Add the veal until it change color (do not leave it too long, it will dry!). Add the Plum Brandy, the wine and in order: salt, pepper, dill and thyme. Set it on the side.

In the other ½ cup of oil, fry the potatoes (one batch at a time - as you do not want to break them) dry them.

Beat the eggs with sour cream, cheese, salt and pepper

Use a large ovenproof pot and butter it generously. Add one layer of potatoes, one layer meat mix and one layer sour cream mix and repeat as needed. The last layer has to be the sour cream mix! Bake it at 350°Ffor 45min - 1 hour.

Separately boil the tomato juice with wine, honey, thyme, salt and pepper. Reduce it to ½ and turn the heat to low. Add the sour cream and mix. Take it off the stove and serve it warm. Serve it with the same dry wine!

ZUCCHINI MOUSSAKA
(musaca de dovlecei)

5-6 big zucchini, same ground mixture as for eggplant moussaka

Peel the zucchini and cut into finger thick slices. Salt and let sit for 10 minutes, then dry with a cloth, dredge with flour and fry. Continue as for potatoes and meat musaca. Instead of tomatoes or tomato sauce, pour a cup of sour cream. Bake until the liquid is substantially reduced.

EGGPLANT PARMIGIANA
(vinete cu brânză)

2 eggplants (peel, slice 1/4" circles), flour, oil, seasoned salt, 1 lb jar meat flavored Prego, ¼ cup grape jelly, 14 oz can sliced style stewed tomatoes, ½ lb shredded mozzarella cheese, ¼ cup grated parmesan cheese, moisten eggplant (milk) and coat lightly in flour.

Quickly brown slices in hot oil, dusting each side generously with seasoned salt. When fork tender and golden brown transfer to a 9x13x2 pan. Cover loosely with foil and bake at 375ºF about 20 to 25 minutes or until tender.

SAUCE: combine sauce, jelly and tomatoes that have been broken up with a fork. Heat on medium until hot, but do not boil. Spread mozzarella cheese over eggplant, and then add sauce. Top with parmesan cheese and return to oven for 5–10 minutes to melt mozzarella. Serve immediately.

ROMANIAN LIVER
(tochitură)
Sent by Nicolae Vidu, Citrus Heights, CA

75g chicken liver, 50g chicken kidneys, 50g pork fillet, 50g Cabanos sausage, 50g onion, 10g garlic, 50ml tomato sauce, 2g salt, 2g pepper, 20ml white wine

Cook onion until golden brown add the liver, kidneys, pork fillet and sausage cook for another 5 min add the wine and cook for another 10 min add tomato sauce, garlic, salt and pepper and bring to a boil. Serve with mămăligă.

ROMANIAN CHICKEN BREASTS
(piept de pui în stil românesc)

3 chicken breasts, halved, ¼ cup oil, salt and pepper, 1 cup diced beef, 1 cup chopped onion, ¾ cup chopped celery, ½ tsp basil, 2 can (6-oz) tomato paste, 1 can (13.75-oz) chicken broth, 1 t parsley, ½ lb spaghetti

Fry the breasts in oil until they become brown. Season the breasts well with salt and pepper. Remove from pan. To oil, add beef, onion, celery and basil; simmer 5 minutes, stirring. Add paste and broth. Return chicken, cover and simmer 1 hour or until done. Turn occasionally. Add parsley and serve over cooked spaghetti.

HERB BACKED CHICKEN
(pui la cuptor)
Sent by Anitta Pat Zala, Sacramento, CA

Chicken is baked with a coating of bread crumbs Parmesan cheese, oregano, thyme, and other seasoning.

3 pounds chicken parts or bone-in breast halves, ½ cup fine dry bread crumbs, ½ cup Parmesan cheese, 2 tsp dried leaf oregano,

crumbled, ½ tsp dried leaf thyme crumbled, ¼ tsp pepper, ¼ cup melted butter, 1 tbsp cold butter, cut in small pieces

Remove skin from the chicken. Combine bread crumbs, Parmesan cheese, parsley flakes, salt, oregano, thyme and pepper. Dip chicken in melted butter then coat with crumb mixture. Arrange chicken in a single layer, without touching, in a greased a baking dish, do not butter. Bake at 350°F for 1 hour, until chicken is tender.

GRILLED MINCED MEAT I
(mititei)

1 lb ground beef, ¼ cup unseasoned beef stock, 1 tbsp finely chopped garlic, 1 tbsp salt, ¼ tbsp ground rosemary, ½ tbsp chopped fresh parsley, ¼ tbsp freshly ground black pepper, 1 pn of cloves

Put all the ingredients except oil into a bowl. Mix into a semi-smooth mass with your hands. Cover the bowel and refrigerator overnight. Remove the bowel from the refrigerator at least 1 hour before you proceed. Roll the mixture by hand into uniform cylindrical sausages measuring approximately 3 inches long by 1 inch thick. Place the sausages in a single, without touching, layer on a barbecue grate 3 inches above the coals (or lightly oiled grate in a pan 3 inches a preheated 550°F oven broiler. Baste them initially and every 2 minutes thereafter. Cook the sausages till their exterior surfaces become crisp and brown, about 6 to 8 minutes. Transfer to a heated dish and serve promptly.

GRILLED MINCED MEAT II
(mititei)

2 lb ground beef, ½ lb suet, ¼ t baking soda, 2 to 3 cloves garlic, salt and pepper, to taste, juniper berries, as desired, caraway seed, to taste, 2 to 3 t beef broth

Grind the meat together with the suet. Add salt, spices, chopped garlic, meat broth and baking soda and mix everything with your hands for 15 minutes, adding two tbsp of water a little at a time. Keep the bowl with this mixture on ice for 5-6 hours. Just before grilling, take tbsp of the mixture and with wet hands, shape the rolls (they are approx. 2-3 inches long and 1 inch thick). Before placing on the grill, grease them with oil and during grilling baste them with a mixture of meat broth and oil.

GRILLED MINCED MEAT III
(mititei)

3 lb meat, 1-1½ lb beef and 1-1½ lb lamb or veal, ½ t baking soda, ½ cup meat stock or bouillon, garlic clove, or more, taste, salt and pepper, to taste.

Mash garlic with a bit of salt and stock. Strain over meat with the other ingredients. Add teaspoon of summer savory chopped and roll as small sausage. Broil over charcoal. Mix day before so flavors will blend. Add bread crumbs if meat is fatty.

GRILLED MINCED MEAT IV
(mititei)

2 pounds lean ground beef, preferably neck, ground together with ¼ pound fresh beef kidney suet, 2 tsp finely chopped garlic, ½ tsp ground allspice, ¼ tsp ground cloves, ¼ tsp crumbled dried thyme, 1½ tsp salt, 1/8 tsp freshly ground black pepper, ½ cup beef stock, fresh or canned, vegetable oil

Combine the beef and suet with the garlic, allspice, cloves, thyme, salt and pepper in a deep bowl. Knead vigorously with both hands until the ingredients are well blended. Then pour in the stock and beat with a wooden tbsp until the mixture is smooth and fluffy. Taste for seasoning. Divide the mixture into 18 equal portions and roll each one into a cylinder about 3½ inches long and 1 inch thick, moistening your hands with cold water as you proceed. Preheat the broiler to its highest setting. Brush the rack of a broiler pan lightly with oil and arrange the sausages side by side on the rack. Broil them about 3 inches from the heat for about 8 minutes, turning them with a spatula or tongs every few minutes until they are crisp and brown on all sides.

Serve the *mititei* at once from a heated platter. Traditionally, the sausages are accompanied by peppers in oil and sour dill pickles.

TONGUE WITH SAUCE
(mâncare de limbă)
Sent by Gabriela Lăzureanu

1 beef tongue, 1 carrot, 1 root parsley, ½ root celery, 1 onion, 100 ml wine, 50 ml tomato juice, 100 g olives, 1 bay leaf, 25 g flour, 50 ml oil, 20 g sugar, salt and pepper to taste

Boil the tongue in the water for 1-1.5 hours, then peel the skin while is still hot (it is easier). Cut the onion, carrot, parsley and celery and fry them in oil, then pour ½ l from the soup that the tongue was boiling in, and boil them for 45 more min. Then drain out the soup and mash the vegetables. Mix the flour with wine and tomato juice and add it to the soup and mashed vegetables. Cut the tongue and add it, too. Caramelize the sugar, add 3 spoons of water and mix it with the sauce. Add salt and put it in the oven for 20 min.

CREAMY CHICKEN ASPARAGUS CASSEROLE
(piept de pui cu sparanghel)
Sent by Anitta Pat Zala, Sacramento, CA

1 tsp unsalted butter, 4 skinless, boneless chicken breast halves, 1 onion, finely diced, 1 pound fresh asparagus, trimmed and cut into 2 ½ inch pieces, 1 tsp dried tarragon, 1 ½ cups cream of chicken soup, ¼ cup sliced almonds, 1 1/3 cups water, 2/3 cup uncooked long grain white rice

Preheat oven to 375°F (190°C). Melt the butter in an ovenproof skillet over medium-high heat, and brown the chicken breasts about 3 minutes on each side. Remove chicken from the skillet, and set aside. Add the onion and asparagus to the skillet; cook for 4 to 5 minutes, or until the onions are tender. Arrange the chicken breasts over the onions and asparagus, and season with tarragon. Pour soup over chicken. Cover the skillet, and bake for 15 minutes in the preheated oven. Remove cover, sprinkle with almonds, and bake for another 5 minutes. Meanwhile, combine water and rice in a saucepan. Bring to a boil. Reduce heat, cover, and simmer for 20 minutes. Serve chicken and asparagus over rice. Tarragon adds a delicate note to this almond-topped casserole.

ZUCCHINI FILLED WITH MEAT
(dovlecei umpluţi cu carne)

6 medium sized zucchini, 14 oz ground meat, 2-3 onions, 2 tbsp rice, chopped parsley and dill, salt, pepper, 2 tbsp lard;

Sauce: 1 lb tomatoes, ½ onions, 1 tsp flour, salt, chopped parsley, 1 tbsp lard, sour cream

Remove the zucchini peel, halve lengthwise and hollow out. Prepare the ground meat mixture as for peppers filled with meat. Fill the zucchini, dredge with flour and fry in lard.

Place in a pan and cover with a sauce prepared as for the peppers filled with meat. Simmer on top of the range, or better yet, in the oven. Serve with sour cream.

EGGPLANTS STUFFED WITH MEAT
(vinete umplute cu carne)

6 small eggplants, 14 oz ground sirloin, 2 onions, 3 tbsp lard, 1 lb parsley and dill, salt, pepper

Remove the stems of the eggplants. Then set to boil for 5-6 minutes in salt water. Remove and keep in cold water until cooled off. Drain well and remove the insides. Do not throw away the insides, but keep in the colander.

To the ground meat add finely chopped raw or fried Onion, 2 tbsp of lard, salt, pepper, chopped parsley and dill and the eggplants' insides.

Mix well and fill the eggplant shells with this mixture. Fry some finely chopped onion with a tbsp of lard, add flour, let it turn yellow, then pour the boiled and strained tomatoes over it.

Add salt and sugar. Place the eggplants in this sauce, spread some chopped parsley and dill and let simmer, covered, until the liquid is reduced somewhat.

STUFFED GREEN PEPPERS
(ardei umpluţi)
Sent by Lucia Tudosa, Austin, TX

12 green (larges) peppers, ½ cup rice, 6 tbsp olive oil, ½ cup chopped onion, salt according with your taste, 6 cups ground beef, 2 eggs, black pepper, dill (chopped).

Cut the tops off peppers and remove the seeds and the ribs do not be hot. Mix all the ingredients well, add 3 tbsp water with 3 tbsp tomato sauce, and mix well, and then fill each green pepper. Do not overstuff peppers. Place peppers in a large pot in a single layer if is possible. Do a sauce from 3 tbsp tomato sauce, 5 tbsp water, 3 tbsp sour cream and 3 tbsp olive oil. Pour this sauce over the stuffed peppers .Cover the pot and cook over a low heat.

PEPPERS FILLED WITH MEAT
(ardei umpluţi cu carne)

12 medium peppers, 1 ¾ lb ground meat, 2 onions, 2 tbsp rice, 1 tbsp, chopped parsley and dill, salt, pepper, 2 tomatoes;

Sauce: 1 lb tomatoes, ½ onion, 1 tsp sugar, ½ tsp flour, salt, chopped parsley, 1 tbsp lard, sour cream

Wash the peppers, dry, core and remove the seeds. Mix the meat with two finely chopped raw or fried onions, a tbsp of lard, rice, chopped parsley and dill, pepper and salt.

Mix everything well and use this mixture to fill the peppers. Put one tomato slice as a lid on each pepper. Arrange in a pan and pour the following sauce on top. Fry the finely chopped onion and flour in lard until golden; add tomato sauce (from boiled and strained tomatoes). Add sugar and salt.

If the sauce does not cover the peppers add some water. Spread some chopped parsley, set to boil for a little while then place in the oven to bake until done. Serve with sour cream.

ROMANIAN PORK CHOPS WITH BEER SAUCE
(cotlete de porc cu bere)

1/4 cup pork fat or drippings, 2 to 3 onions, finely sliced, 3 lb tart apples, peeled and sliced, 1 to 2 clove garlic chopped, 4 thick pork chops, salt and pepper to taste

Beer Sauce: 2 tbsp butter, 2 tbsp flour, 1 cup mild beer, salt, cayenne pepper, finely chopped parsley or chives, 1 tbsp brown sugar

Heat the fat in a pan, spread with half the onions, and add the apples, the remaining onion and garlic. Cook gently on top of the stove until the onions are soft and the apples cooked.

In the meantime prepare the chops. With a small knife score them in two or three places around the edges to prevent curling and cook them quickly in a dry pan or under the broiler until brown on both sides.

When the chops are brown, place them on top of the simmering onions and apples. Sprinkle with salt and pepper, cover and cook over a low heat until the chops are tender (about 30 minutes). Meanwhile prepare the sauce.

Melt the butter, add the flour, stir well to make a roux, and then gradually add the beer to make a thick sauce. Add salt and pepper, parsley or chives, and sugar; stir well.

Serve the chops with the onion and apple mixture on a hot dish; and serve the beer sauce either separately or poured over the chops.

ROMANIAN CHICKEN WITH APRICOTS
(mâncare de pui cu caise)

3 lb chicken (cut into 4), oil for frying, 1 ¼ tbsp flour, 2 cups chicken stock, 1 onion (minced, 1 to 2 tsp brown sugar, salt and pepper, 1 lb fresh apricots.

Heat just enough oil in a large pan to fry and brown the chicken pieces. Remove them from the pan, but keep hot. Pour off all but about 1 tbsp of the oil, add the flour to the pan, stirring all the time, and, still stirring, and gradually add the stock. When the sauce has thickened, add the onion and continue cooking until it has almost disappeared. Return the chicken pieces to the pan, add the sugar, salt, pepper and apricots, cover and cook gently until the chicken is tender.

ROMANIAN RAGOUT OF MUSHROOMS
(ghiveci de ciuperci)

5 bacon slices, chopped, 1 bunch of scallions, trimmed and chopped, chopped parsley, salt and pepper, 2 lb whole mushrooms, 1 tbsp flour, 1 cup sour cream or yogurt

Heat a shallow pan, add the bacon and fry it until the fat runs freely. Add the scallions, parsley, salt and pepper. Cover and simmer for a few minutes, then add the whole mushrooms, cover again and continue simmering for 10 minutes.

Beat the flour into the sour cream and gradually pour this mixture over the mushrooms. Stir gently and cook until the mushrooms are tender.

It's usually served as a main dish, often with the cornmeal staple, *mămăligă*. All types of mushroom can be used and if scallions are not available, use coarsely chopped onion.

MUSHROOM AND GIZZARD DISH
(mâncarică de pipote cu ciuperci)
Sent by Doina Brownell, West Sacramento, CA

2 lbs chicken gizzard, 2 cans of mushrooms or 2 lbs fresh mushrooms, salt, pepper, 1 tbsp Vegeta (soup mix), ½ lbs sour cream, 1 tbsp oil, parsley

Sauté chopped mushrooms, add salt. Add the chicken gizzard and add water to cover mushrooms. Boil in a covered pan until the water decreased and the chicken gizzard is well done. Add Vegeta, salt, pepper, and parsley. Serve it with sour cream over backed potatoes.

CHICKEN PAPRIKAS
(papricaş de pui)
Sent by Katica Goț, Oliverhurst, CA

1 cut-up frying chicken, 2 tbsp paprika, 2 tbsp shortening (lard or oil), 1 small onion, 1 garlic clove, salt, black pepper, 1 tbsp sour cream, 1 tbsp flour

In a large skillet heat shortening and add chopped onion and garlic. Cook just until transparent. Add pieces off chicken and paprika. Cook over medium heat, stirring occasionally for 8-10 min. Add water or chicken broth until chicken is covered. Cook for about half an hour stirring occasionally until chicken is tender. Separate, in a small bowl combine flower, milk (1 cup) and sour cream, and then whisk it until smooth. Add paprika to the chicken and stir gently. Cook for another 2-3 min. Serve with noodles or mashed potato.

ROMANIAN GARLIC SKIRT STEAK
(friptură cu usturoi)

1 ½ lbs skirt steaks, pepper, fresh ground, to taste, 1 pinch kosher salt, 2 garlic cloves, minced, 1 tbsp vegetable oil, 1 onion, sliced, salt and pepper, ½ tsp paprika.

Preheat your broiler to high. Season with pepper and broil steak for 3-5 minutes per side. This can be tough if it is overcooked, cut into slices across the grain. Meanwhile, heat the oil in a fry pan and add onion slices, garlic, and paprika, salt and pepper. Sauté until slightly browned on both sides. Serve onions over steak. (Optional - smear some deli mustard on steak before broiling).

BRAISED DUCK WITH CABBAGE
(rață pe varză)

1 pound white cabbage, ¼ pound lean bacon, cut into ¼-inch dice, 5-pound duck, cut into 8 serving pieces, ¼ cup finely chopped fresh, fennel, or substitute ½ tsp powdered fennel, 2 tbsp finely chopped shallots, or substitute 2 tbsp finely chopped scallions, white parts only, ½ tsp finely chopped garlic, ½ tsp, crumbled dried thyme, ¼ tsp crumbled dried sage, ¼ tsp crumbled dried marjoram, 1½ cups sauerkraut juice

Remove the tough outer leaves of the cabbage, wash the head under cold running water, and cut it into quarters. Shred the cabbage by cutting out the core, then slicing the quarters crosswise in 1/8-inch-wide strips. In a heavy 4- to 6-quart casserole, fry the bacon over moderate heat, stirring frequently until the bits are brown and crisp and have rendered most of their fat. With a slotted spoon, transfer the bacon bits to paper towels to drain. Pour all but 2 tbsp of the fat remaining in the casserole into a cup or bowl and set aside. With paper towels pat the pieces of duck completely dry. Then brown them in the casserole, 3 or 4 at a time, turning them frequently with tongs. As they brown, transfer the pieces of duck to a plate. Preheat the oven to 425. Discard all the fat in the casserole and in its place add the reserved bacon fat. Drop in the shredded cabbage, fennel, shallots or scallions, garlic, thyme, sage and marjoram. Stirring frequently, cook uncovered over moderate heat until the cabbage is limp but not brown. Add the sauerkraut juice and stir until it comes to a boil.

Arrange the pieces of duck on top of the cabbage, pour in the liquid that has accumulated around them, and scatter the reserved bacon bits over the top. Cover the casserole tightly and braise in the lowest part of the oven for 15 minutes. Lower the heat to 325°F and continue to braise for about 1 hour longer or until the duck is tender. With a long tbsp skim off and discard all the surface fat and serve the duck and cabbage directly from the casserole. Or mound the cabbage on a deep heated platter and arrange the duck pieces over or around it.

ROMANIAN DUCK WITH CABBAGE
(rață pe varză)

4 lb duck, salt and paprika, 2/3 cup butter or other cooking fat, 1 firm heat white cabbage, 6 to 8 peppercorns, 1 tbsp tomato puree

Rub the duck liberally inside and out with salt, paprika and half the butter. Place the duck, breast up, on a rack in a roasting pan, and cook uncovered in a preheated moderate oven 350°F for 30 minutes. Prick the skin from time to time to release the fat.

While the duck is cooking, wash and shred the cabbage, discarding any old leaves and hard stalk. Melt the remaining butter in a saucepan and add the cabbage, turning it from time to time until it browns. Add salt and peppercorns. Dilute the tomato puree with a little water or, better still, stock and add this to the cabbage. Leave to cook over a moderate heat until the cabbage is soft.

Take the duck from the oven and out of the roasting pan. Remove the rack and pour off excess fat.

Spread the cabbage on the bottom of the pan, place the duck on top, return the pan to the oven and continue roasting until the duck is tender about another hour, or longer if a larger duck is used.

FRESH VEGETABLE STEW WITH VEAL AND GRAPES
(ghiveci national)

¾ pound fresh pork fat, cut into small dice, or 8 tbsp melted butter combined with 4 tbsp vegetable oil, 3 pounds boneless breast of veal, cut into 1-inch chunks, 2 tbsp salt, freshly ground black pepper, ½ cup flour, 3 medium-sized onions, peeled and cut into ¼-inch-thick slices, 2 tsp coarsely chopped garlic, 4 cups freshly made beef stock, or substitute 2 cups condensed canned

beef stock combined with 2 cups cold water, 2 tbsp tomato paste, 1 small eggplant (about ¾ to 1 pound), peeled, 6 medium-sized boiling potatoes (about 2 pounds), peeled, ½ small white cabbage (about ½ pound), trimmed and cored, 1 pound acorn squash, peeled and seeded, 3 medium-sized carrots (about ½ pound), peeled, 1 large green bell pepper, stemmed, deribbed and seeded, 1 medium-sized celery root (celeriac), about ½ pound, peeled, 1 small cauliflower (about ¾ to 1 pound), trimmed and washed, ¼ pound green string beans, trimmed, and cut in half lengthwise, 1 cup dry red wine, 2 tsp finely chopped parsley, ½ tsp crumbled dried, marjoram, ½ tsp crumbled dried thyme, 4 medium-sized firm ripe tomatoes, peeled, cut into quarters and seeded (see bigos), ¼ pound seedless green grapes, washed, ¼ cup fresh green peas, shelled.

Preheat the oven to 350°. In a heavy 12-inch skillet, fry the pork fat (you are using it) over moderate heat, stirring frequently, until it is crisp, delicately browned, and has rendered all its fat. Remove the crisp bits with a slotted tablespoon and discard them. Pour the rendered fat into a measuring cup; there should be about ¾ cup. Pour 4 tbsp of the fat back into the skillet and set aside off the heat. Pat the chunks of veal completely dry. Season them on all sides with 1 teaspoon of the salt and a liberal grinding of pepper. Dip them in the flour and, when they are evenly coated, shake vigorously to recover the excess flour. Heat the pork fat in the skillet over high heat until a drop of water flicked into it splutters and evaporates instantly. Or, pour 4 tbsp of the butter-and-oil mixture into a 12-inch skillet and place over high heat until the foam begins to subside. Brown the veal chunks the hot fat, 7 or 8 at a time, turning them frequently with tongs or a spatula. Add more fat or butter and oil to the skillet as needed. As the veal browns, transfer the chunks to a heavy 6-to8-quarts casserole. Add the onion slices and garlic to the fat remaining in the skillet and, stirring frequently, cook for about 5 minutes, until they are soft and translucent. With a slotted tablespoon transfer the onions and garlic to the casserole and spread them over the veal. Pour off all the fat from the skillet and in its place add 1 cup of the stock (or the stock-and-water mixture) and the tomato paste. Stirring constantly, bring to a boil over high heat. Pour the mixture into the casserole. Cut the eggplant, potatoes, cabbage and squash into 1½-inch cubes, and cut the carrots, green pepper and celery root into strips about 2 inches long and ¼ inch wide. Separate the cauliflower into small flowerets. Put 6 tbsp of pork fat or butter and oil in the skillet and place it over moderate heat. Adding them to the skillet in separate batches and frying each batch just long enough to color the pieces lightly and evenly, fry the eggplant, potatoes, carrots, string beans, green pepper, celery root, squash, cauliflower and cabbage. As they brown, transfer the vegetables to the casserole with a slotted spoon, arranging each one in a separate layer. Add more fat to the skillet when necessary. Pour off any fat remaining in the skillet, then add the remaining 3 cups of stock (or stock and water), the wine, parsley, marjoram, thyme and remaining salt. Bring to a boil over high heat, scraping in any browned particles clinging to the bottom and sides of the skillet. Pour the mixture down the sides of the casserole. Bring to a boil over high heat, then cover tightly and bake in the middle of the oven for 45 minutes. Add the tomatoes, grapes and peas, and bake covered for 15 minutes longer. Taste for seasoning, then serve directly from the casserole.

Note: Although the Romanians traditionally use a great variety of colorful vegetables in their national stew, you may, if you wish, eliminate some, increasing the quantity of others. For example, you may omit the acorn squash or cauliflower and double the amount of potatoes or eggplant.

MIXED VEGETABLES AND VEAL STEW
(ghiveci)

1/3 cup all-purpose flour, 2½ tsp salt, ¼ tsp freshly ground black pepper, 2 pounds boneless veal shoulder, cut into 1-inch cubes, 2½ tbsp butter, ¼ cup olive oil, 2 medium yellow onions, peeled and sliced, 3 cloves garlic, peeled and finely chopped, 1 cup Beef Stock or use canned, 1 cup dry red wine, 3 tbsp finely chopped parsley, 2 tbsp tomato paste, 1 cup sliced carrots, 2 cups coarsely chopped tomatoes, fresh or canned, 1½ cups green bell pepper, cored, seeded, and cut into ¼-inch strips, 4 cups cubed eggplant (½-inch cubes), 2 cups cubed zucchini (½-inch cubes), 2 cups cleaned and thinly sliced leeks (white parts only), 2 cups peeled and chopped turnips, 2 cups peeled and chopped celery root, 2 cups peeled and chopped parsnips, 3 cups thinly sliced green cabbage, 1 cup trimmed and julienned string beans, ½ cup seedless green grapes, ½ tsp dried marjoram, ½ tsp dried thyme, whole, Salt and freshly ground pepper to taste.

Garnish: plain yogurt or sour cream

In a bowl combine the flour, ½ teaspoon of the salt and ½ teaspoon of the pepper, or more to taste. Add the veal and toss until the cubes are completely coated. Remove the meat from the flour, sifting it through your hands to shake off the excess flour. Sauté the veal in the butter and oil in an 8- to 10-quart Dutch oven over medium-high heat, stirring frequently, until brown on all sides, about 5 minutes. Add the onions and garlic and cook, stirring frequently, until the onions are soft, about 5 minutes. Add all of the remaining ingredients, except the yogurt or sour cream, and stir until well mixed. Cook covered, over high heat until the liquid boils. Season them with salt and pepper to taste. Place in a preheated 350°F oven. Bake stirring several times during cooking, until the vegetables are very tender, about 1 hour. Serve hot. Garnish each serving with yogurt or sour cream.

LOIN OF PORK WITH FENNEL
(ruladă de porc cu fenel)
Sent by Dorel Andriuca, Roseville, CA

1 tbsp unsalted butter, 2 cups sliced yellow onions (2 onions), 2 cups sliced fennel (1 large bulb), salt, freshly ground black pepper, 2 tsp minced garlic (2 large cloves), 1 tbsp minced fresh thyme leaves, ¼ cup white wine, 3 cups fresh bread crumbs, olive oil, 1 (3 ½ lb) loin of pork, butterfiled.

For the stuffing, heat 1 tbsp of olive oil and the butter in a large (12-inch) sauté pan. Add the onions and fennel with 1 teaspoon salt and ½ teaspoon pepper. Cook over low to medium-low heat for 15 minutes, stirring occasionally, until the onions and fennel are tender and lightly browned. Add the garlic and thyme and cook for 1 more minute. Add the wine and cook for another minute, deglazing the pan. Cool slightly. Add the bread crumbs and 1 teaspoon of salt to the stuffing mixture. Lay the pork on a board with the fat side down, and sprinkle with salt and pepper. Spread the stuffing evenly on the pork and roll up lengthwise, ending with the fat on the top of the roll. Tie with kitchen string, rub with olive oil, and sprinkle liberally with salt and pepper.

Preheat the oven to 425 °F. Place the rolled pork loin on a baking rack on a sheet pan and roast for 30 minutes. Lower the heat to 350°Fand roast for another 20 to 30 minutes, until the interior of the pork is 137F. (If the thermometer hits stuffing rather than pork, it will register a higher temperature, so test the meat in several places.) Remove from the oven and cover tightly with aluminum foil. Allow to rest for 15 minutes. Remove the strings, slice thickly, and serve.

GROUND-PORK CASSEROLE WITH NOODLES AND CHEESE
(musaca cu tăiţei)

4 tbsp butter, softened, 2 slices homemade-type white bread with crusts removed, cut ½ inch thick and torn into small pieces, ½ cup milk, 2 tbsp salt, 1 pound fine egg noodles, 6 eggs, 2 pounds lean ground pork, 2 tbsp finely chopped leeks, white part only, thoroughly washed to rid them of all sand, 2 tbsp finely chopped fresh parsley, 2 tbsp finely cut fresh fennel leaves or ¼ tsp powdered fennel, Freshly ground black pepper, 6 tbsp butter, cut into ¼-inch bits, ½ cup heavy cream, ¼ cup finely grated Kashkaval cheese, or substitute sweet Munster or Provolone.

Preheat the oven to 400 ºF. With a pastry brush, spread the softened butter evenly over the bottom and sides of a heavy 3-quart casserole. Combine the bread bits and milk in a bowl and set aside. Bring 4 quarts of water to a boil in a 6- to 8-quart pot. Add 1 tbsp salt, drop in the noodles, and stir with a fork to prevent the strands from sticking to one another or to the bottom and sides of the pot. Stirring occasionally, boil briskly, uncovered, for 6 to 8 minutes, or until the noodles are tender but still slightly resistant to the bite. Drain the noodles in a large colander, lifting the strands with two forks to make certain all the water drains off. Then, in a deep bowl, beat 4 of the eggs and 2 teaspoons of salt with a whisk or a rotary beater for 1 to 2 minutes. Add the noodles and turn them about with a fork until they are evenly coated. Set aside. Meanwhile, combine the pork, the bread and milk, the leeks, parsley, fennel, 1 teaspoon of salt and a few grin dings of pepper in a large bowl. Knead vigorously with both hands, and then beat with a wooden tablespoon until the mixture is smooth and fluffy. To assemble the musaca, spread about one third of the noodles evenly in the bottom of the buttered casserole. Spread with a tablespoon half of the meat mixture over the noodles, smoothing the top with a spatula. Sprinkle with 2 tablespoons of the butter bits, and then add one half of the remaining noodles. Cover the noodles with the rest of the meat mixture, scatter 2 tablespoons of butter bits over it, and add the remaining noodles. Top with the rest of the butter bits, and then cover the casserole with its lid. Bake in the middle of the oven for 30 minutes. Beat the remaining 2 eggs, the heavy cream and grated cheese together with a whisk or fork, and when they are well mixed pour them evenly over the musaca. Cover again and bake for 1 hour longer, removing the cover for the final 30 minutes to allow the top to brown. To unmold and serve the musaca, run a thin knife all around the sides of the casserole. Place an inverted serving plate over the top and, grasping plate and casserole together firmly, carefully turn them over. The musaca should slide out easily. Serve at once.

GROUND-VEAL CASSEROLE WITH POTATOES
(musaca cu cartofi)

6 tbsp butter, softened, 2 tbsp soft fresh crumbs, made from homemade-type white bread, pulverized in a blender or finely shredded with a fork, 8 medium-sized boiling potatoes (about 2½ pounds), 1 cup finely chopped onions, 1 pound lean ground veal, 2 tbsp flour, ¼ cup dry white wine, ¼ cup finely chopped fresh parsley, 2 tbsp finely cut fresh fennel eaves, ¼ tsp crumbled dried thyme, 1 tsp salt, ½ tsp freshly ground black pepper, 2 egg yolks, lightly beaten, plus 2 eggs, 2 tbsp butter, cut into ¼-inch bits, 1 cup heavy cream.

With a pastry brush, spread 2 tbsp of the softened butter over the bottom and sides of a 2-quart casserole 3 inches deep. Add the bread crumbs and tip the casserole from side to side to spread them evenly. Set aside. With a small, sharp knife or swivel-bladed vegetable purer, peel the potatoes, dropping them into cold water as you proceed. Then, cut the potatoes into ¼-inch-thick slices and return them to the water. In a heavy 10- to 12-inch skillet, heat 2 tbsp of butter over moderate heat. When the foam begins to subside, pat a handful of potatoes completely dry with paper towels and drop them into the skillet. Turn them frequently with a spatula, fry the potatoes for 4 or 5 minutes, until they are golden brown on both sides. As they brown, transfer the slices to paper towels to drain while you dry and fry the remaining potatoes, adding more butter to the skillet when necessary. When the potatoes are browned, add 2 more tbsp of butter to the skillet and drop in the onions. Stirring frequently, cook for about 5 minutes, or until they are soft and translucent but not brown. Add the veal and, mashing it frequently with the back of a tbsp to break up any lumps, cook until no trace of pink remains. Stir in the flour and cook for a minute or two, then remove from the heat and beat in the wine, parsley, fennel, thyme, salt and pepper. Let the mixture cool for about 5 minutes and stir in the egg yolks one at a time, stirring until no trace of yolk is visible. Taste for seasoning. Preheat the oven to 400°F. Assemble the casserole in the following fashion: spread about one third of the potato slices on the bottom of the casserole, overlapping them neatly. Spread half the meat mixture evenly over the potatoes, add another layer of potato slices, and then add the rest of the meat, spreading it out as before. Cover with the remaining potato slices and scatter the 2 tbsp of butter bits on top. Bake covered in the middle of the oven for 30 minutes. Then beat the 2 eggs and the cream together with a whisk or a rotary beater and pour evenly over the musaca. Bake uncovered for 30 minutes longer, or until the top is golden brown. Serve at once, directly from the casserole.

ROMANIAN VEGETABLE STEW
(ghiveci românesc)

2 lbs eggplants, 2 ¼ lbs fresh ripe tomatoes, 2 tbsp fresh parsley, 2 tbsp fresh dill, 2 onions, 3 garlic cloves, 3/4 lb leek, white part only, 3 scallions, 1 green pepper, 5 tbsp olive oil, 2 bay leaves, 1 tbsp tomato paste, 1 tbsp sugar, 2 slices lemon zest.

Preheat the oven to 325°F. Cut the eggplant into large dice, sprinkle lightly with salt and set aside for at least half an hour, then rinse and squeeze out excess moisture. Meanwhile, plunge the tomatoes into boiling water, then rapidly into cold. Skin and chop them. Roughly chop the fresh herbs, onion, and garlic, white of leek, scallions and green pepper. Soften the chopped onion and garlic in half the oil in a heavy-bottomed pan. Add the eggplant, leeks, green pepper, dill and half the parsley, and cook for a few minutes, stirring constantly. Add the bay leaves, tomatoes, lemon zest, tomato paste and sugar and stir again. Pour over the remaining oil and transfer, if necessary, to an ovenproof casserole dish with a tight-fitting lid. Cook in the oven, tightly covered, for 1 ½ hours or until they perfectly tender. This magnificent vegetable mixture can be served hot, garnished with the remaining herbs, but it shows off its flavors best when cold. Try it with cold chicken or turkey, or warm cornbread.

LINGUINI WITH SHRIMP AND LEMON OIL
(paste cu creveți si lămâie)
Sent by Dorel Andriuca, Roseville, CA

1 (8 ounce) package linguine pasta, 1 tbsp extra virgin olive oil, 6 cloves garlic, minced, 2 shallots, 1 lemon, juiced, ½ tsp lemon zest,

salt to taste, 2 tsp freshly ground black pepper, 1 pound fresh shrimp, peeled and deveined, ¼ cup butter, 3 tbsp chopped fresh parsley, 1 tbsp chopped fresh basil

Bring a large pot of lightly salted water to a boil. Add linguine, and cook for 9 to 13 minutes or until al dente; drain.

Heat oil in a large saucepan over medium heat, then sauté the shallots and garlic about 1 minute. Mix in lemon juice, lemon zest, salt, and pepper. Reduce heat, and simmer until liquid is reduced by about 1/2. Mix shrimp, butter, parsley, and basil into the saucepan. Cook 2 to 3 minutes, until shrimp is opaque. Stir in the cooked linguine, and continue cooking 2 minutes, until well coated.

CHICKEN RAGOUT
(ostropel de pui)
Sent by Mihaela Iosif, Sacramento, CA

6-8 chicken thighs and /or drumsticks, 1 cup oil, 1 clove garlic, 3 cups crushed tomatoes, parley, salt to taste

In a large saucepan, fry the chicken. Take them out. Add 1 crushed clove of garlic to the boiling oil. Then, add tomatoes and sauté. Add 1 cup water and let boil 10-15 minutes. Add back the chicken and let boil for 15 more minutes. If water level drops, add more water to maintain level. At the end, turn off fire and sprinkle parsley on top.

TOCHITURA
(tochitură)
Sent by Mihaela Iosif, Sacramento, CA

½ lb pork liver, ½ lb pork kidneys, ½ lb pork heart, ½ lb pork tongue, ½ lb pork meat, 1 cup oil, 2-3 onions, 3 cups crushed tomatoes, ½ tbsp salt

Cut the meat in cubs of 1 in3. Boil all the meat in water with salt. Add the meat in this order: kidney, heart, tongue, meat and leaver, at about 5 minutes intervals. In a separate saucepan, sauté the onion till golden-brown. Add boiled meats. Then add 1 ½ water (or broth) and 3 cups of chopped tomatoes. Let it boil till water level drops almost completely. Serve with mămăligă.

ROMANIAN CHICKEN BREASTS
(piept de pui)

3 whole chicken breasts, halved, ¼ cup oil, salt and pepper, to taste, 1 cup diced beef, 1 cup onion, chopped, 3/4 cup celery, chopped, ½ tsp basil, 2 (6 ounce) cans tomato paste, 1 (13 ¾ ounce) can chicken broth, 1 tbsp parsley, ½ lb spaghetti,

Brown the chicken breasts in oil. Season them well with salt and pepper. Remove from pan. To oil, add beef, onion, celery and basil; simmer 5 minutes, stirring. Add tomato paste and broth. Return chicken, cover and simmer 1 hour or until done. Turn occasionally. Add parsley and serve over cooked spaghetti.

BEEF TOCANITA
(tocăniţă)
Sent by Liana Ciontoş, Roseville, CA

1 lb beef meat (stew meat) washed and dried in a paper towel, salt, pepper, paprika, 3 tbsp flour

Condiment the meet with salt, pepper and paprika, roll the meat in flour. In a deep pan heat 1/3 oil and fry the meat for 3-4 minutes, add 4 cups water and bring that to slow boiling. When the meat is tender, add 1/2 onion cut in thin slices, 1/2 red pepper. Let it boil for about 15 minutes, and if sour cream is to your liking add that before turning off the heat, and served right the way with mashed potatoes or any kind of pasta.

ROMANIAN STEW
(tocăniţă moldovenească)
Sent by George Muntean Sr., Muntean Bistro, Sacramento, CA

1/2 cup vegetable oil, 1 lb onion, chopped, 2 lb boneless chicken thigh meat, 8 ribs celery, cut small chunks, 2 carrots cut small chunks, 1 tbsp Hungarian paprika, ½ tbsp black pepper, ½ tbsp chopped parsley, ¼ tbsp salt, 1 ½ cups of brown rice, ¼ cup of chicken base.

Take the oil and put it in a saucepan and let it warm for 10 minutes. Add the chopped onion and simmer for 10 - 15 minutes. Add chopped celery and carrots, parsley, black pepper, salt and simmer for other 10 minutes.

Add the chicken meat and paprika for other 10 minutes. Take medium saucepan put the chicken base and add 2 cups of hot water and mix it than pour the mix over the meat. Let it cook until it comes to a boil and then add brown rice and simmer until rice is cook the way you want. This will be Romanian Stew. If you want it to be more soupee add more water the way you want.

MOLDAVIAN STEW
(tocăniţă moldovenească)

home made pork sausages, smoked smaller sausages, beef and chicken meat, onion and garlic, tomato sauce, water, salt and pepper

Fry the ingredients separately. I fried the sausages completely and the meat 80-90%. As a sign of the pork sausages quality they left a very clean sauce which I then used partially to cook the onion and the eggs.

In the same time prepare a traditional "*mămăligă*" (polenta) made of corn flour and water. Sometimes the stew is served with extremely hot mămăligă but I do not like extremely hot dishes so I prepare the mămăligă from time so it has the time to cool down.

Brown the onion and when ready add salt, pepper, tomato sauce, water and add all the meat ingredients fried before. The sauce must cover the ingredients. Then boil everything for 10 minutes on a low flame such that all the smells and tastes can mix together for the delicious result.

Then, in some traditional clay dishes add the mămăligă, then the stew and on the top add a fried egg for each dish and enjoy.

RICE, COUNTRY STYLE
(pilaf tărănesc)
Sent by Bianca Iosif, Sacramento CA

½ **cup olive oil, 2 onions, 2 green peppers, 1 red pepper, 1 ½ cups rice, 4 cups water, 2 cups crushed tomatoes, 1 tsp salt, pepper to taste**

Thinly slice onions and peppers. In a large saucepan, heat oil and add onions and peppers. Cook, stirring occasionally, until onions are transparent and peepers are tender. Add rice into saucepan and sauté for 1-2 minutes. Add water. Stir once or twice. Cover and cook for 15-20 minutes on a low heat until the liquid has been absorbed. Add tomatoes and bring to boil. Add salt and pepper to taste and serve.

SHUBEREK
(şuberek)
Sent by Eugen Georgescu, Orangevale, CA

Dough: 2.2 lb flour, 0.66 lb melted fat (baked) or 0.44 lb, 0.88 lb hot water, 1 tsp sea salt

Filling: 0.44 lb melted fat, 1.1 lb chopped white onions, 2.2 lb chopped meat, 0.22 lb dried grapes, 6 boiled eggs, chopped, 0.44 lb of green olives, salt and black pepper

Dough Preparation: Add the salt to the hot water, and stir until it is completely dissolved. Let it cool. Arrange the flour as a ring (like a volcano, with a hole in melted fat/lard (fried) the middle) on your counter. Incorporate the warm melted fat/lard by putting it in the middle of the flour and mixing with your fingers. Once the flour and fat are mixed, slowly add the salted water, a bit at a time, kneading the dough until it is smooth and shiny. Put the dough in a covered bowl and let rest in the refrigerator for one half to one hour. Take the dough from the refrigerator and shape it on the counter with a rolling pin until it is approximately 2 mm thick. Cut in circles 13 -15 cm diameter.

Filling Preparation: Add the melted fat and chopped onions to a pan with a lid, and sauté until slightly brown. Keep the onions moving. Do not let them burn. Add the chopped meat and the salt. Cook until the meat is no longer pink. Add pepper to taste. Remove from the oven and let it to cool.

Put a generously filled tbsp of filling on each dough disk, and then add some raisins, one olive, and a teaspoon of chopped boiled egg. Moisten the edges of the disks with water; fold each one over the filling to form a half moon. Seal the edges by gently pressing with a fork.

Arrange the empanadas on a clean metal dish or baking sheet.

Let your oven reach maximum temperature and bake the empanadas for ten minutes. At that point, take a look. If the dough is pale brown with dark spots, they're ready.

SALT ENCRUSTED PORK LOIN OVER LEEKS
(pork la tavă cu praz)
Sent by Eugen Georgescu, Orangevale, CA

2 to 3 lb pork tenderloin (one piece), 15 leek leaves, 1/4 cup grated onion, 6 cloves garlic, ½ cup olive oil, fresh ground pepper, 4-6 rosemary stems, 6 basil leaves, 3 lbs coarse salt, 1 to 1 ¼ cup water, rock salt to cover

Line a shallow roasting pan with aluminum foil and lay in a bed of rock salt approximately 1/2" deep. Layer clean Leek leaves onto the salt bed. Combine the oil, onion, 2 cloves of crushed garlic and 1/4 teaspoon pepper in a large plastic bag. Toss the roast in the bag to coat it thoroughly with the oil and spice marinade. Combine coarse salt with 1 cup of water to form a thick paste. Add more water as needed to make a workable paste. Take 1 ½ cups of this paste and form into a rectangle larger than the pork roast on the leek leaves. Layer 3 stems of rosemary and 2 cloves of garlic slivered onto the salt paste. Remove the roast from the marinade bag and place it on the salt bed. Layer remaining rosemary, basil, and slivered garlic cloves onto the pork roast. Take the remaining salt paste and spread it on the meat to seal it well. Fill the pan with rock salt to surround and cover the meat. Cover with aluminum foil.

Cook for 15 minutes per pound. When the cooking time is reached, check with a meat thermometer before removing from the oven and allow resting for 10 minutes. Remove from the pan and discard the salt crust.

CHICKEN WITH WHITE WINE
(pui în vin alb)
Sent by Eugen Georgescu, Orangevale, CA

1 lb (or how much you want) chicken legs and thighs, 1 onion, diced, ¼ cup good olive oil, 1 cup white wine, ¼ cup pine nuts, ¼ cup olives

Fire your oven until hot, and let the temperature fall a little, as you need the heat of the oven to brown your chicken. Place the onions and olive oil in either stainless steel or terracotta pot that has a lid. The chicken should fit on one layer. Sauté the onion until it is translucent, which should be pretty quick. Then add the chicken and brown. Depending on your oven, you could do this without turning the chicken. Add the wine and pine nuts and cover. Bake until the chicken falls from the bone—it should feel stewed. Add the olives at the end to heat through. Serve with lentils in vinaigrette and white beans.

ROAST RED ONIONS IN HONEY BALSAMIC
(garnitură de ceapă cu miere si oțet)
Sent by Eugen Georgescu, Orangevale, CA

6-8 red onions, halved, 1 cup white wine, ½ cup honey, 4 tbsp thyme, 4 tbsp Balsamic vinegar, salt and pepper

Fire your oven until it reaches 500°F, and then allow the temperature to fall to about 450°F. Clean onions by cutting off each end and the outer skin, then cut the onions in half so they rest on the cleaned ends. Place them in an oiled baking dish with the center up, and level if you can slice carefully. Then, make up a sauce using white wine, honey, thyme and balsamic vinegar. Reduce this mixture, either on a cook top, until it thickens. Pour half this mixture over your onions and put in the oven. The onions will open up as they bake and I add the second half of the honey balsamic mixture. They will bake for about 30 to 45 minutes. These are good when placed between the eggplant and red peppers – with a little olive oil drizzled on top. And awesome cold the next day too!

ROMANIAN POT ROAST
(friptură la cuptor)

3-4 lbs rib roast or rolled roast, 1 tbsp butter, 1 garlic clove, chopped, 1 tbsp parsley, chopped, 4-6 medium sized potatoes, 4-6 carrots (shaved & cut in half), 3-4 stalks celery (cut in quarters), 2 chopped onions, salt & pepper

Preheat oven to 325°F. Mix: 1 tbsp of butter, 1 chopped garlic clove, 1 tbsp of chopped parsley with ¼ teaspoon each of salt & pepper. Poke holes in roast and put the above mixture into holes. Place roast into a shallow roasting pan with a small amount of water fat side up. Place the cut up vegetables around the roast. Bake 2 to 2 ½ hours or until meat thermometer inserted into thickest part of meat registers 130°F to 135°F for medium-rare doneness. Remove from oven. Cover and let stand 20 minute before carving.

ROSEMARY ROAST POTATOES
(cartofi la cuptor)
Sent by Eugen Georgescu, Orangevale, CA

1 lb potatoes, washed, scrubbed and cut into 1" cubes, 4 tbsp olive oil, 2 tsp rosemary, salt and pepper

Add the potatoes, chopped rosemary leaves and olive oil to a terracotta baking dish. Roast in a moderately hot oven for 30-40 minutes, stirring periodically to prevent sticking. You want a hot enough oven to brown your potatoes, without burning at the bottom. Stir to coat the potatoes. Roast in a moderately hot oven for 30-40 minutes, stirring periodically to prevent sticking.

CHICKEN ESCALOPE
(pui escalop)
Sent by Eugen Georgescu, Orangevale, CA

1 lb boneless chicken breasts, 2 tbsp olive oil, juice of 1 lemon, 1 tbsp wine vinegar, 1 tbsp balsamic vinegar, 1 tbsp capers, salt and pepper

Place the breasts between two pieces of waxed paper and pound flat with a rolling pin to a thickness of about 1/4". Put the olive oil into a stainless steel or aluminum pan, add the chicken and turn to coat. Pour the lemon juice, vinegar, and capers over the meat; season with salt and pepper. Fire your oven until hot. Cook the chicken in a hot oven, without turning. The top of the chicken should be brown and bubbly, and the inside should be cooked through, but not dry. Place one escalope on each plate and cover with cooking juices. Or, put the entire dish on a warm serving platter. Top with fresh lemon slices and serve immediately.

ROMANIAN BAKED WHITE FISH
(peşte alb la cuptor)

2 lbs any white fish fillets, 2 carrots, chopped, ¼ cup parsley, ½ celery root, chopped, 1 green pepper, chopped, for mushroom sauce, 2 tbsp butter, 2 tbsp mushroom soup mix (or flour), 1 cup white wine, 1 cup cooking water, from the fish, ½ cup grated cheese, 4 ounces sour cream, 8 ounces sliced mushrooms, 2 tbsp chopped dill

To poach the fish, fill a large sauce pan with plenty of water with plenty of salt. Drop all the chopped carrots, parsley, 1/3 celery root, 1 green pepper into the water. Cook the vegetables ingredients for about 15 minutes, and then add fish to the water. Continue poaching the fish until veggies are done, and the carrot is very soft. Keep about 1 cup of the cooking water, and allow the vegetables to cool. Remove the fish with a slotted tbsp and place in a large pan (9"x 13"). Baste with lemon juice. Remove the cooked veggies, chop, and sprinkle over the fish. Prepare mushroom sauce: in a large skillet over medium heat, melt butter, and cook the mushrooms until slightly cooked, add mushroom soup powder (or flour) while stirring. Gradually add the liquids while whisking constantly, and cook until slightly thickened. During the stirring add the grated cheese and the sour cream. Remove from heat and add the dill. Pour the sauce evenly over the fish. Bake in oven at 350 until cheese is melted, and slightly browned, about 20 minutes.

FRIED SALMON
(peşte prăjit)

1 large salmon cleaned and skinned (you can also use salmon steaks) about 3 lbs, salt, 200g cornmeal, 6 spoons butter, 3 spoons oil (sunflower), 5-6 garlic cloves (or 7-8 pieces spring green garlic) diced, 1 cup of diced parsley, 1 cup sour cream, white crusty bread.

Clean the fish and dry it with paper towel. Rub it well with salt. Dredge the fish through cornmeal to cover it well. In a pan, heat the butter and oil and fry the fish covered with a lid until it changes color and looks done (about 10 - 15 min.) Arrange it on a plate.

Heat the sour cream at low heat for 2 - 3 min and add the diced garlic and parsley. Pour it over the fish. Eat it with bread. Serve it with a glass of Sauvignon.

ROMANIAN VEGETABLE STEW
(ghiveci)

2 large onions, chopped, 4-5 medium carrots, peeled and sliced, 3-4 medium bell peppers, seeded and chopped (any color), 3 garlic cloves, minced, 2 tbsp vegetable oil (I use olive oil.), 1 small

cabbage, sliced thinly, 3 fresh tomatoes, peeled and chopped or 1 (14 ounce) can tomatoes, chopped and juices reserved, 2 cups water, 3-4 medium potatoes, peeled and chopped, 1 (12 ounce) package frozen peas, ½ tsp thyme, 2 tbsp fresh dill, minced, 2 tbsp fresh parsley, minced, ½ lemon, juice of 1-2 tsp paprika, salt, pepper.

Optional seasonal veggies: 1 large eggplant (cubed, salted, and rinsed), 1 large zucchini (sliced), 1 small head cauliflower (broken into flowerets), 1 kohlrabi (peeled and cubed)

Heat the oil in a large stewpot or Dutch oven. Add the onion, carrots, and peppers. Sauté over medium heat until onions are transparent. (About 5 minutes). Add garlic, potatoes, and cabbage. If using kohlrabi add it now. Sauté them for about 3 minutes. Add water and tomatoes, salt and pepper, and thyme and paprika. Bring to a boil. Cover and simmer for about 15 minutes, or until the potatoes are almost tender. Add the other optional veggies (eggplant etc.) of your choice. Return to a boil, cover and simmer. Simmer, covered for about 20 more minutes or until the vegetables are soft and flavors have blended. Add frozen peas, fresh herbs, and lemon juice. Cook for five minutes with the cover on. Serve hot with rice.

CABBAGE WITH PORK
(varză dulce cu carne de porc)

1 lb pork, 1 medium cabbage, 2 onions (optional), 2 peppers, 1 ½ tbsp lard, 1 cup borş, 5-6 big tomatoes, salt

Cut the meat in bite sizes, fry in lard until it starts to brown, cover with tepid water and let it boil slowly about an hour. During this time, chop the cabbage, add a little salt and squeeze all excess water. Place on top of the meat. Add the thinly sliced peppers, onions and tomatoes. Add the borş. Let it bake in the oven at least one hour. If necessary, add a little water or tomato sauce.

BREADED PORK CHOPS
(cotlete de porc pane)

6 pork chops, 2 eggs, 2 tbsp lard, 2 tbsp flour, pepper

Pound the chops with the pounder, salt, pepper, dredge with the beaten egg, then flour, then egg and finally breadcrumbs. Fry in hot lard, at low heat. Serve with French fries, with some salad or pickles.

GREEN BEANS WITH PORK
(fasole verde cu carne de porc)

1 ¾ lb pork, 2 lbs green beans, 2 onions, 1 tbsp lard, 4-5 tomatoes, ½ tsp flour, salt, minced parsley and dill

Cut the meat in bite sizes and fry in the lard. Add the finely chopped onions and let it fry very little. Add the flour and mix well. Pour tepid water to cover the meat. Add the salt and let it boil at slow heat for half an hour. Add the beans and let boil another 15 minutes. Then add the separately boiled and drained tomatoes and the chopped parsley and dill. Place in the oven until the liquid is almost entirely gone. Instead of fried onions you can use grated raw onions. In this case, add with the water.

CUCUMBERS WITH PORK
(castraveti cu carne de porc)

1 lb pork, 8 medium sized pickles, 2 tbsp lard, 1 tbsp tomato sauce, 1 onion, ½ tsp flour, salt, chopped dill

Cube the meat and fry it in lard until it starts to brown. Add the chopped onion and flour and let fry a little longer. Then add warm water to cover the meat. Cover and simmer for half an hour. Prepare 2 inch long pieces of pickle. To the meat add pickles, tomato sauce, sugar, chopped dill and simmer until the meat is done and the liquid is reduced. You can also use raw onion instead of fried. In this case, add it with the warm water.

MUSHROOMS WITH PORK
(ciuperci cu carne de porc)

1 lb pork, 1 lb mushrooms, 2 onions, 2 tbsp sour cream, 1 tbsp lard, salt, pepper, flour

Cube the meat, salt and let sit for 30 minutes. In the meantime, clean the mushrooms and cut in pieces. Dredge the meat with flour and fry in hot lard, add chopped onion and the mushrooms. Fry everything at very low heat for 20 minutes. Add sour cream, pepper and salt if needed. Let simmer, covered, until the meat is tender. If there is not enough sauce, add a little water.

LEEKS WITH PORK
(praz cu carne de porc)

1 lb pork, 1 bunch leeks, 1 tbsp tomato paste, ½ tsp sugar, 2 tbsp lard, salt

Fry the meat pieces until brown. Cover with water; add a little salt and let boil until the meat is tender. During this time, clean the leeks slice them and blanch. Arrange the drained leeks on top of the meat add the tomato paste and Sugar and let boil for 10-15 minutes on top of the range. Then place in the oven and leave it until the sauce is thickened.

PEAS WITH PORK
(mazăre cu carne de porc)

1 lb pork, 2 lbs shelled peas, 1 onion, 1 tbsp lard, ½ tsp flour, ½ tsp sugar, salt, chopped dill, 1 tbsp sour cream, 2 tbsp milk, 1 cup beef broth or water

Cut the meat in bite size pieces, fry in lard, then add a finely chopped onion and let it fry just a little. Add the flour, mix, so that it does not fry and then add the beef broth or water. Cover and let boil at slow temperature until the meat is almost tender. Add the peas, salt, sugar, dill, sour cream or milk and let boil at slow temperature until most of the liquid is gone. You can replace the fried onion with grated raw onion. In this case, add with the broth or water.

POTATOES WITH PORK
(cartofi cu carne de porc)

1 lb pork, 2 tbsp lard, 2-3 onions, 1 lb potatoes, 2 tbsp tomato paste, 1 tsp paprika, salt, a little thyme (optional)

Cut the meat in bite sizes, salt and fry in lard. When it starts to brown, add the finely chopped raw onion or let the onion fry until it turns yellow. Add water to cover the meat. Cover and let boil at slow temperature until the meat is almost tender. Then add the tomato paste, paprika, salt, a little thyme and the halved or quartered potatoes (depending on size). If necessary, add more water to cover. Let boil at slow temperature until the potatoes are done and the liquid is almost completely gone.

SAUERKRAUT WITH PORK
(varză acră cu carne de porc)

1 lb pork, 1 medium cabbage, 2 ½ tbsp lard, 1/2 tsp paprika, 1 tbsp tomato paste

Cut the meat in bite size pieces and fry very little in lard. Add water to cover and let boil, covered, about a half hour. During this time, chop the sauerkraut. Then add it to the meat, also adding paprika, tomato paste, and a little water. Let boil, at slow temperature for another hour. If the liquid evaporates, add a little warm water. Then bake in the oven for another hour. Serve with mămăligă.

SUCKLING PIG, BAKED
(purcel de lapte la tavă)

1 suckling pig, salt, 1/2 cup rum, 1 tbsp oil

As soon as the piglet was slaughtered, place in a large basin, spray some rosin on it and then pour some hot water. Turn the piglet on all sides so that it softens. Then remove from the basin onto a cutting board and remove all hairs. (It will be very easy.) Rub with a clean cloth and then singe over an open flame. Then place in a basin with tepid water. Wash and scrape with a knife. Rinse with cold water, then slit open on the belly, from the tail to the neck. Remove the intestines and innards, taking care not to break the bile. Wash well in 2-3 changes of water, drain for 10 minutes, then place on a cutting board with the four legs bent (kneeling). Refrigerate until the following day. One hour before roasting, do this. Wash the piglet; rub with a dry cloth, inside and outside. Rub with one tbsp of salt and let sit for 30 minutes. Place in the roasting pan with the knees bent and set on sticks and the ears wrapped in white paper. Grease with lard and place a red apple in its mouth. Add 2-3 tbsp of water and set in the oven at low heat to start with, then higher and higher. During roasting, occasionally baste with a little rum mixed with oil. When it starts to brown, increase the heat, do not baste and cook until done. Serve with French fries, sautéed sauerkraut, roasted Apples or pickled peppers.

SUCKLING PIG, STUFFED WITH ORGAN MEAT
(purcel de lapte umplut cu mǎruntaie)

1 suckling pig, 3 eggs, 2 white bread slices, 2 tbsp lard, 1 onion, 4 oz raisins (to taste), chopped parsley, salt, pepper

Grind the heart, liver and spleen from the piglet, with a raw onion and the crustless bread slices (previously soaked and squeezed). Beat three eggs in a bowl; mix with the ground meat, adding salt and pepper, chopped parsley, the raisins (to taste) and a finely chopped lard fried onion. Fill the piglet with this filling, sew it and place in the oven. Instead of raisins, you can add 2-3 tbsp rice boiled in salt water, then rinsed in cold water and mixed with a tbsp of butter and a little pepper.

PORK HOTCHPOTCH
(ghiveci din carne de porc)

1 ¾ lb pork, 2 tbsp lard, 1 parsnip, 1 carrot, 2 peppers, 1 eggplant, 1 zucchini, a handful of okra, a handful of green beans, a handful of wax beans, a handful of string beans, ½ lb peas, 1 small cauliflower, 2 big onions, 3 potatoes, 1 small celery root, 5-6 big tomatoes, 2 garlic cloves (optional), minced parsley and dill, salt

Cut the meat into bite sizes and fry in lard until they start to brown. Add salt and tepid water to cover. Let boil on slow heat, covered, an hour to an hour and a half. During this time, prepare the vegetables. Clean, wash and cut in bite sizes. Arrange the vegetables on top of the meat, add the sliced, peeled and seeded tomatoes, the parsley and dill and salt. Let boil on top of the range for a few minutes, then place in the oven. Shake the pot from time to time so that they do not stick. Bake until the liquid evaporates.

BAKED PORK LEG
(pulpǎ de porc la tavǎ)

A piece of the leg (about 2-4 lbs), salt, a little lard

Salt the meat and let sit for 30 minutes. Place in the lard greased pan, add 3-4 tbsp of water and set in the oven, first at high heat until it starts to brown, then reduce heat. During the roasting, baste with the liquid in the pan. Keep in the oven for 1 to 1 ½ hours. Serve sliced, with sautéed cabbage. Pour some sauce from the pan over the slices.

PORK SCHNITZEL
(şniţel din carne de porc)

1 ¾ lbs pork, 1 tsp oil, 2 eggs, 2-3 tbsp lard, flour, bread crumbs, pepper, salt

Cut the meat in medium sized pieces, about a finger thick. Lightly pound with the wooden hammer, salt and pepper. Dredge each veal slice with the eggs beaten with a teaspoon of oil, flour, egg again and finally, bread crumbs. Fry on both sides in hot lard. Serve with French fries, sautéed vegetables or a salad.

PORK STEW
(tocană de carne de porc)

2 lbs pork, 4-5 onions, 2 tbsp lard, 1 tbsp tomato paste or 4-5 tomatoes, salt, pepper

Cut the meat in bite sizes, fry a little in lard, add the chopped onion, let it fry a little, add a little water and then let it boil covered at slow heat. Add a little water from time to time until the meat is tender. Add the tomato paste or peeled and seeded tomatoes (in small chunks), salt and pepper. Cover the pot and let boil at slow heat until the liquid evaporates almost entirely. Serve with mămăligă.

BAKED PORK
(ceafă de porc (garf) la cuptor)

one piece of pork (approx. 4 lbs), 3-4 juniper berries, 1 garlic clove, ½ tsp paprika, a few coriander Berries, salt, a little shortening

Do not wash the meat but dry it with a wet cloth. Salt it; rub with minced garlic and the spices. Set in a bowl and leave for 3-4 hours. Then spread some paprika on top of the meat and place in a lard greased pan. Place in the oven at high heat for 30 minutes, and then reduce the heat to medium. Keep in the oven for 1 ½ hours. During roasting, baste with the liquid in the pan. Slice, arrange on the serving platter, pour some liquid from the pan (strained) over it and serve with French fries, lettuce or pickled peppers or cucumbers. It may be served cold, sliced more thinly.

BAKED PORK CHOPS
(cotlete de porc la cuptor)

pork chops (in a whole rack), salt, a little lard

Use the cleaver to cut the backbones, salt and place the whole meat piece in the roasting pan that was greased with a little lard. Add 2-3 tbsp of water. Leave it in the oven for 1 1/2 to 2 hours, basting every now and then with the liquid in the pan. When ready, slice and serve with French fries or mashed potatoes or sautéed cabbage. It may also be served cold, sliced thinly.

WINTER ROLL
(ruladă de iarnă)

2 lbs ground sirloin, 5 oz bacon, 2 onions, 1 crustless white bread slice, 1 raw egg, salt, pepper, 1 tsp chopped parsley and dill, 1 tbsp bread crumbs, 5-6 juniper berries, 2-3 cloves, ½ tsp thyme, 10 pepper Berries, 3 tbsp meat broth or water

Grind the meat with the finely chopped raw or lard fried onions, the soaked and squeezed bread. Add salt, pepper, chopped parsley and dill and raw egg. Add to the ground meat mixture the cubed bacon and the finely ground spices. Mix well. Place the meat mixture on a wooden cutting board on which you spread some bread crumbs. Shape it like a roll. Place in a bread baking dish which you greased with lard. Spread some bread crumbs on top. Pour a little melted lard over it and bake. Serve sliced, with sautéed cabbage. It is very tasty served cold. This roll is very good if prepared with half pork and half beef.

BEEF HOTCHPOTCH
(ghiveci din carne de vacă)

1 ¾ lb fatty beef, 3 tbsp lard, 1 parsnip, 1 carrot, 2 peppers, 1 eggplant, 1 zucchini, a handful of okra, a handful of green beans, a handful of wax beans, a handful of string beans, ½ lb peas, 1 small cauliflower, 2 big onions, 3 potatoes, 1 small celery root, 5-6

big tomatoes, 2 garlic cloves (optional), minced parsley and dill, salt

Cut the meat into bite sizes and fry in lard until they start to brown. Add salt and tepid water to cover. Let boil on slow heat, covered, an hour to an hour and a half. During this time, prepare the vegetables. Clean, wash and cut in bite sizes. Arrange the vegetables on top of the meat add the sliced, peeled and seeded tomatoes, the parsley and dill and salt. Let boil on top of the range for a few minutes, then place in the oven. Shake the pot from time to time so that they do not stick. Bake until the liquid evaporates.

BIGUS
(bigus)

1 medium sour cabbage, 5 oz smoked bacon, cubed, 5 oz hot dogs cut in pieces, 5 oz smoked salami, cubed, 2 tbsp lard, pepper

Cut julienne the cabbage. If it is too sour or too salty, wash it. Fry it in hot lard, together with small cubes of bacon, salami and hot dogs. Fry them and keep stirring and adding a tbsp or two of water and pepper. When everything is fried, put in the oven for half an hour.

BOILED BEEF
(rasol de carne de vacă)

2 lbs beef, 3 qts water, 2 potatoes, 2 carrots, 1 parsnip, 1 celery root, 1 pepper, 1 onion, 5 juniper berries (optional), 1 bay leaf (optional), salt

Drain the meat that has boiled with the beef soup and cut in bite sizes. Place on a plate and garnish with the vegetables: potatoes, carrots, parsnip. Pour a little oil, vinegar/lemon juice and a tbsp of the boiling liquid. Add a little pepper (to taste) and serve with a salad or pickles.

BEEF STEW
(tocană de carne de vacă)

2 lbs beef, 4-5 onions, 2 tbsp lard, 1 tbsp tomato paste or 4-5 tomatoes, salt, pepper

Cut the meat in bite sizes, fry a little in lard, add the chopped onion, let it fry a little, add a little water and then let it boil covered at slow heat. Add a little water from time to time until the meat is tender. Add the tomato paste or peeled and seeded tomatoes (in small chunks), salt and pepper. Cover the pot and let boil at slow heat until the liquid evaporates almost entirely. Serve with mămăligă.

BOILED BEEF WITH SOUR CREAM AND HORSERADISH
(rasol de carne de vacă cu smântână si hrean)

2 lbs boiled beef, 1 cup sour cream, 1 tbsp horseradish sauce, 1 tsp vinegar, ½ tsp sugar, salt

Cut the cold meat in bite sizes, place on a platter and cover with the following sauce: mix the horseradish sauce with the vinegar, sugar and salt. Add sour cream and mix well.

BOILED BEEF WITH TOMATO SAUCE
(rasol cu sos de roşii)

2 lbs kg boiled beef, 2-3 onions, 1 tbsp tomato paste or 1 lb boiled and strained tomatoes, 1 cup beef broth or milk, 1 tbsp butter, 1 tbsp vinegar, a little sugar, salt, flour

Cut the cold meat in bite sizes, place on a platter and cover with the following sauce: fry the chopped onion in butter until softened. Add the flour, mix well and pour the broth or milk on top. Add the tomato paste or chunks of peeled and seeded tomatoes, salt and pepper. Cover the pot and let it boil at slow heat until the liquid is entirely gone. Serve with mămăligă.

BOILED BEEF WITH SOUR CREAM AND MUSTARD
(rasol de carne de vacă cu smântână şi muştar)

2 lbs boiled beef, 1-2 tbsp mustard, 1 tsp vinegar, ½ tsp sugar, salt

Cut the cold meat in bite sizes, place on a platter and cover with the following sauce: mix the mustard with the vinegar, sugar and salt. Add sour cream and mix well.

BOILED TONGUE
(limbă fiartă)

1 beef or 3-4 pork tongues (approx 2 lbs), 2 onions, 1 parsley root, 1 carrot, 1 bay leaf, 4-5 juniper berries, salt, horseradish sauce, mustard or tomato sauce

Wash the tongue in several changes of water, scrape with a knife, remove the fatty parts, set in a pot with cold water and simmer. Remove foam; add onion, soup vegetables, juniper berries, bay leaf and salt. Cover and simmer for 3 hours. Remove from the water, place on a cutting board and peel with the help of a knife, pulling the skin from the tip to the root. Slice, arrange on a platter and pour horseradish or mustard or tomato sauce over it.

BRAINS IN DOUGH
(creier în aluat)

1 beef or 2 veal or pork brains, 5 oz flour, 1 cup milk, 1 egg, 2 tbsp club, soda, 2 tbsp lard, salt, green lettuce

Boil the brain. Let cool off, and then cut into finger thick slices and salt. Make dough out of flour, milk, beaten egg, salt and club soda. The dough must have a sour cream thickness. Dredge the brain slices in this dough and fry in hot lard. Serve with green lettuce.

BULGARIAN PILAF (WITH LAMB ORGAN MEAT)
(pilaf bulgăresc cu măruntaie de miel)

innards and intestines from a medium lamb, 2 tbsp lard, 1 ½ cup rice, 2 onions, 3 cups water, salt, ½ tsp pepper

Wash the intestines, scrape them, turn inside out, wash a few more times, rub with salt and wash again. Then cut in small pieces. Cut the heart, liver, lungs and kidneys (after you washed and removed the inside fat) the same way. Set everything to boil with a finely chopped onion, salt, pepper and water. When it comes to a boil, remove foam and add the rice which was slightly fried in lard. After a few minutes of boiling, put in the oven to bake until the rice is done.

BREADED BRAINS
(creier pane)

1 beef or 2 veal or pork brains, 2 eggs, 2 tbsp flour, 4 tbsp bread crumbs, salt, 2 tbsp butter or lard, sauté of green peas or carrots or green beans

Boil the brain, let cool off, then cut into finger thick slices, salt, dredge with egg, then flour, egg again and finally bread crumbs. Fry in hot lard or butter. Serve with a sauté of greens Peas, carrots or green beans.

BREADED UDDER
(uger pane)

1 lb udder, vegetables for soup, 1 egg, 1 tbsp milk, 1 tbsp lard, salt, pepper, 2 tbsp flour, and bread crumbs

Boil the udder with the vegetables and a little salt. When it is soft, remove, let cool off, then cut into medium thick slices (as for schnitzel). Salt, pepper, dredge with egg beaten with milk, drain well, dredge with flour, again with egg and finally bread crumbs. Fry in hot lard like schnitzel. Serve hot with boiled vegetables or lettuce.

CABBAGE WITH BEEF
(varză dulce cu carne de vacă)

1 lb fatty beef, 1 medium cabbage, 2 onions (optional), 2 peppers, 2 ½ tbsp lard, 1 cup borş, 5-6 big tomatoes, salt

Cut the meat in bite sizes, fry in lard until it starts to brown, cover with tepid water and let it boil slowly about an hour. During this time, chop the cabbage, add a little salt and squeeze all excess water. Place on top of the meat. Add the thinly sliced peppers, onions and tomatoes. Add the borş. Let it bake in the oven at least one hour. If necessary, add a little water or tomato sauce.

FRIED LIVER
(ficat prăjit)

1 3/4 lbs beef, pork or veal liver, 3 tbsp oil, 2 tbsp flour, salt

Wash and dry the liver, cut into finger thick slices, dredge with flour, shake well and fry in hot oil. Do not salt until after frying, just before serving. Serve with assorted vegetables.

GREEN BEANS WITH BEEF
(fasole verde cu carne de vacă)

1 ¾ lb beef, 2 lbs green beans, 2 onions, 2 tbsp lard, 4-5 tomatoes, ½ tsp flour, salt, minced parsley and dill

Cut the meat in bite sizes and fry in the lard. Add the finely chopped onions and let it fry very little. Add the flour and mix well. Pour tepid water to cover the meat. Add the salt and let it boil at slow heat for half an hour. Add the Beans and let boil another 15 minutes. Then add the separately boiled and drained tomatoes and the chopped parsley and dill. Place in the oven until the liquid is almost entirely gone. Instead of fried onions you can use grated raw onions. In this case, add with the water.

GRILLED MINCED MEAT ROLLS
(mititei)

2 lbs ground beef, ½ lb suet, ¼ tsp baking soda, 2-3 garlic cloves, some ground pepper, juniper berries and caraway, 2-3 tbsp meat broth, salt

Grind the meat together with the suet. Add salt, spices, chopped garlic, meat broth and baking soda and mix everything with your hands for 15 minutes, adding two tbsp of water a little at a time. Keep the bowl with this mixture on ice for 5-6 hours. Just before grilling, take tbsp of the mixture and with wet hands, shape the rolls (they are about 2-3 inches long and 1 inch thick). Before placing on the grill, grease them with oil and during grilling baste them with a mixture of meat broth and oil.

GROUND MEAT, BREADED
(şniţel din carne tocată)

1 ¼ lb ground sirloin, 2 tbsp butter or lard, ½ cup bread crumbs, salt, pepper

Mix the ground meat with salt and pepper. From this paste, shape 6 flat patties about ½ inches thick. Dredge with bread crumbs and fry in hot shortening. Serve with French fries, mashed potatoes or boiled vegetables with melted butter on top of them.

HEART GULASH
(gulaş de inimă)

1 ¾ lbs beef heart, ½ tbsp flour, 1 onion, 2-3 tbsp lard, butter or oil, 1 tbsp tomato paste, pepper, salt

Wash and cube the heart, fry slightly in a pan with shortening and finely chopped onion, add flour, mix well and cover with warm water. Cover and simmer for ½ hour. Add tomato paste, salt, pepper and let simmer until the sauce thickens. Serve with hot mashed or boiled potatoes.

HOT DOGS WITH MASHED POTATOES
(cremvurşti cu piure cu cartofi)

1 lb hot dogs, mashed potatoes

Boil the hot dogs for a few minutes. Arrange the mashed potatoes on a plate and the hot dogs on top of them. Serve with a salad. You may also serve the hot dogs with boiled potatoes that had melted butter poured on them.

KIDNEY DISH
(mâncare de rinichi)

1 beef or 2 veal or pork kidneys, 3 onions, 1 tbsp lard, 1 tbsp tomato sauce, 1 tsp paprika, ½ tsp flour, 2-3 tbsp wine, 1 cup meat broth or water, salt, pepper

Remove the outer membranes from the kidney, split in half lengthwise, remove all fatty tissues inside, slice thinly and set to boil starting with cold water. After coming to a boil, drain and wash well with tepid water. Finely chop the onion, fry in lard until yellowish, add flour, let it fry a little, and then add meat broth or water. Add tomato sauce, paprika, wine, salt and pepper. Let boil until the kidneys are done.

KIDNEYS WITH SOUR CREAM
(rinichi cu smântână)

1 beef or 2 veal or pork kidneys (approx 1 ¼ lbs), 1 small onion, 1 tbsp butter, 1 cup sour cream, 1 level tsp flour, ½ cup meat broth, salt

Prepare the kidneys as for kidney dish. Fry the onion with the butter until yellow, add flour, mix, and then add meat broth. To this sauce, add sour cream, salt and kidney pieces. Simmer until the kidneys are done.

LAMB HAGGIS
(drob de miel)

organ meat (heart, kidneys, liver, tongue, spleen) from a lamb, 2 big onions, 2 eggs, 1 tbsp mixed chopped parsley and dill, 1 tbsp chopped green onions (green parts), salt, pepper, 1 tbsp lard, 1 bread slice

Grind the organ meat with the finely chopped raw or slightly fried onion, lard and crustless slice of bread (previously soaked and squeezed dry). Add salt, pepper, chopped parsley and dill, chopped green onions, beaten eggs and mix everything well. In a well greased pan, set the washed Lamb stomach so as to cover the bottom and sides of the pan with room to spare. Arrange the ground meat mixture, cover with the sides of the stomach and bake. When ready, turn onto a plate and serve with green lettuce.

LAMB HAGGIS IN DOUGH
(drob de miel în aluat)

Meat mixture: organ meat (heart, kidneys, liver, tongue, spleen) from a lamb, 2 big onions, 2 eggs, 1 tbsp mixed chopped parsley and dill, 1 tbsp chopped green onions (green parts), salt, pepper, 1 tbsp lard, 1 bread slice

Dough: 1 egg, 1 tbsp lard, 1 tsp sour cream, 1 tsp vinegar, salt, 6 oz flour

Make dough from 1 egg, lard, sour cream, vinegar, salt and flour. The dough should not be too hard. Roll the dough into a round sheet, place in a greased pan to cover the bottom and sides of the pan with room to spare like for the Lamb haggis. Place the ground meat mixture inside and cover with the edges of the dough. Grease with lard and bake. When ready, turn onto a plate and serve with green lettuce.

LAMB IN YOGURT SAUCE
(miel în sos de iaurt)

1 ¾ lbs lamb, 1 lb yogurt, ½ tbsp flour, 2 tbsp butter (or lard), 1 tbsp chopped dill, salt

Fry the Lamb pieces in butter. When golden brown, add a few tbsp of water and simmer, covered, until the meat is almost done (if necessary, add some more water). Make a paste from yogurt and flour, adding the yogurt a little at a time and stirring. Pour this paste over the Lamb pieces. Add the dill and salt and let simmer a little longer until the meat is done. Serve with mămăligă.

LAMB ONION AND GARLIC STEW
(stufat de miel)

1 lb Lamb, 30 green onions, 30 green garlic, 3 tbsp lard, ½ tsp flour, 2 tbsp tomato sauce (or 1 lb tomatoes), 1 tbsp vinegar, salt, sugar

Cut the meat in pieces and fry it with a tbsp of lard. Then add the flour, let it fry a little and remove from heat. Cut the green onions and garlic in two inch pieces and fry separately in the remaining lard until slightly softened. Then place over the meat pieces. Add salt, tomato sauce or boiled and strained tomatoes, sugar and 2-3 tbsp of water. Boil for a few minutes then set in the oven until the liquid is substantially reduced.

LAMB PILAF
(pilaf de miel)

1 lb lamb, 1 cup rice, 2 cups water, 1 big onion, salt, chopped dill, 2 tbsp lard

Cut the meat in pieces and fry with a tbsp of lard. When becomes golden brown, add finely chopped onion, water and salt. Cover the pan and let simmer for 5 minutes. In the meantime, slightly fry the rice with a tbsp of lard. Place over the meat, add chopped dill and cover with a lid that was covered in a soaked and squeezed cloth. Bake in the oven until the rice is cooked.

LAMB ROAST
(friptură de miel la tavă)

3 lbs lamb meat (from legs), 1-2 tbsp lard, salt, a few garlic cloves

Wash and dry the meat, salt and let sit for a half hour. Grease a roasting pan with lard, arrange the meat in, pour 2-3 tbsp of water and place in the oven, first at low temperature, then increase the heat. When it is roasted, place on a platter. Pour a few tbsp of water in the roasting pan, add a few chopped garlic cloves and set it on top of the range where it should be allowed to come to a boil. Strain the liquid and pour it over the roast. Serve with French fries and salad to taste.

LAMB SCHNITZEL
(şniţel de miel)

lamb leg (in 6 pieces), 1 egg, 2 tbsp milk, 2 tbsp lard, 1 tbsp oil, 2 tbsp flour, bread crumbs, salt

Use only leg meat, cut into finger thick slices and flattened with the wooden hammer. Beat the egg and mix with milk. Dredge the meat with the egg mixture, then flour, then egg again and finally breadcrumbs. Fry in lard mixed with oil at low heat. Serve with French fries and green lettuce or pickles.

LAMB WITH SOUR CREAM
(miel cu smântână)

1 ¾ lbs Lamb, 1 tbsp lard, 1 cup sour cream, 1 tsp flour, salt, chopped dill

Cut the meat and fry in lard until brown. Add the flour, mix well, fry only slightly, then pour the sour cream, add salt and simmer for 15-20 minutes. Add chopped dill and set in the oven so that the liquid is reduced. (Keep the pan covered.) Serve with mămăligă.

LAMB WITH MUSHROOMS
(miel cu ciuperci)

1 lb lamb, 1 lb mushrooms, 2 onions, 2 tbsp sour cream, 1 tbsp lard, salt, pepper, flour

Cube the meat, salt and let sit for 30 minutes. In the meantime, clean the Mushrooms and cut in pieces. Dredge the meat with flour and fry in hot lard, add chopped onion and the Mushrooms. Fry everything at very low heat for 20 minutes. Add sour cream, pepper and salt if needed. Let simmer, covered, until the meat is tender. If there is not enough sauce, add a little water.

LAMB WHITE SAUCE STEW
(ciulama de miel)

1 ¾ lbs Lamb, 2 tbsp lard, 1 onion, 2 tbsp flour

Cut the meat and set in a pan adding water to cover. Add one whole onion and salt. Remove foam and simmer until done. Throw away the onion. Separately, slightly fry the flour in lard. Add the meat boiling liquid, stirring quickly and then pour over the meat pieces. Let boil for a few minutes longer. The stew is tastier if you add a cup of milk to the sauce.

LAMB WITH SPINACH
(miel cu spanac)

1 lb lamb, 3 lbs spinach, 1 big onion, ½ tsp flour, 2 tbsp lard, 1 tbsp tomato sauce, salt, lemon juice

Fry the meat pieces in lard, add finely chopped onion, flour, washed, blanched and drained spinach, a tbsp of tomato sauce, 2-3 tbsp water and salt. Cover the pan and bake until the liquid is reduced. When you serve, add lemon juice.

LAMB WITH TARRAGON
(miel cu tarhon)

20 oz lamb, 1 tbsp lard, 1 onion, 4-5 tomatoes, ½ tsp flour, tarragon, salt

Fry the lamb pieces in lard until yellow. Add the finely chopped onion and flour. When the onion starts to turn yellow, add 3-4 tbsp of water, juice from 4-5 tomatoes, salt and tarragon. The quantity of tarragon is to taste. Cover and simmer. When the meat is almost done, set into the oven for 15-20 minutes. You may prepare this with raw onion. In this case, add it with the water.

LAMB, BREADED
(miel pane)

lamb breast (in 6 pieces), 1 egg, 2 tbsp milk, 1 tbsp lard, 1 tbsp oil, 2 tbsp flour, bread crumbs, salt

Cut the breast (rib) part into medium sized pieces, salt and let sit for 10-15 minutes. Beat the egg and mix with milk. Dredge the meat with the egg mixture, then flour, then egg again and finally breadcrumbs. Fry in lard mixed with oil at low heat. Serve with green lettuce or pickles.

LEEKS WITH BEEF
(praz cu carne de vacă)

1 lb beef, 1 bunch leeks, 1 tbsp tomato paste, ½ tsp sugar, 2 tbsp lard, salt

Fry the meat pieces until brown. Cover with water; add a little salt and let boil until the meat is tender. During this time, clean the leeks slice them and blanch. Arrange the drained leeks on top of the meat add the tomato paste and sugar and let boil for 10-15 minutes on top of the range. Then place in the oven and leave it until the sauce is thickened.

LEEKS, STUFFED WITH MEAT
(praz umplut cu carne)

1 ¾ lb ground meat (mixture of beef and pork recommended), 4 big onions, 2 tbsp rice, 1 slice bread, 3 tbsp lard, 5-6 tomatoes, or 1 tbsp tomato sauce, salt, pepper, chopped dill, sour cream

Prepare the ground meat mixture as for Regular cabbage rolls. Cut the leeks into 3 inch pieces blanch and remove the insides so as to get tubes. Fill with the ground meat mixture and place in a pan. Over a layer of stuffed leaks place a layer of finely chopped leeks (remaining from when you made tubes). Pour boiled and strained tomatoes (or tomato sauce) and add water so as to barely cover the leeks. Set to boil and when almost ready, place in the oven until the liquid is reduced well. Serve with sour cream.

MACARONI OR HOME MADE PASTA MOUSSAKA
(musaca de macaroane sau de tăieţei de casă)

Meet mixture: 1 ¾ lb ground sirloin, 3 big onions, 3-4 tbsp lard, pepper, salt

1 lb macaroni or homemade pasta, 2 eggs, salt, 2 tbsp butter or lard, bread crumbs

Finely chop an onion, fry slightly with a tbsp of lard, add the ground meat, pepper and salt and let fry lightly. Do not over fry.

Boil the macaroni in salt water, rinse with cold water, drain well and mix with two beaten eggs and two tbsp of butter or lard. In a well greased and covered with bread crumbs pan, arrange half of the macaroni, then the ground meat mixture and then the other half of macaroni. Spread bread crumbs, melted butter or lard and bake until golden-brown. Before serving, turn onto a round platter.

MARINADE FOR VENISON
(marinată pentru vânat)

1.5 qts l water, 1 qt wine vinegar, ½ tsp ground juniper berries, ½ tsp ground pepper, 5-6 bay leaves, peel from ½ lemon, 1 tbsp salt, 5-6 cloves, 2-3 garlic cloves

Boil the water with the wine vinegar, juniper berries, pepper, bay leaves, cloves, garlic, and peel from ½ lemon (in pieces) and a tablespoon of salt in a non-reactive pot. Boil everything for 5 minutes. Let cool and pour over the venison placed in a bowl. Keep it like this for 24 hours. The liquid must cover the venison. If not, you have to turn the venison every 5-6 hours.

MEAT BALLS, PICKLED
(chiftele marinate)

Meat mixture: 1 lb ground meat, 3 onions, 1 egg, 2 slices white bread

4-5 tomatoes or 1 tbsp tomato sauce, 1 small onion, 2-3 juniper berries, 1 bay leaf, 1/2 tsp sugar, 1-2 tbsp vinegar, salt, chopped parsley and dill, lard for frying, flour (1-2 tbsp)

Make meat balls out of the ground meat mixture, dredge with flour and
fry lightly in a pan with hot lard. Fry quickly at hot temperature, on all
sides. Arrange the fried meat balls in a pan and cover with the following
sauce. Put a finely chopped onion in the pan where the meat balls were
fried and fry it with 1/2 teaspoon flour and then add the boiled and
strained tomatoes. Add salt, sugar, juniper berries, bay leaf, vinegar and
chopped parsley and dill. Simmer by shaking the pan from time to time.

MOLDAVIAN CROQUETTES
(pârjoale moldovenești)

**1 lb ground meat, 3 onions, 1 egg, 2 slices white bread, 1 tbsp lard,
chopped parsley and dill, salt, pepper, lard for frying, bread
crumbs**

Grind the meat with a raw onion, soaked and squeezed bread and two
finely chopped and lightly fried (in a tbsp of lard) onions. Place the
mixture in a bowl, and add an egg, salt, pepper and chopped parsley and
dill. Mix everything well. Take tbsp of the mixture and with wet hands
shape into round or oval patties. Then bread them and fry in hot lard on
both sides. For the meat you can use beef, pork, mutton, chicken breast or
mixed beef and pork. You may replace the chopped parsley and dill with
chopped garlic. Serve hot, with mashed potatoes, vegetable sautés, lettuce
or pickles.

BAKED MUTTON LEG
(pulpă de berbec la tavă)

**1 leg of mutton ¼ lb bacon, 1 head of garlic, 1 tbsp lard, ½ cup
wine or vinegar, salt**

Wash and remove excess fat. De-bone the meat. Rub it with salt and let
sit for 30 minutes. Then interlard with pieces of Bacon and garlic cloves.
Roll the meat and tie with string. Place in the roasting pan which was
greased with lard, add 2-3 tbsp of water, a tbsp of lard, wine or vinegar
and set in the oven at high heat until it starts to brown. Then reduce heat
to medium. Every now and then, baste with the liquid in the pan. When
the meat is cooked, take out of the pan, remove the strings and cut into
medium thick slices. Add 2-3 tbsp of water to the sauce in the pan, let boil

for a couple of minutes and then pour over the meat. Serve with mashed potatoes and sautéed carrots. This roast is also excellent cold.

MUTTON STEW
(tocană de berbec)

2 lbs mutton, 4-5 onions, 2 tbsp lard, 1 tbsp tomato paste or 4-5 tomatoes, salt, pepper

Cut the meat in bite sizes, fry a little in lard, add the chopped onion, let it fry a little, add a little water and then let it boil covered at slow heat. Add a little water from time to time until the meat is tender. Add the tomato paste or peeled and seeded tomatoes (in small chunks), salt and pepper. Cover the pot and let boil at slow heat until the liquid evaporates almost entirely. Serve with mămăligă.

OKRA WITH BEEF
(bame cu carne de vacă)

1 lb beef, 1 lb okra, 1 onion, 2 tbsp lard, 4-5 tomatoes, 1 tbsp vinegar, salt, a little sugar, minced parsley and dill

Cut the meat in bite sizes and fry in lard. Then add water to cover and a finely chopped onion. Cover and let boil at slow temperature until the meat is almost tender. Add the okra that was previously washed after sitting for a while in water with 2 tbsp of vinegar, salt, sugar, quartered peeled and seeded tomatoes, a tbsp of vinegar and the minced parsley and dill. Let boil until the okra is almost boiled, then place in the oven for 10-15 minutes.

PEAS WITH BEEF
(mazăre cu carne de vacă)

1 lb beef, 2 lbs shelled peas, 1 onion, 2 tbsp lard, 1/2 tsp flour, 1/2 tsp sugar, salt, chopped dill, 1 tbsp sour cream, 2 tbsp milk), 1 cup beef broth or water

Cut the meat in bite size pieces, fry in lard, then add a finely chopped onion and let it fry just a little. Add the flour, mix, so that it does not fry and then add the beef broth or water. Cover and let boil at slow temperature until the meat is almost tender. Add the peas, salt, sugar, dill, sour cream or milk and let boil at slow temperature until most of the liquid is gone. You can replace the fried onion with grated raw onion. In this case, add with the broth or water.

POTATOES AND MEAT MOUSSAKA
(musaca de cartofi cu carne)

1 lb ground sirloin, 1 ¾ lb potatoes, 2 onions, 3 tbsp lard, salt, pepper, chopped parsley and dill, 1 tbsp tomato sauce or 3-4 tomatoes, bread crumbs

Peel the potatoes and cut into finger thick slices. Salt them and let sit for a few minutes. Then dry and fry on both sides. Grind the meat with two raw onions and then set in a pan to fry with a tbsp of lard. Add salt and pepper and fry lightly (do not overfry). In a pan greased with lard and covered with bread crumbs, arrange a layer of potatoes and then a layer of the meat mixture. Do this until all potatoes and all meat are used up, taking care that the last layer is potatoes. Spread chopped parsley and dill between all layers. Pour a tbsp of tomato sauce mixed with a cup of meat broth (or arrange tomato slices) over the potatoes. If using tomato slices do not use tomato sauce. Bake in the oven until the liquid is substantially reduced.

RABBIT CROQUETES
(pirjoale de iepure)

1 lb ground rabbit meat, 3 onions, 1 egg, 2 slices white bread, 1 ½ tbsp lard, chopped parsley and dill, garlic, salt, pepper, lard for frying, bread crumbs

Grind the meat with a raw onion, soaked and squeezed bread and two finely chopped and lightly fried (in a tablespoon of lard) onions. Place the mixture in a bowl, and add an egg, salt, pepper and chopped parsley and dill. Mix everything well. Take tablespoon of the mixture and with wet hands shape into round or oval patties. Then bread them and fry in hot lard on both sides. For the meat you can use Beef, Pork, mutton, Chicken breast or mixed Beef and Pork. You may replace the chopped parsley and dill with chopped garlic. Serve hot, with mashed potatoes, vegetable sautés, lettuce or pickles.

POTATOES WITH BEEF
(cartofi cu carne de vacă)

1 lb beef, 2 tbsp lard, 2-3 onions, 1 lb potatoes, 2 tbsp tomato paste, 1 tsp paprika, salt, a little thyme (optional)

Cut the meat in bite sizes, salt and fry in lard. When it starts to brown, add the finely chopped raw onion or let the onion fry until it turns yellow. Add water to cover the meat. Cover and let boil at slow temperature until the meat is almost tender. Then add the tomato paste, paprika, salt, a little thyme and the halved or quartered potatoes (depending on size). If necessary, add more water to cover. Let boil at slow temperature until the potatoes are done and the liquid is almost completely gone.

POTATOES STUFFED WITH MEAT
(cartofi umpluţi cu carne)

12 medium potatoes, 12 oz ground sirloin, 2 tbsp lard, 2 onions, 1 tbsp mixed chopped parsley and dill, 1 tbsp flour, 1 tbsp tomato sauce or 1 lb tomatoes, 1/2 tsp sugar, salt, pepper, 1 cup sour cream

Peel the potatoes and with a thin knife hollow them out. Mix the ground meat with finely chopped raw or fried onion, a tbsp of lard, salt, pepper and chopped parsley and dill. Fill the potatoes with this mixture. Dredge with flour and fry in lard, turning on all sides. Arrange the browned potatoes in a pan and cover them with the following sauce. In the lard remaining from frying the potatoes, fry 1/2 teaspoon flour and add tomato sauce or juice. Add sugar, salt and water (if preparing with tomato sauce). The sauce must cover the potatoes. Simmer the pan on top of the range for a few minutes, pour the sour cream and then bake in the oven until the potatoes are tender.

RABBIT PAPRIKASH
(papricaş de iepure)

fore legs, ribs, neck and innards from one rabbit, 2 tbsp lard, 2-3 onions, 1 tsp paprika, 2-3 tbsp sour cream, juice from 1/2 lemon, salt and pepper

Cut the rabbit into small pieces and fry in a pan with the lard and chopped onion. When the meat is golden brown, add paprika, salt, lemon juice and water to cover. Simmer until the liquid is half reduced, and then put into the oven, uncovered, until the remaining liquid is again halved. Before serving, add 2-3 tablespoons of sour cream. Serve with Cream of Wheat dumplings, boiled macaroni or mashed potatoes.

RABBIT PATE
(pastă din carne de iepure)

2 lbs rabbit meat, ½ lb butter, 2 onions, 1 tbsp lard, 1 cup milk, 2-3 juniper berries, 20 pepper Berries ground with 1 clove, a pinch of ground nutmeg, salt, 1 egg, pickles, red beets

Slightly fry the meat pieces with a tbsp of lard, add 2-3 tbsp of water, salt, a cup of milk and the quartered onions. Boil them, covered, at very low heat, until the liquid is reduced and the pieces are nicely golden brown. Set aside and after cooling off, grind three times. Put the butter in a bowl and beat until creamy, adding the nutmeg, juniper berries, pepper, cloves, then the ground meat. Mix them until homogeneous and very creamy. Arrange on a platter and garnish with slices of hard-boiled egg, sliced pickled cucumbers and red beets.

RABBIT ROAST
(friptură de iepure)

back and hind legs of one rabbit, salt, bacon, garlic, lard, 1 tbsp vinegar

After taking the meat out of the marinade, wash with cold water, rub with salt and let sit for about 1 hour. Then dry and interlard with pieces of Bacon and garlic cloves. Grease a pan with lard, set the meat inside, pour ½ cup water, and add a little salt and a tbsp of vinegar or better yet ½ cup wine. Place 1 tbsp lard over the meat and roast at medium heat, taking care to baste every 10-15 minutes with the pan drippings. When ready, slice, arrange on the platter and pour the pan dripping over the meat. If there is too little sauce, after the meat is removed, add 2 tbsp of water and let come to a boil on top of the range. The sauce may be served separately in a gravy boat. Serve the meat with beet salad.

RABBIT WITH OLIVES
(iepure cu măsline)

fore and hind legs and neck from one rabbit, ½ cup oil, 5-6 large onions, 2 tbsp tomato sauce, 5-6 juniper berries, 1 bay leaf, 7 oz olives, ½ tsp sugar, 1 cup wine (or 1 cup water with one tbsp vinegar), salt and pepper

Fry the rabbit pieces in a pan with hot oil, add chopped onion, wine, 2-3 tbsp of water, tomato sauce, salt, sugar, juniper berries, bay leaf and the washed and pricked olives. Mix everything carefully, cover and simmer until ready (sauce well reduced). Mix every now and then while the dish is cooking.

RABBIT WITH SOUR CREAM
(iepure cu smântână)

6 pieces (portions) of rabbit meat, 1 tbsp lard, 1 tsp flour, 1 tbsp butter, 1 cup sour cream, 2-3 juniper berries, ½ chopped onion, salt

Lightly fry the rabbit pieces in a pan with oil, add 1/2 cup water, chopped onion and juniper berries. Cover and simmer for 1/2 hour. If the liquid is too much reduced, add 1-2 tbsp of water. Mix the sour cream with flour and pour over the meat. Add 2 tbsp of water, butter and salt. Cover and simmer at very low heat for another 15-20 minutes. Serve with warm mămăligă.

REGULAR CABBAGE ROLLS
(sarmale cu varză dulce)

1 large cabbage, 1 ¾ lb ground meat (mixture of pork and beef is recommended), 4 large onions, 2 tbsp rice, 1 bread slice, 3 tbsp lard, 5-6 tomatoes or 1 tbsp tomato sauce, salt, pepper, chopped dill, 1 qt borş, sour cream

Grind the meat with the crustless bread slice (previously soaked and squeezed dry) and a raw onion. Place in a bowl and mix with rice, dill, pepper, salt and finely chopped onion slightly fried in two tbsp of lard. Mix everything well. Core the cabbage with a sharp thin knife and then blanch it with borş. Then carefully remove the cabbage leaves, one by one, so that they do not tear. Cut larger leaves in 2 or 3 and then place a little meat in each cabbage piece and roll in. The smaller the rolls are, the tastier they are. Place a layer of rolls in the pan (take a deep one), then cover with a layer of chopped (julienned) cabbage, then a layer of thinly sliced tomatoes. Do this layering until all the rolls are made. The last layer must be tomato slices or add tomato sauce. Add a heaping tbsp of lard, pour the borş and let simmer on top of the range for 30 minutes. Then place in the oven so that the liquid is reduced. Serve with sour cream.

RIZZOTO WITH KIDNEYS
(rizoto cu rinichi)

1 beef or 2 veal or pork kidneys, 1 cup rice, 2 cups meat broth or water, 3 tbsp lard, 3 onions, 2 tbsp tomato sauce, ½ tsp paprika, salt, pepper, a little sugar, grated parmesan to taste, chopped parsley

Remove the outer membranes from the kidneys, split in half lengthwise, remove the interior fatty tissues and slice thinly. Set to boil starting with cold water. After it comes to a boil, drain and wash the kidneys with tepid water. Finely chop the onion, fry in 2 tbsp of lard until softened, and add tomato sauce, paprika, one cup meat broth or water, salt, pepper, sugar and the kidneys. Simmer until the kidneys are done. In the meantime, fry the rice in one tbsp of lard, add a cup meat broth. Place the rice in a greased Bundt pan (hole in the middle), cover and set into the oven to bake. When the rice is done, turn onto a plate, spread some grated parmesan on top and place the kidneys and sauce in the middle hole. Spread some chopped parsley on top and serve hot.

ROLLED MEAT LOAF STUFFED WITH MACARONI
(ruladă de carne tocată umplută cu macaroane)

Meat mixture: 2 lbs ground sirloin, 5 oz bacon, 2 onions, 1 crustless white bread slice, salt, pepper

7 oz macaroni, 1 tbsp butter, 1 egg, pepper

Boil the macaroni in salt water, drain, rinse with cold water, drain, and then mix with the beaten egg, pepper and melted butter. On a clean, wet cloth spread the meat mixture uniformly, in a ½ inch layer. Place the macaroni in the middle of the meat mixture. Roll the meat loaf with the aid of the cloth, so that the meat encloses the macaroni. Place the rolled meat loaf on a lard greased baking sheet, glaze with egg, cover with bread crumbs and bake at medium heat for 30-40 minutes. Serve cut into finger thick slices with green lettuce, red beet salad or carrot sauté.

SAUERKRAUT WITH MUTTON
(varză acră cu carne de berbec)

1 lb mutton, 1 medium cabbage, 4 tbsp lard, ½ tsp paprika, 1 tbsp tomato paste

Cut the meat in bite size pieces and fry very little in lard. Add water to cover and let boil, covered, about a half hour. During this time, chop the sauerkraut. Then add it to the meat, also adding paprika, tomato paste, and a little water. Let boil, at slow temperature for another hour. If the liquid evaporates, add a little warm water. Then bake in the oven for another hour. Serve with mămăligă.

STUFFED CABBAGE WITH...CABBAGE
(varză cu varză)

One large cabbage, 2 eggs, 2slices od bread, 3 table spoons of cooking oil, ¼ tsp dill weed, ¼ tsp oregano, ¼ tsp salt, and ¼ tsp pepper, one can of slied tomatoes in tomatoe juice

Remove the center of the cabbage with a knife and place cabbage in boiling water with a pinch of salt (the boiling water should cover the cabbage). Leave cabbage in boiling water enough for the outer leaves to become soft, then remove cabbage from water and allow it to cool off and dry. Mince 1-2 onions and fry them gently in oil. Add a little water, the two eggs (minced), salt, pepper, oregano.

Moist the two slices of bread in water and puree the bread

Mix a couple of cabbage leaves with the bread and the fried onion and add the mixture into the de-stemmed cabbage.

Place the cabbage upside down into a pot sprinkled with oil, add the slices tomatoe and tomatoe juice and place in the own at 350 degrees for about 30 minutes.

Remove from owen and sprinkle with dill weed. Serve the cabbage with sour cream.

ROLLED MEAT LOAF
(ruladă de carne tocată)

2 lbs ground sirloin, 5 oz bacon, 2 onions, 1 crustless white bread slice, 1 raw egg, 4 hard-boiled eggs, salt, pepper, 1 tsp chopped parsley and dill, 1 tbsp bread crumbs, green lettuce or red beets

Grind the meat with the finely chopped raw or lard fried onions, the soaked and squeezed bread and the Bacon. Add salt, pepper, chopped parsley and dill and raw egg. Mix everything well. Roll out a clean wet cloth and place the mixture on it, in the shape of a rectangle with the length triple the width. Arrange the hard-boiled eggs in a row along the middle of the rectangle. Start rolling the meat with the aid of the cloth, so that the eggs are enclosed in the meat. Place the rolled meat loaf on a lard greased baking sheet, grease the top with melted lard, spread some bread crumbs on top and bake for 45 minutes. Serve cut into finger thick slices, garnished with green lettuce or red beet salad.

RUSSIAN BEEFSTEAK
(biftec rusesc)

1 ¼ lb sirloin, 3 big onions, salt, pepper, 2 tbsp lard

Cut the sirloin in one inch thick slices. Pound them slightly, salt, pepper and fry in hot lard on both sides at high heat. Remove the meat from the pan but keep warm while you fry the chopped onion in the fat remaining from frying the meat. The onion must be browning. Arrange the meat on a platter, arrange some fried onion on top of each slice and pour a little fat from the pan on them. Serve immediately with French fries and some salad (either lettuce or cucumber).

ROLLED MEAT LOAF STUFFED WITH RICE
(ruladă de carne tocată umplută cu orez)

Meat mixture: 2 lbs ground sirloin, 5 oz bacon, 2 onions, 1 crustless white bread slice, salt, pepper

5 oz rice, 1 tbsp butter, 1 egg, pepper

Boil the rice in salt water (one part rice to 2 parts water), then mix with the beaten egg, pepper and melted butter. On a clean, wet cloth spread the meat mixture uniformly, in a 1/2 inch layer. Place the rice in the middle of the meat mixture. Roll the meat loaf with the aid of the cloth, so that the meat encloses the rice. Place the rolled meat loaf on a lard greased baking sheet, glaze with egg, cover with bread crumbs and bake at medium heat for 30-40 minutes. Serve cut into finger thick slices with green lettuce, red beet salad or carrot sauté.

SAUERKRAUT WITH BEEF
(varză acră cu carne de vacă)

1 lb fatty beef, 1 medium cabbage, 4 tbsp lard, ½ tsp paprika, 1 tbsp tomato paste

Cut the meat in bite size pieces and fry very little in lard. Add water to cover and let boil, covered, about a half hour. During this time, chop the sauerkraut. Then add it to the meat, also adding paprika, tomato paste, and a little water. Let boil, at slow temperature for another hour. If the liquid evaporates, add a little warm water. Then bake in the oven for another hour. Serve with mămăligă.

SMOTHERED ROAST BEEF II
(friptură înăbuşită) II

3 lbs lean meat, 1 onion, 2-3 garlic cloves, 1 medium carrot, 1 cup wine, 2 tbsp lard, salt, pepper, 1 tsp paprika

Brown the meat a little on all sides, using hot lard. Add a halved carrot, an onion, salt, garlic, pepper, wine and warm water to cover the meat. Cover and let boil until the meat is tender and there are only 2-3 tbsp of liquid left. Remove the carrot, onion and garlic, sieve them and add them back to the pot. Add one tbsp of tomato paste, 2-3 tbsp of water and let come to another boil, turning the meat on all sides. Slice the meat, pour the sauce on top and serve with potatoes, boiled rice or boiled vegetables. Pour some melted butter on top of the side dish.

SMOTHERED ROAST BEEF I
(friptură înăbuşită) I

3 lbs beef, 1/3 lb bacon, one head of garlic, 2 tbsp lard, salt, pepper

Rub the entire piece of meat with salt and then, after making some slits in the meat, place garlic cloves and pieces of Bacon in them. Fry the meat on all sides in hot lard, add broth or water, pepper, cover and let boil, at slow temperature until the liquid is gone and the meat is tender. If necessary, during the boiling add some more warm broth or water. Slice the meat in one inch thick slices, place on a platter and serve with mashed potatoes, vegetable saute, lettuce or pickles.

TOMATOES STUFFED WITH MEAT
(roşii umplute cu carne)

12 big tomatoes, 1 ¾ lb ground meat, 2 onions, 2 tbsp rice, 1 tbsp lard, chopped parsley and dill, salt, pepper, 2 tomatoes;

Sauce: 1 lb tomatoes, ½ onion, 1 tsp sugar, ½ tsp flour, salt, chopped parsley, 1 tbsp lard, sour cream

Wash the tomatoes, dry, core and remove the seeds. Mix the meat with two finely chopped raw or fried onions, a tbsp of lard, rice, chopped parsley and dill, pepper and salt. Mix everything well and use this mixture to fill the tomatoes. Put one tomato slice as a lid on each tomato. Arrange in a pan and pour the following sauce on top. Fry the finely chopped onion and flour in lard until golden; add tomato sauce (from boiled and strained tomatoes). Add sugar and salt. If the sauce does not cover the peppers add some water. Spread some chopped parsley, set to boil for a little while then place in the oven to bake until done. Serve with sour cream.

TONGUE WITH OLIVES
(limbă cu măsline)

1 beef or 3-4 pork tongues (about 2 lbs), vegetables for soup, 7 oz olives, 3-4 onions, 1 bay leaf, 2-3 juniper berries, 2 tbsp tomato sauce, 1 tbsp vinegar, 3 tbsp oil, ½ tsp sugar, salt, 1 lemon, chopped parsley

Boil the tongue with the vegetables. When the tongue is almost done, remove from the broth, clean and cut into finger thick slices. Fry the finely chopped onion in oil until softened, and add tomato sauce, vinegar, sugar, juniper berries, salt and a cup of the tongue boiling liquid. (You must first remove the fat from liquid.) Add olives that were well washed and previously kept in warm water for 2-3 hours and the tongue slices. Cover and let boil until done. You may serve it warm or cold, garnished with chopped parsley and a few lemon slices.

TONGUE IN SOUR CREAM SAUCE
(limbă în sos de smântână)

1 beef or 3-4 pork tongues (about 2 lbs), vegetables for soup, 1 cup sour cream, 1 tbsp butter, ½ tbsp flour, ½ cup of the tongue boiling liquid, ½ onion, chopped dill

Boil the tongue and cut into finger thick slices. Melt the butter in a pan and fry a half of a grated onion, add the flour, the tongue boiling liquid, then add the sour cream and tongue slices. Simmer for 10-15 minutes, add chopped dill and then let simmer for a couple of minutes. Serve hot.

VEAL ROAST
(friptură de vițel la tavă)

2-4 lbs veal, salt, a little lard

Salt the meat and let sit for 30 minutes. Place in the lard greased pan, add 3-4 tbsp of water and set in the oven, first at high heat until it starts to brown, then reduce heat. During the roasting, baste with the liquid in the pan. Keep in the oven for 1 to 1 1/2 hours. Serve sliced, with sautéed cabbage. Pour some sauce from the pan over the slices.

BOILED HEN
(găină rasol)

1 medium hen, 2 carrots, 1 parsley root, 1 celery root, 1 parsnip, 1 onion, 2 juniper berries (optional), 1 bay leaf (optional), 3-4 potatoes, 3 qts water, salt

Clean and wash the hen and set it to boil at low heat with 3 qts/3 l water. Remove foam, and then add the vegetables, onion, juniper berries, bay leaf and salt. Cover and simmer until the hen is almost done. Add the halved (lengthwise) potatoes and let simmer until done. Remove the hen, cut in pieces, arrange on a platter and garnish with boiled potatoes and sliced carrot and celery. Spray with a few tbsp of the boiling liquid. Serve to taste with oil and lemon juice or vinegar, horseradish sauce or garlic juice.

VEAL SCHNITZEL
(şniţel de viţel)

1 ¾ lbs leg meat, 1 tsp oil, 2 eggs, 2-3 tbsp lard, flour, bread crumbs, pepper, salt

Cut the meat in medium sized pieces, about a finger thick. Lightly pound with the wooden hammer, salt and pepper. Dredge each Veal slice with the eggs beaten with a teaspoon of oil, flour, egg again and finally, bread crumbs. Fry on both sides in hot lard. Serve with French fries, sautéed vegetables or a salad.

CHICKEN PILAF
(pilaf de pui)

1 large chicken, 2 tbsp butter or lard, 1 cup rice, salt

Clean and wash the chicken, cut into pieces, salt and set into a pan with water to cover. Let boil for 15 minutes. Remove foam. Fry the rice with the lard. The rice must be dry without becoming brown. Arrange the chicken pieces on top of the rice and add two cups of the chicken broth. Let it come to a boil on top of the range and then place in the oven until the rice is done.

HEN WITH OLIVES
(gaină cu măsline)

6 hen portions (breast, thighs, etc.), 4 tbsp oil, 7 oz olives, 1 tbsp tomato sauce, 1 tsp flour, 3 onions, 1 tsp vinegar, or ½ cup wine, sugar, salt, 1 bay leaf

Fry the hen pieces in 2 tbsp of oil, add 3-4 tbsp of water and simmer. Every now and then, turn the pieces, adding 2-3 tbsp of water. When the meat is half done, add washed and pricked olives. Separately, fry the chopped onion in two tbsp of oil until yellow. Add the flour, let fry a little longer, then add a cup of chicken broth or water, tomato sauce, salt, sugar, bay leaf and wine or vinegar. Pour this sauce over the meat and let boil until the meat is done. You may serve this warm or cold.

CHICKEN WHITE SAUCE STEW
(ciulama de pui)

1 chicken, 1 onion, 1 tbsp butter, 1 ½ tbsp flour, salt

Cut the meat and set in a pan adding water to cover. Add one whole onion and salt. Remove foam and simmer until done. Throw away the onion. Separately, slightly fry the flour in butter. Add the meat boiling liquid, stirring quickly and then pour over the meat pieces. Let boil for a few minutes longer. The stew is tastier if you add a cup of milk to the sauce.

CHICKEN WITH CAULIFLOWER
(pui cu conopidă)

1 medium chicken, 1 medium cauliflower, 1/2 tsp flour, 2-3 tbsp white wine or 1 tbsp lemon juice, 1 cup water, 2 tbsp butter, salt, pepper

Clean and wash the chicken, cut into pieces and fry them in a pan with a tbsp of butter. Add the flour and then pour a cup of water. Add wine, salt and pepper. Clean the cauliflower and divide into flowerets. Fry it slightly with a tbsp of butter and then arrange over the chicken pieces. Let simmer, covered, until the liquid is much reduced.

CHICKEN WITH EGGPLANT
(pui cu vinete)

1 Chicken, 3 medium eggplants, 1 onion, 1 tbsp flour, 3-4 tbsp oil, salt, chopped parsley

Cut the eggplants in quarters, lengthwise, and then halve each quarter. Salt it and let sit for at least a half hour. Then slightly squeeze each piece, dredge with flour and fry in oil. Sauté the chicken pieces, covered, in a tablespoon of oil. Add the grated onion and 2-3 tbsp of water. Arrange the eggplant pieces over the chicken, add the parsley, cover and let boil, at low heat, for 10-15 minutes. Then move the pan to the oven and let it bake until ready.

CHICKEN WITH GREEN PEAS
(pui cu mazăre verde)

1 medium chicken, 1 ¾ lbs green pea, 1 tbsp butter, ½ tsp flour, ½ tsp sugar, chopped dill, salt

Clean and wash the chicken and cut into pieces. Fry in butter until yellow. Add the flour and fry until yellow. Then add ½ cup water, salt, sugar and peas. Let simmer, covered, and when almost ready, add the chopped dill.

CHICKEN WITH OKRA
(pui cu bame)

1 chicken, 1 tbsp lard, 1 lb okra, 5-6 tomatoes, 1 onion, chopped parsley and dill, 1 tbsp vinegar, ½ tsp sugar, salt

Clean and wash the okra. Keep okra in water with salt and vinegar for one hour. Fry the chicken pieces in butter until yellow. Add grated onion, boiled and strained tomatoes, salt, sugar and the okra (which were rinsed several times after removal from the salt-vinegar water). Simmer, covered, until the okra are almost done. Add a tbsp of vinegar and the chopped greens and set in the oven for a little while.

CHICKEN WITH SOUR CREAM
(pui cu smântână)

1 chicken, 1 tbsp butter, 1 tsp flour, 1 cup sour cream, salt

Sauté the chicken pieces in melted butter, adding 1-2 tbsp of water if necessary. When the chicken is almost done, add salt and then sour cream well mixed with flour. Simmer for 10-15 minutes. Keep warm until serving.

CHICKEN WITH GREEN BEANS
(pui cu fasole verde)

1 chicken, 1 ¾ lbs green beans, 2 tbsp lard, 1 onion, ½ cup chicken broth or water, 5-6 tomatoes, 1 tsp chopped parsley and dill, salt, 1 tsp flour

Slightly fry the chicken pieces in lard until they turn yellow. Add the finely chopped onion, a teaspoon of flour, mix and let fry for a little while. Add a half cup of chicken broth (or water), the cleaned green beans and the peeled, seeded and cut tomatoes. Add salt and chopped greens and let simmer, covered, for a half hour. Then set in the oven until the liquid is greatly reduced. You can also use raw onion. In this case, add it with the chicken broth.

CHICKEN WITH TARRAGON
(pui cu tarhon)

1 medium chicken, 1 tbsp lard, 1 onion, 4-5 tomatoes, 1/2 tsp flour, tarragon, salt

Fry the chicken pieces in lard until yellow. Add the finely chopped onion and flour. When the onion starts to turn yellow, add 3-4 tbsp of water, juice from 4-5 tomatoes, salt and tarragon. The quantity of tarragon is to taste. Cover and simmer. When the meat is almost done, set into the oven for 15-20 minutes. You may prepare this with raw onion. In this case, add it with the water.

PARTRIDGES, STUFFED
(potârnichi umplute)

6 partridges, 1 onion, 4 oz fresh bacon, 2 crustless slices of white bread soaked in milk, 1 egg, gizzards from 4 partridges, 1 tbsp butter, 1 tbsp lard, ground pepper and juniper berries, salt, chopped parsley

Wash and salt the partridges. Let them sit until you prepare the following stuffing. Chop the gizzards and sauté in a tbsp of lard, with the finely chopped onion. Remove from heat, add the cubed Bacon, bread, salt, pepper, parsley and mix everything well with an egg. Stuff the partridges with this stuffing and then fry in a pan with a tbsp of butter, until golden-brown. Add 2-3 tbsp of water, cover and simmer at low heat until done. Keep turning them and add a little water from time to time, as needed.

QUAILS WITH SOUR CREAM
(prepelițe cu smântână)

6 quails, 1 tbsp butter, 1 cup sour cream, 1 tsp flour, salt

Wash and halve the quails lengthwise. Cover and let sit for 15-20 minutes. Then fry with the butter. Then pour the sour cream which was well mixed with the flour, add 1-2 tbsp of water, salt, cover and simmer for 15-20 minutes. Serve with warm mămăligă.

FRIED QUAILS, HUNTER STYLE
(prepeliţe fripte vânătoreşte)

6 quails, 3 tbsp butter or lard, salt

Place a tbsp of lard in a Dutch oven and let it get hot. Place the previously salted quails inside and cover. Turn the quails every 2-3 minutes. After they are golden brown, add 2 tbsp of water and simmer at very low heat, for 10-15 minutes. When ready, pour a little melted butter or lard over them. Serve hot.

ROASTED QUAILS
(prepeliţe fripte)

6 quails, 6 slices fresh bacon, 1 tsp lard, salt, 3-4 tbsp wine

Wash the quails, salt and wrap with thin slices of fresh bacon. Place in a pan, add a teaspoon of lard and the wine and roast, at medium heat, turning them a few times and basting with the pan drippings.

CHICKEN WITH TOMATOES
(pui cu roşii)

1 chicken, 1 tbsp butter, 1 onion, ½ tsp flour, 1 ¾ lbs tomatoes, ½ tsp paprika, salt, sugar

Sauté the chicken pieces in butter. When almost ready, add the finely chopped onion and flour, mixing continuously. Then add the halved and seeded tomatoes, paprika, salt and sugar. Cover and simmer until the tomatoes are done. Do not stir during simmering. Shake the pan instead.

BAKED CHICKEN
(pui la tavă)

1 big chicken, ½ tbsp lard, salt

Salt the chicken, let sit for 15-20 minutes, then place in the roasting pan, add the lard and 2-3 tbsp water and set in the oven. During roasting, baste with the pan drippings. Serve with French fries and green lettuce or cucumber salad.

BREADED CHICKEN
(pui pane)

1 medium chicken, 1 egg, 2 tbsp flour, 1 tbsp lard, salt

Section the chicken, salt. Lightly pound with the wooden hammer, salt and pepper. Dredge each chicken slice with the eggs beaten with a teaspoon of oil, flour, egg again and finally, bread crumbs. Fry on both sides in hot lard. Serve with French fries, sautéed vegetables or a salad.

SMOTHERED CHICKEN
(pui înăbuşit)

1 big chicken, 1 tbsp lard, salt, a little garlic

Salt the chicken and place in a pan with melted lard. Fry on all sides, add 4-5 tbsp of water or chicken broth, cover and simmer. Occasionally turn the chicken and if the liquid is too reduced, add 1-2 tbsp of water. At the end, you may add a little crushed garlic. Serve with French fries and green lettuce or cucumber salad.

DUCK ROAST WITH BAKED APPLES
(friptură de raţă cu mere coapte)

1 duck, 12 big apples, 1 tbsp lard, salt

Clean, wash and salt the duck. Introduce 2 small apples in its cavity. Place in the roasting pan with a tbsp of lard and a few tbsp of water. Set in the oven at high temperature and keep basting with the pan drippings. When the duck starts to brown, place the washed and dried apples around it and reduce the heat. As they bake, remove the apples from the pan, letting the duck in until done. When it is done, remove from the pan, slice, arrange on a platter with the apples around the meat. Put two tbsp of water in the pan and let boil on top of the range. Stir. Strain this sauce and pour over the meat.

DUCK WITH OLIVES
(raţă cu măsline)

6 duck portions (breast, thighs, etc.), 4 tbsp oil, 7 oz olives, 1 tbsp tomato sauce, 1 tsp flour, 3 onions, 1 tsp vinegar, or ½ cup wine, sugar, salt, 1 bay leaf

Fry the duck pieces in 2 tbsp of oil, add 3-4 tablespoons of water and simmer. Every now and then, turn the pieces, adding 2-3 tbsp of water. When the meat is half done, add washed and pricked olives. Separately, fry the chopped onion in two tbsp of oil until yellow. Add the flour, let fry a little longer, then add a cup of chicken broth or water, tomato sauce, salt, sugar, bay leaf and wine or vinegar. Pour this sauce over the meat and let boil until the meat is done. You may serve this warm or cold.

DUCK WITH PICKLED CUCUMBERS
(rață cu castraveți acri)

1 small duck, 8 medium pickles, 2 tbsp lard, 1 tbsp tomato sauce, 1 onion, ½ tsp flour, salt, chopped dill

Fry the duck pieces in lard until it starts to brown. Add the chopped onion and flour and let fry a little longer. Then add warm water to cover the duck pieces. Cover and simmer for half an hour. Prepare 2 inch long pieces of pickle. To the meat add pickles, tomato sauce, sugar, chopped dill and simmer until the meat is done and the liquid is reduced. You can also use raw onion instead of fried. In this case, add it with the warm water.

DUCK WITH SOUR OR SWEET CABBAGE
(rață cu varză acră sau dulce)

1 duck, 1 large can sauerkraut or 1 cabbage (sliced), 3 tbsp lard, 1 tbsp tomato sauce, ½ tsp paprika, a few pepper berries, salt

Clean, wash and salt the duck. Let it sit for one hour. In the meantime, fry the sauerkraut or the cabbage in lard, adding paprika, tomato sauce, pepper and salt (if needed). Arrange the cabbage in a uniform layer in a roasting pan and place the duck on top. The duck was previously dried and then greased with lard. Set into the oven and baste occasionally with the liquid in the pan. After the duck has been roasted on one side, turn onto the other side.

DUCKLING ON CABBAGE
(boboc de rață pe varză dulce)

1 duckling, 1 large cabbage (sliced), 3 tbsp lard, 1 tbsp tomato sauce, ½ tsp paprika, a few pepper berries, salt, some borş and some unripe tomatoes

Clean, wash and salt the duckling. Let it sit for one hour. In the meantime, fry the cabbage in lard, adding paprika, tomato sauce, borş and some unripe tomatoes, pepper and salt (if needed). Arrange the sauerkraut in a uniform layer in a roasting pan and place the duckling on top. The duckling was previously dried and then greased with lard. Set into the oven and baste occasionally with the liquid in the pan. After the duckling has been roasted on one side, turn onto the other side.

DUCKLING ON SAUERKRAUT
(boboc de raţă pe varză acră)

1 duckling, 1 large can sauerkraut, 3 tbsp lard, 1 tbsp tomato sauce, ½ tsp paprika, a few pepper berries, salt

Clean, wash and salt the duckling. Let it sit for one hour. In the meantime, fry the sauerkraut in lard, adding paprika, tomato sauce, pepper and salt (if needed). Arrange the sauerkraut in a uniform layer in a roasting pan and place the duckling on top. The duckling was previously dried and then greased with lard. Set into the oven and baste occasionally with the liquid in the pan. After the duckling has been roasted on one side, turn onto the other side.

GOOSE ON CABBAGE
(gâscă pe varză)

1 goose, 1 large can sauerkraut or 1 cabbage (sliced), 3 tbsp lard, 1 tbsp tomato sauce, 1/2 tsp paprika, a few pepper Berries, salt

Clean, wash and salt the goose. Let it rest for one hour. In the meantime, fry the sauerkraut or the cabbage in lard, adding paprika, tomato sauce, pepper and salt (if needed). Arrange the cabbage in a uniform layer in a roasting pan and place the goose on top. The goose was previously dried and then greased with lard. Set into the oven and baste occasionally with the liquid in the pan. After the goose has been roasted on one side, turn onto the other side.

GOOSE ROAST
(friptură de gâscă la tavă)

1 goose, 1 tbsp lard, salt

Clean, wash and salt the goose. Place in the roasting pan with a tbsp of lard and a few tbsp of water. At the beginning, keep the heat low and then increase it. Roast it for 1 ½ hours. When it is done, remove from the pan, slice, arrange on a platter with the apples around the meat. Serve either with baked apples like the duck or with French fries and a salad, pickles or sautéed cabbage.

Put two tbsp of water in the pan and let boil on top of the range. Stir. Strain this sauce and pour over the meat.

GOOSE WITH OLIVES
(gâscă cu măsline)

6 goose portions (breast, thighs, etc.), 4 tbsp oil, 7 oz olives, 1 tbsp tomato sauce, 1 tsp flour, 3 onions, 1 tsp vinegar, or ½ cup wine, sugar, salt, 1 bay leaf

Fry the goose pieces in 2 tbsp of oil, add 3-4 tbsp of water and simmer. Every now and then, turn the pieces, adding 2-3 tbsp of water. When the meat is half done, add washed and pricked olives. Separately, fry the chopped onion in two tbsp of oil until yellow. Add the flour, let fry a little longer, then add a cup of chicken broth or water, tomato sauce, salt, sugar, bay leaf and wine or vinegar. Pour this sauce over the meat and let boil until the meat is done. You may serve this warm or cold.

GRAPE LEAF ROLLS WITH LAMB
(sarmale cu foi de viţă şi carne de miel)

1 ¾ lb ground lamb, 4 large onions, 2 tbsp rice, 1 bread slice, 3 tbsp lard, 5-6 tomatoes or 1 tbsp tomato sauce, salt, pepper, chopped dill, 1 qt borş, sour cream, ½ lb grape leaves, 2 tbsp chopped dill, 0.5 qt borş, salt, 1 cup sour cream or plain yogurt

Grind the meat with the crustless bread slice (previously soaked and squeezed dry) and a raw onion. Place in a bowl and mix with rice, dill, pepper, salt and finely chopped onion slightly fried in two tbsp of lard. Mix everything well.

The grape leaves must be young. Wash a few times and scald with water. Place a little meat in each grape leaf and roll in. The smaller the rolls are, the tastier they are. Place a layer of rolls in the pan (take a deep one), then cover with a layer of thinly sliced tomatoes. Do this layering until all the rolls are made. The last layer must be tomato slices. Add a heaping tbsp of lard, pour the borş and let simmer on top of the range for 30 minutes. Then place in the oven so that the liquid is reduced. Serve with sour cream.

HEN BREAST MEAT BALLS
(chifteluțe din piept de gaină)

1 lb ground hen breast, 3 onions, 1 egg, 2 slices white bread, 1 tbsp lard, chopped parsley and dill, lard for frying, bread crumbs

Grind the meat with a raw onion, soaked and squeezed bread and two finely chopped and lightly fried (in a tbsp of lard) onions. Place the mixture in a bowl; add an egg, salt, pepper and chopped parsley and dill. Mix everything well. Take tbsp of the mixture and with wet hands shape into round or oval patties. Then bread them and fry in hot lard on both sides. You may replace the chopped parsley and dill with chopped garlic. Serve hot with sautéed peas or carrots

HEN PILAF
(pilaf de găină)

1 large hen, 2 tbsp butter or lard, 1 cup rice, salt

Clean and wash the hen, cut into pieces, salt and set into a pan with water to cover. Let boil for about 1 hour. Remove foam. Fry the rice with the lard. The rice must be dry without becoming brown. Arrange the hen pieces on top of the rice and add two cups of the chicken broth. Let it come to a boil on top of the range and then place in the oven until the rice is done.

LEMON SAUCED CHICKEN
(anghemaht de pui)

1 chicken, 1 tbsp butter, 1 tsp flour, 1/2 lemon, salt

Boil the chicken pieces as for chicken pilaf. Fry the flour in butter until yellow, add a cup of the chicken broth, salt, chicken pieces and the peeled and sliced lemon. Simmer for 5-10 minutes. The sauce must be much thinner than for the chicken white sauce stew. Therefore, add some more chicken broth if necessary.

TURKEY ROAST
(friptură de curcan la tavă)

1 turkey, 2 tbsp lard, salt

Clean, wash and salt the goose. Place in the roasting pan with a tablespoon of lard and a few tbsp of water. At the beginning, keep the heat low and then increase it. Roast it for 1 ½ hours. When it is done, remove from the pan, slice, arrange on a platter with the apples around the meat. Serve either with baked apples like the duck or with French fries and a salad, pickles or sautéed cabbage.

Put two tbsp of water in the pan and let boil on top of the range. Stir. Strain this sauce and pour over the meat.

TURKEY WITH CHESTNUTS
(mâncare de curcan cu castane)

12 little turkey pieces, 1 tbsp lard, 1 tsp butter, 1 tsp flour, 1 small onion, 1 ¾ lbs chestnuts, 1 ½ tsp sugar, salt

Fry the turkey pieces with lard until yellow. Pour chicken broth or water to almost cover, add salt and a whole onion and simmer, covered, until the meat is almost done. Remove the onion. Separately fry the flour until yellowish, add the turkey boiling liquid and caramelized sugar (1 teaspoon) to which a little more of the turkey boiling liquid has been added. Pour this sauce over the turkey pieces; add ½ teaspoon sugar, salt, butter and the boiled and peeled chestnuts. Be careful to keep the chestnuts whole. Simmer until the sauce is greatly reduced. (The dish must have very little sauce.)

PHEASANT ROAST
(friptură de fazan)

1 pheasant, 5 oz bacon for interlarding, 2 tbsp butter, salt

Remove feathers, singe, wash several times and keep in cold water for half an hour. Then remove, dry, rub with some salt and interlard the breast and legs with pieces of bacon. Then let sit for 20-30 minutes. Set in a roasting pan with 2 tbsp of butter and 2-3 tbsp of water. Turn several times while roasting, basting with the liquid in the pan. Serve with fried small whole potatoes, sautéed cauliflower or baked small apples.

TURKEY WITH DRIED APRICOTS
(curcan cu caise uscate)

12 little turkey pieces, 1 tbsp lard, 1 tsp butter, 1 tsp flour, 1 small onion, 1 ¾ lbs dried apricots, 1 ½ tsp sugar, salt

Fry the turkey pieces with lard until yellow. Pour chicken broth or water to almost cover, add salt and a whole onion and simmer, covered, until the meat is almost done. Remove the onion. Separately fry the flour until yellowish, add the turkey boiling liquid and caramelized sugar (1 teaspoon) to which a little more of the turkey boiling liquid has been added. Pour this sauce over the turkey pieces; add ½ teaspoon sugar, salt, and butter. Add the apricots when the meat is almost done, taking care to keep them whole. Simmer until the sauce is greatly reduced. (The dish must have very little sauce.) If you wish, you may add a little more sugar.

TURKEY WITH OLIVES
(curcan cu măsline)

6 turkey portions (breast, thighs, etc.), 4 tbsp oil, 7 oz olives, 1 tbsp tomato sauce, 1 tsp flour, 3 onions, 1 tsp vinegar, or ½ cup wine, sugar, salt, 1 bay leaf

Fry the turkey pieces in 2 tbsp of oil, add 3-4 tbsp of water and simmer. Every now and then, turn the turkey pieces, adding 2-3 tbsp of water. When the meat is half done, add washed and pricked olives. Separately, fry the chopped onion in two tbsp of oil until yellow. Add the flour, let fry a little longer, then add a cup of chicken broth or water, tomato sauce, salt, sugar, bay leaf and wine or vinegar. Pour this sauce over the meat and let boil until the meat is done. You may serve this warm or cold.

TURKEY WITH QUINCES
(curcan cu gutui)

6 turkey portions (breast, thighs, etc.), 4 medium quinces, 2 tbsp flour, 2-3 tbsp lard, 2 tsp sugar, salt

Fry the hen pieces with a tbsp of lard until yellow. Add ½ teaspoon of flour and salt, cover with water and simmer, covered. In the meantime, peel the quinces, cut into thick slices, remove seeds, dredge with flour and fry in lard on both sides. When the meat is almost done, add 1 teaspoon of caramelized sugar to which a little chicken broth or water was added and 1 teaspoon of regular sugar. Place the quinces over the meat, cover the pan and simmer. Do not stir, but shake the pan occasionally. The sauce must be greatly reduced.

WILD DUCK ROAST
(friptură de rață sălbatică)

1 wild duck, 2-3 tbsp lard, 5 oz bacon (for interlarding), 4-5 tbsp wine, salt to taste

Keep the wild duck in the marinade at least 12 hours. Then wash, dry, salt, interlard with pieces of bacon and set in a pan with lard. Fry on all sides, add 2-3 tbsp of wine and let simmer, covered, for 45 minutes. Add 1 tbsp of wine every now and then and turn the roast. Then set the roast into the oven, uncovered, until done. Serve with beet or red cabbage salad.

CARP ON RICE
(crap pe orez)

2 lbs carp, 1 cup rice, 1 tsp flour, 2 tbsp vinegar, salt, pepper, 4 tbsp oil, onion

Clean and wash the fish, then split lengthwise and cut in 1 1/2" wide pieces; salt and let sit for a half hour. In the meantime, start frying the chopped onion until half done. Add the washed and dried rice and let fry until it starts turning yellow. Then pour water to cover the rice and let it boil for 5-6 minutes. Place the rice-onion mixture in a baking dish; add salt and pepper and then the fish pieces on top. Make a sauce out of a teaspoon of flour mixed with two tbsp of vinegar, pour over the fish and place in the oven. Add some water every now and then, as needed. Serve warm or cold.

FRIED CARP
(crap prăjit)

2 lbs carp, 3 tbsp oil, 2 tbsp flour, lemon juice, salt

Clean, wash and cut the fish salt it and let it sit for 10-15 minutes. Then dry each piece with a clean cloth, dredge with flour and fry in hot oil, on both sides. Serve warm, with French fries and green lettuce. You may add some lemon juice to taste.

CARP STEW
(plachie de crap)

2 lbs carp, 4 tbsp oil, 5-6 big onions, 1 tbsp tomato sauce, 2 tbsp flour, 2-3 pepper berries, 2-3 juniper berries, 1 cup wine, a few lemon slices, salt

Clean and wash the fish, cut into pieces, salt and let sit for 15-20 minutes. Then dry each piece with a clean cloth, dredge with flour and fry in hot oil on both sides. Fry the chopped onion in the oil that remained from the fish frying. When the onion starts to turn yellow, add the tomato sauce, wine, salt, pepper, juniper berries, lemon slices and fish pieces. Place in the oven at low temperature and let it bake until the liquid is reduced. You may serve it warm or cold.

CARP WITH MAYO
(crap cu maioneză)

2 lbs carp, soup vegetables (carrots, parsnips, parsley roots), 3-4 juniper berries, 1 bay leaf, 1 onion, salt, lettuce

Boil the carp with the vegetables as for carp, poached. Let it cool off in the liquid it boiled in. Then remove carefully and set on a platter. Split it lengthwise; remove the backbone and all other bones. Do this carefully so that the fish maintains its shape. Place one half over the other, cut into pieces and cover with mayo. Garnish the edges of the platter with finely chopped lettuce. Every here and there make mounds of finely chopped carrot (carrot that boiled with the fish). Place an olive on top of each mound.

MARINATED CARP
(marinată de crap)

2 lbs carp, 3 tbsp oil, 2 tbsp flour, salt, 1 cup vinegar, 1 cup water, 3-4 juniper berries, 2-3 bay leaves, 2 lumps of sugar

Clean and wash the carp, cut into pieces, salt and let sit for a half hour. Pat dry each piece, dredge with flour and fry in hot oil on both sides, at low temperature. Arrange the nicely fried pieces in a bowl or jar and then pour over them the vinegar which was boiled with water, salt, juniper berries, bay leaves and sugar. When the vinegar is added to the fish, it has to be cold. Serve after 2-3 days.

POACHED CARP
(crap rasol)

2 lbs carp, 1 onion, 1 carrot, 1 parsley root, 2-3 pepper Berries, 1 bay leaf, 2 tbsp lemon juice, 2 tbsp oil, 2-3 potatoes, salt

Clean, wash, salt the fish and let it sit for 10-15 minutes. In the meantime, set the vegetables to boil with 1 qt/1 l of water, some salt, pepper and bay leaf. Let boil until the vegetables are tender. Then remove from heat, add the quartered potatoes and let boil for a few minutes. Then add the fish pieces. Let everything simmer, covered, until the fish and potatoes are done. After the fish has cooled off, remove from the pot and place in the middle of a platter, surrounded by vegetables and potatoes. Mix the oil with the lemon juice and 2-3 tbsp of the poaching liquid and pour over the fish and vegetables. Then spread some chopped parsley on top of that.

HERRING IN OIL
(scrumbii în ulei)

2 lbs herrings, 3-4 lemons, 2 bay leaves, 5-6 juniper berries, 2 tsp salt, oil as needed

Clean, wash the herrings remove the heads and tails and cut in medium sized pieces. Salt and let it sit for an hour. Place the fish pieces in a dry bowl, pour the lemon juice over them and let sit for another 20-30 minutes. Then start putting the fish pieces in a jar, layering fish pieces with a bay leaf, 2-3 juniper berries, some lemon juice and oil so as to cover each fish layer. Do this until all fish pieces are used up. Pour a two finger wide layer of oil, cover the jar with a plate and steam it for 25-30 minutes (counting from when the water starts boiling). Serve cold. This can be kept over the winter; in this case, tie the jar with cellophane first and then steam. You may prepare a soup (sour) for two out of the heads and tails.

BREADED PERCH (SMALL)
(şalău mic pane)

2 lbs small perch, 2 tbsp flour, 2 eggs, 1 tbsp milk, bread crumbs, salt, 1 lemon, 4-5 tbsp oil

Clean and wash the fish, salt and let sit for a half hour. Dry each fish with a clean cloth, dredge first with the eggs beaten with the milk, then with the flour, then again with the eggs and then with the bread crumbs. Hold the fish's head with one hand and the tail with the other, while dredging with the bread crumbs so that it is uniformly covered. Fry in hot oil, at low temperature, so that it does not burn. Arrange on a platter and garnish with the quartered lemon.

PERCH WITH MAYO
(şalău cu maioneză)

2 lbs perch, soup vegetables (carrots, parsnips, parsley roots), 3-4 juniper berries, 1 bay leaf, 1 onion, salt, lettuce

Boil the fish with the vegetables. Let it cool off in the liquid it boiled in. Then remove carefully and set on a platter. Split it lengthwise remove the backbone and all other bones. Do this carefully so that the fish maintains its shape. Place one half over the other, cut into pieces and cover with mayo. Garnish the edges of the platter with finely chopped lettuce. Every here and there make mounds of finely chopped carrot (carrot that boiled with the fish). Place an olive on top of each mound.

PERCH WITH RICE IN DOUGH
(şalău cu orez în aluat)

Dough: 2 oz yeast, 1 egg, 1 cup milk, ½ tbsp sugar, ½ tsp salt, ½ cup melted butter (or lard or oil), flour as needed;

Filling: 1 cup rice, 2 cups milk, 1 cup water, 3 tbsp butter, 3 hard-boiled eggs, 1 lb perch, ¼ tsp pepper, salt

Prepare the starter with yeast, 2-3 tbsp tepid milk and a little flour. When it has risen, mix in the egg, sugar, salt and shortening and make medium soft dough. While the dough rests, set to boil, at low temperature, the rice with the milk, water and salt. When the liquid is almost completely reduced, add pepper and butter and let it cool.

Completely debone the Perch, cut into strips, salt and let it sit until the dough has risen and the rice has cooled off. Divide the dough into two equal parts. Roll into two sheets about a finger thick. Place one sheet to cover the bottom and sides of a buttered dish. Then cover with a uniform layer of rice. After that, put rounds of hard-boiled eggs, and to top those, the Perch strips. Finally, cover with the second sheet of dough, drape with a cloth and let rise for a little while. Then use some egg to glaze. Place in the oven to bake. Serve warm, cut into squares.

POLISH STYLE PERCH
(şalău polonez)

2 lbs perch, 1 carrot, 1 parsley root, 1 onion, 2-3 juniper berries, 3-4 potatoes, 2 eggs, 1 tbsp sour cream, butter, 1 tsp flour, chopped parsley, salt, lemon juice, red beets

Clean and wash the fish. Boil with the carrot, onion, parsley root and juniper berries. When boiled, let it cool a little in its own liquid, then remove carefully and debone while keeping its shape intact. Arrange on a long platter and pour some lemon juice over it. Remove the vegetables from the liquid where they boiled with the fish and boil the potatoes in the same liquid. After they are done, cube them.

Take a pan and fry the flour with the butter and then pour a cup of the fish liquid over it. Let it boil for a few minutes, stirring continuously, then add the yolks mixed with the sour cream. Remove from heat, add the cubed potatoes, salt and mix. Then pour over the fish. Garnish with some chopped parsley. Around the fish, arrange sliced boiled red beets that were kept in vinegar.

FRIED PERCH
(şalău prăjit)

2 lbs perch, 3 tbsp oil, 2 tbsp flour, lemon juice, salt

Clean, wash and cut the fish salt it and let it sit for 10-15 minutes. Then dry each piece with a clean cloth, dredge with flour and fry in hot oil, on both sides. Serve warm, garnished with lemon slices.

POACHED PERCH
(şalău rasol)

2 lbs perch, 1 onion, 1 carrot, 1 parsley root, 2-3 pepper berries, 1 bay leaf, 2 tbsp lemon juice, 2 tbsp oil, 2-3 potatoes, salt

Clean, wash, salt the fish and let it sit for 10-15 minutes. In the meantime, set the vegetables to boil with 1 qt/1 l of water, some salt, pepper and bay leaf. Let boil until the vegetables are tender. Then remove from heat, add the quartered potatoes and let boil for a few minutes. Then add the fish pieces. Let everything simmer, covered, until the fish and potatoes are done. After the fish has cooled off, remove from the pot and place in the middle of a platter, surrounded by vegetables and potatoes. Mix the oil with the lemon juice and 2-3 tbsp of the poaching liquid and pour over the fish and vegetables. Then spread some chopped parsley on top of that.

FRIED PIKE
(ştiucă prăjită)

2 lbs pike, 3 tbsp oil, 2 tbsp flour, lemon juice, salt

Clean, wash and cut the fish salt it and let it sit for 10-15 minutes. Then dry each piece with a clean cloth, dredge with flour and fry in hot oil, on both sides. Serve warm, garnished with lemon slices and lettuce.

POACHED PIKE
(ştiucă rasol)

2 lbs pike, 1 onion, 1 carrot, 1 parsley root, 2-3 pepper berries, 1 bay leaf, 2 tbsp lemon juice, 2 tbsp oil, 2-3 potatoes, salt

Clean, wash, salt the fish and let it sit for 10-15 minutes. In the meantime, set the vegetables to boil with 1 qt/1 l of water, some salt, pepper and bay leaf. Let boil until the vegetables are tender. Then remove from heat, add the quartered potatoes and let boil for a few minutes. Then add the fish pieces and let simmer, covered, until the fish and potatoes are done. After the fish has cooled off, remove from the pot and place in the middle of a platter, surrounded by vegetables and potatoes. Mix the oil with the lemon juice and 2-3 tbsp of the poaching liquid and pour over the fish and vegetables. Then spread some chopped parsley on top of that.

STUFFED (AND BOILED) PIKE
(știucă umplută (fiartă))

1 pike (approx. 2 lbs), crustless slice of white bread, 2 onions, 3 tbsp oil, 3 eggs, salt, pepper, 1 carrot, 1 onion, 1 beet, 2 qts water, 1 tsp chopped parsley, lemon, mustard sauce

Clean and wash the pike and remove its head. Starting from the head, skin the fish carefully. If there remains any meat sticking to the skin, scrape with a knife. Salt and skin and leave aside. De-bone the fish and grind it with the milk (or water) moistened bread and with the finely chopped and oil fried onion. Add salt, pepper, a teaspoon of chopped parsley and two beaten eggs to the mixture. Mix well and stuff the pike skin (do not overstuff or it may burst while boiling). Make small fish balls from the remaining mixture. Take a pot and put a whole onion, the thinly sliced carrot and beet, as well as the fish bones into it. Then add the stuffed fish, head, small fish balls and 2 qts of water. Let boil covered at low temperature. When it is done, remove the stuffed fish, arrange in the middle of a long platter, cut into finger thick slices and place the head where it belongs to make it look like a whole fish again. Arrange the fish balls and a few lemon slices around it. Serve with mustard sauce.

BAKED AND STUFFED PIKE
(știucă umplută la cuptor)

1 pike (approx. 2 lbs), crustless slice of white bread, 2 onions, 3 tbsp oil, 3 eggs, salt, pepper, 1 carrot, 1 onion, 1 beet, 2 qts water, 1 tsp chopped parsley, lemon, mustard sauce, 2 tbsp oil

Prepare like the pike, stuffed (and boiled). Arrange the stuffed fish and head in the baking dish. Add 2 tbsp of oil and set in the oven to bake. Every now and then, baste with the oil in the dish. When ready, remove from the baking dish, arrange on a long platter, and after it has cooled off, slice into finger thick slices and put them all together to give the illusion of a whole fish. Place the fish in its place and garnish with slices of hardboiled egg. Serve with mustard sauce.

SHEAT FISH WITH MAYO
(somn cu maioneză)

2 lbs sheat fish, soup vegetables (carrots, parsnips, and parsley roots), 3-4 juniper berries, 1 bay leaf, 1 onion, salt, lettuce

Boil the fish with the vegetables. Let it cool off in the liquid it boiled in. Then remove carefully and set on a platter. Split it lengthwise; remove the backbone and all other bones. Do this carefully so that the fish maintains its shape. Place one half over the other, cut into pieces and cover with mayo. Garnish the edges of the platter with finely chopped lettuce. Every here and there make mounds of finely chopped carrot (carrot that boiled with the fish). Place an olive on top of each mound.

SHEAT FISH WITH TOMATOES
(mâncare de somn cu roşii)

2 lbs sheat fish, 4 tbsp oil, 2 tbsp flour, 1 big onion, tomatoes, ½ tsp sugar, 3-4 juniper berries, 1 bay leaf, salt

Clean and wash the fish, cut into pieces, salt and let sit for a half hour. Fry the finely chopped onion in oil until yellow, add 1/2 teaspoon flour, salt, sugar, juniper berries, bay leaf and the boiled and strained tomatoes. Let boil for a few minutes and remove from heat. Dredge the fish pieces with flour and fry on both sides. Then place in the pan with the sauce and bake in the oven until the liquid is reduced.

FRIED SHEAT FISH
(somn prăjit)

2 lbs sheat fish, 3 tbsp oil, 2 tbsp flour, lemon juice, salt

Clean, wash and cut the fish salt it and let it sit for 10-15 minutes. Then dry each piece with a clean cloth, dredge with flour and fry in hot oil, on both sides. Serve warm, with French fries and green lettuce.

TOMATOES STUFFED WITH FISH
(roşii umplute cu peşte)

12 big tomatoes, 1 ¾ lb boiled fish (after all bones have been removed), 2 onions, 2 tbsp rice, 1 tbsp lard, chopped parsley and dill, salt, pepper, 2 tomatoes;
Sauce: **1 lb tomatoes, ½ onion, 1 tsp sugar, ½ tsp flour, salt, chopped parsley, 1 tbsp lard, sour cream**

Wash the tomatoes, dry, core and remove the seeds. Mix the fish with two finely chopped raw or fried onions, a tbsp of lard, rice, chopped parsley and dill, pepper and salt. Mix everything well and use this mixture to fill the tomatoes. Put one tomato slice as a lid on each tomato. Arrange in a pan and pour the following sauce on top. Fry the finely chopped onion and flour in lard until golden; add tomato sauce (from boiled and strained tomatoes). Add sugar and salt. If the sauce does not cover the peppers add some water. Spread some chopped parsley, set to boil.

TURBOT IN RED WINE
(calcan în vin roşu)

2 lbs turbot, 1 cup red wine, 1 tsp flour, 1 tbsp butter, 1 parsley root, 1 carrot, 1 onion, 2 cloves, 2-3 juniper berries, 1 bay leaf, salt, 1 lb potatoes

Clean, wash the fish, cut into pieces, salt and let sit for a half hour. Place the thinly sliced carrot, parsley root and onion on the bottom of a pan. Arrange the fish pieces, cloves, juniper berries and bay leaf on the vegetables. Pour the wine and 3-4 tbsp of water in and set to boil at high temperature. When it actually starts boiling, reduce the heat, cover the pan and let simmer. When the fish is done, carefully drain all liquid into another pan, add the butter beaten with the flour to this liquid, mix and let it simmer until the sauce starts to thicken a little. Arrange the fish on a serving platter, the quartered potatoes (boiled separately) around it and pour the strained sauce on top of the potatoes. You may also prepare Perch and Pike this way.

DESSERT

COUNTRY STILE PASTRY WITH FARMER'S CHEESE AND RAISINS
(plăcintă fără aluat cu brânză de vaci)
Sent by Katica Got, Oliverhurst, CA

2 margarine sticks, 200 g flour, 5 tbsp sugar +1 cup more, 1 tsp of baking soda, 500 g farmer's cheese, 200 g raisins, 5 eggs, aromas as preferred (vanilla sugar, lemon zest)

Combine flour with 5 tbsp of sugar and baking soda (1). Use 1 stick of un-melted margarine to coat a baking pan (19/24 cm). Put half of the combination of flour sugar and baking soda in the pan make sure it is even on the bottom. Separately, combine the farmer's cheese with 2 eggs, raisins, 1 cup sugar and aromas (2). Carefully, with a tablespoon put (2) on (1). Make sure (2) is evenly on (1). Sprinkle the remaining flour (1) on the top of (2). Whisk 3 eggs and pour it on the top. Cut the remaining stick of margarine in small pieces and put it on the top- over the whisked eggs. Bake 30-40 min until see a nice crust.

PLUM DUMPLINGS
(găluşte cu prune)
Sent by Ligia Lazar, Davis, CA

125g margarine, 200 ml water, salt, 1 lbs small plums (1 inch diameter) 2 lbs potatoes, 150 plain breadcrumbs and ½ cup of sugar. Dough: 80g flour (four tbsp full), 2 eggs,

First boil the potatoes in skin and then peel them. Smash really well, add the flour, the egg yolk and the salt. The mixture should be well worked. Take a small piece of dough, spread it as a square. In the middle of this square you put a pitted plum or half of a plum and roll the dough over to cover the entire plum with dough. Submerge the dumplings in a pot with boiling water with a little bit of salt and boil them for 10 minutes.

Brown the breadcrumbs in a pot. Put a drop of oil on the bottom of the pot beforehand, so the breadcrumbs won't stick and burn. Make sure you stir occasionally for that purpose as well. After the breadcrumbs cool, add ½ cup of sugar. Roll the dumplings in the breadcrumb and sugar mixture and serve hot or cold.

DAY AND NIGHT
(prăjitura Zi și Noapte)
Sent by Veronica Solomon, Antelope, CA

250g butter, 360g sugar, 560g-cake flour, 6 eggs, 1 cup warm milk, vanilla, 1 tbsp baking powder

Cream together the butter, sugar and egg yolks. Then add cake flour and warm milk. Whip up egg whites and fold in cream. Divide de sponge in two, one leave white and in second add cocoa powder. Brush with melted butter one sheet pan 6"x9"and add the sponge: 1 tablespoon white, one tbsp dark until the sheet is cover. Second layer add on top of white sponge dark sponge and on top of dark sponge white sponge until all sponge is on sheet. Bake at 35°F about 25-30 minutes.

ROMANIAN APPLE CAKE
(prăjitură de mere)
Sent by Ligia Lazar, Davis, CA

5 apples (Golden Delicious, preferred), peeled and cored, 3 eggs, 1 ½ cups white sugar, ¾ cup vegetable oil, 1 tsp baking soda, 1 tsp ground cinnamon, 1 tbsp vanilla extract, 2 cups all-purpose flour, ¾ cup chopped walnuts, ½ cup milk and ¼ cup of lemon juice.

Preheat oven to 350°F (175ºC). Grease and flour a 9x13 inch pan. Cut the apples into 1 inch wedges. Set aside. In a large bowl, whisk together the eggs and sugar until blended. Mix in the baking soda, oil, cinnamon and vanilla. Stir in the flour, just until incorporated; add the milk and the lemon juice. Fold in the apples and walnuts.
Pour batter into prepared pan. Bake in the preheated oven for 55 minutes, or until a toothpick inserted into the center of the cake comes out clean.

Allow to cool slightly. May be served warm or at room temperature. Makes 1 - 9x13 inch pan.

LITTLE POCKETS FILLED WITH CHEESE
(plăcintă cu poalele în brâu)
Sent by Ligia Lazar, Davis, CA

500g flour, 10g yeast (the fresh kind), 2 eggs, 1 tbsp butter, 1 tbsp oil, milk, 1 tsp sugar, salt,

Filling: 150g cheese (probably something like ricotta would work, or maybe farmer's cheese), fresh butter (about the size of a walnut), 1 egg, 1 tsp flour, 2 tbsp milk, 1 tsp sugar, salt

Soften the yeast in a pot with a little bit of warm water. Add about a handful of flour little by little, stirring until it reaches the consistency of thick sour cream. Dust the top with a little bit of flour and then put it somewhere warm to rise.

Put the rest of the flour into a large bowl and make a well in the middle, add the eggs (slightly beaten) and the butter (melted) and the oil. Also add the mixture from above and mix it all well, and knead it very well until the dough comes off your hands and the bowl (it stops sticking to you and the bowl.) While beating, add milk, or warm water just enough to reach the "proper" softness.

For the filling: Mix the cheese with the butter, add the egg, milk, flour, sugar and salt to taste. Mix well.

Roll out the dough, and then cut it into small squares.

Place some cheese in the middle and then fold the edges to the middle, folding it like an envelope. Make sure to seal it well, so none of the cheese will leak out. Brush with an egg wash and then bake. Serve warm.

ROMANIAN CHEESE PIE
(plăcintă cu brânză)
Sent by Pia Lazar, Davis, CA

500 g flour, 24 oz water, ½ tea tbsp salt, 250 g cottage cheese, 250 g feta cheese, 4 eggs, 2 tea spoons lemon peel, 2 tea spoons rum essence, 5 oz. vegetable oil

In a medium bowl mix the flour, water and the salt until all the flour is incorporated and soft dough is obtained. You divide the dough in four parts. Use a rolling pin to spread each of the four parts in a thin sheet, and let each sheet dry on the horizontal surface. In another bowl mix the cottage cheese, feta cheese, eggs, lemon peel and rum.

Take a sheet of dough and with a brush spread a thin layer of vegetable oil on the whole surface of the sheet. Spread some of the cheese mixture on half of the sheet, and folding it with the other half. Then gathered it from the opposite sides, and put it in the pan. The pan needs to be covered with a thin layer of vegetable oil. Each of the four sheets filled with cheese will be placed in the pan and baked at 400 °F for 45 minutes. Take it out, spray it with a little bit of water and cover it with a towel. Let it sit for 20 min, cut it in 2 inch square pieces and serve it warm is preferred.

If, it is too difficult to make the dough, replace it with the fillo dough that you can buy it from the grocery store (find it in the freezer section). Usually, the box contains 20 sheets, and you can use five sheets for each piece. Between each sheet you need to spread vegetable oil, with the cheese filling in the center and then gathered.

BERRY STRATA
(plăcintă cu mure, zmeură, căpşuni şi fragi)
Sent by Dorel Andriuca, Roseville, CA

2 tbsp butter, 3 tbsp honey, 4 large eggs, ½ cup whole milk ricotta, 3 tbsp sugar, 1 cup whole milk, ¼ cup orange juice, 4 slices of bread, torn into 1 inch pieces (about 4 cups), 1 (10-ounce) bag frozen mixed berries, thawed and drained

Melt the butter in a small saucepan over low heat. Turn off the heat, add the honey, and stir to combine.

Meanwhile, in a large bowl combine the eggs, ricotta, and sugar. Using a fork, mix to combine and beat the eggs. Add the milk, orange juice, butter and honey mixture, and bread. Stir to combine. Gently fold in the berries.

Place the ingredients in a 10-inch round (2-quart) baking dish. Cover with plastic wrap and place in the refrigerator for at least 2 hours and up to 12 hours.

Preheat the oven to 350ºF. Bake the strata until golden on top and baked through, about 40 minutes. Let stand for 5 minutes before serving. Tablespoon into dishes and serve.

FRIED DOUGH
(gogoşi)

½ cup warm water, 5 tsp yeast, pinch of sugar, 1 cup warm milk, 1/3 cup sugar, 1 ½ tsp salt, 1 tsp vanilla, 2 eggs, 1/3 cup oil, 2 cups unbleached all purpose flour, 3–4 cups unbleached bread flour (or all-purpose), oil for frying, granulated sugar for dusting

In a large mixing bowl, stir together the yeast, warm water and a pinch of sugar. Allow to stand a couple of minutes to allow yeast to swell or dissolve. Stir in the remaining sugar, milk, vanilla, eggs, oil, salt, all-purpose flour and most of bread flour (if using) to make a soft dough. Knead 5 to 8 minutes by hand or with a dough hook, adding flour as needed to form firmer smooth and elastic dough. Place in a greased bowl. Place bowl in a plastic bag and seal. If not using right away, you can refrigerate the dough at this point. Let rise about one hour. Gently deflate dough. If dough is coming out of the refrigerator, allow to warm about 40 minutes before proceeding. Cut off portions of dough (about the size of a mandarin orange). Stretch or roll into large, thin oblong shapes and place on waxed paper lined baking sheet. Prepare all dough this way, layering more paper between the stretched pieces of dough. Cover with a wet towel and let rest 15 minutes. When oil is hot (385ºF) fry slabs, one or two at a time. Turn them over as soon as they puff up and fry on other side for a few seconds to complete.
Drain on paper towels. Prepare a bowl with a cup or two of white sugar. Toss in one at a time and coat well, shaking off excess in the bowl.
You can also serve these with pie toppings or a dollop of strawberry or raspberry jam.

BUTTERMILK BISQUITS
(biscuiţi cu lapte bătut)
Sent by Ruxandra Vidu, Citrus Heights, CA

½ cup butter, 2 ½ tbsp sugar, 1 egg, beaten, ¾ cup buttermilk, ¼ cup club soda, 1 tsp salt, 5 cup flour

Preheat oven to 450 ºF. Combine all of the ingredients. Knead the dough by hand until smooth. Flour your hands. Pat the dough flat to ¾ inch thick on waxed paper. Cut out biscuits. Bake for 12 minutes or until golden brown. Makes about 18 biscuits.

WALNUT CRESCENTS

Dough: 1 8-ounce package Philadelphia cream cheese, room temperature, 16 tbsp (2 sticks) butter or margarine, room, temperature, 1 egg, 1 tbsp sugar, 6 cups all-purpose flour, ½ tsp salt, ½ cup plus 3 tbsp cold water

Filling: 4 tbsp (½ stick) stick butter or margarine, ½ pound walnuts, ground, ½ cup sugar, ½ cup milk, 1 tsp vanilla,

Dusting: Confectioners' sugar

To make the dough: Place the cream cheese and butter in a bowl with the egg, sugar, flour, salt, and water. Mix well (you can also mix by hand). Roll the dough into a log, 10 inches long. Wrap in plastic wrap and refrigerate the dough for at least 1 hour. Working with ¼ of the dough at a time, place it on a floured countertop, turning it over to coat well so that it does not stick. Roll the dough out very thin. Using a fluted pastry cutter (a pizza cutter works too), cut the dough into strips 2 inches wide. Then cut the dough across again to make 2-inch squares. Place ½ teaspoon filling on each square, using the back of a teaspoon to spread it. Roll up the square diagonally, from one corner to the opposite corner, or from one side to the opposite side. Form either into a crescent shape, or leave it straight, and place the filled dough on an ungreased cookie sheet. Bake for 15 or 20 minutes in a preheated 350°F oven until the cookies are light brown. Sprinkle with confectioners' sugar immediately. Let cool. More powdered sugar can be added when serving. Store them in a covered container. These freeze well.

To make the filling: In a saucepan, place the butter, ground nuts, sugar, and milk and cook until thick, stirring to prevent sticking. Add the vanilla. Cool slightly before using on the dough. Sugar may be increased according to taste but do not make the filling too sweet.
Note: If all the dough is not used at one time, it can be stored in the refrigerator for several days. Do not freeze the dough.

HOMEMADE CHOCOLATE
(ciocolată de casă)

200 ml water, 375 g sugar, 50 grams cocoa, 1 stick butter, 500 g powder milk

Mix water and sugar together. Cook for 8 minutes. Remove from heat add butter. Then add cocoa and stir slightly. Add milk mix well. Pour into 13"x9" pan and let cool.

SEMOLINA PUDDING
(budică de griş)

2½ cups milk, ¼ cup butter, 1½ cups Roman Meal Cereal (instant or quick-cooking), ¼ cup sugar, Pinch of salt, ¼ cup raisins, stewed fruit

Mix all the ingredients except the stewed fruit in a covered casserole. Cook in the microwave oven, stirring from time-to-time, until the milk is absorbed and the cereal is cooked. Put into serving bowls or dishes and top with your choice of stewed fruit-such as plums, rhubarb sauce, apple sauce, or sweet cherries.
Tip: For a special treat, top with a little thick cream or whipped cream. This pudding is usually served warm.

LEMON RUM SOUFFLE
(tortă Românească)

14 tbsp unsalted butter, softened, 1½ cups confectioners' sugar

8 eggs, separated, ¼ cup strained fresh lemon juice, 1 tbsp finely grated fresh lemon peel, ¼ cup dark rum, or substitute cognac, 2 tbsp soft fresh bread crumbs (made from homemade type white bread, trimmed of crusts and pulverized in a blender or finely shredded with a fork).

Preheat the oven to 350°F. Fold a 24-inch-long piece of wax paper lengthwise in half and again lengthwise in half. With a pastry brush, spread 2 tablespoons of the softened butter evenly on one side of the folded strip, and over the bottom and sides of a 2-quart soufflé dish. Then wrap the paper strip, buttered side in, around the outside of the soufflé dish to make a collar extending about 2 inches above the top edge of the dish. Tie the paper in place with string. Set aside. In a deep mixing bowl, cream the remaining 12 tablespoons of butter and the sugar together, beating and mashing them against the sides of the bowl with a large tablespoon until the mixture is light and fluffy. Beat in the egg yolks, one at a time, then stir in the lemon juice, lemon peel and rum. Continue to beat until the ingredients are thoroughly combined. With a wire whisk or a rotary or electric beater, beat the egg whites until they are stiff enough to stand in unwavering peaks on the beater when it is lifted from the bowl. Fold the egg whites gently into the lemon mixture with a rubber spatula, using an over-under cutting motion rather than a stirring motion. Finally fold in the bread crumbs. Ladle the soufflé into the buttered and collared dish, spreading it evenly and smoothing the top with the spatula. Bake in the middle of the oven for 45 minutes, or until the soufflé puffs up above the rim of the collar and the top is lightly browned. Carefully remove the wax paper and serve the soufflé at once.

COTTAGE CHEESE SWEET PIE
(plăcintă de brânză dulce)

Pastry: 500 g flour, 500 g butter, 1glass water, 2-3 tsp melted butter, 1/4 tbsp salt, 1 tsp lemon juice

Filling: 2 lbs cottage cheese, 1/2 cup butter, 6 -8 spoons sugar, 4 eggs, 1 lemon zest grated, 1/2 cup raisins, 1/2 cup rum or cognac (Metaxa), 4 tbsp flour or 5 tbsp cream of wheat

Pastry: You have to make everything fast and in a cold area. On the table, dust the flour and make a whole in the middle, put inside the water, melted butter, lemon juice and salt. Work the dough to get a medium soft consistency. Leave it for 15 -20 min. Try to sleep - as the hard work is starting now! Roll out the dough to a 1 cm thick. Put slices of cold butter and cover on top and cover with dough, closing it like an envelope. Cover and let it cool 10 min. Roll the dough and fold it in 3 to 4 times. You have to keep on folding it, this way, the pastry is formed by placing pats of chilled butter between layers of pastry dough, rolling it out, folding it in thirds, and letting it rest. Repeat at least 8 times - you will have a pastry with many layers of dough and butter.

Filling: Leave raisins 1/2 hour in the cognac or rum. Beat the eggs with sugar, lemon zest; add the butter and the cottage cheese. Add the flour or the cream of wheat. At the end, mix in the raisins.

Use half of the pastry layered (after you rolled it, of course) at the bottom of the pan. Pour the cheese filling. Add the other half of rolled pastry. Bake at 375°F for 45 min. Keep an eye on it after 30 min, each oven bakes differently.

FROTHY WINE DESSERT
(şatou)

5 egg yolks, ½ cup sugar, 1 tbsp finely grated fresh lemon peel, 1 cup white muscatel or other sweet white wine, 2 tbsp fresh or frozen raspberries thoroughly defrosted and drained (optional).

Place the egg yolks, sugar and lemon peel in the top of an enameled or stainless-steel double boiler set over barely simmering water. Beat with a whisk or a rotary beater or an electric hand mixer for 15 to 20 minutes, or until the mixture becomes a thick custard. In a separate pan, quickly bring the wine to a boil. Then pour it into the custard in a slow thin stream, beating all the while. Continue beating for another 10 minutes or so, until the cream is thick enough to coat a tablespoon heavily. Tablespoon the cream into 4 individual dessert dishes or stemmed glasses and serve at once, while hot. If you like, you may rub 2 tbsp of raspberries through a fine sieve with the back of a tablespoon and fold the puree into the dessert just before serving.

CHEESE-AND-SOUR-CREAM SOUFFLE
(alivenci)

1 tbsp butter, softened, 3 tbsp flour, 8 ounces pot cheese, ½ cup sour cream, 3 eggs, ½ cup milk, ½ tsp salt, Confectioners' sugar

Preheat the oven to 350°F. With a pastry brush, spread the tablespoon of softened butter over the bottom and sides of an 8-inch-square baking dish at least ½ inches deep. Add 2 tablespoons of the flour and tip the dish back and forth to spread it evenly. Invert the dish and rap it on a table to remove the excess flour. Set aside. Force the pot cheese through a food mill into a deep bowl, or rub it through a fine sieve with the back of a spoon. Stir in the sour cream with a whisk or large spoon, and then beat in the eggs, one at a time. Add the milk and salt, and the remaining 1 tablespoon of flour and continue to beat until the flour is completely absorbed. Pour the soufflé into the baking dish and bake in the middle of the oven for about 30 minutes, or until the top puffs and is lightly browned. Sprinkle lightly with confectioners' sugar and serve at once.

SOUR CHERRY FILLO PASTRY PIE
(plăcintă cu vişine)

1 package fillo pastry or puff pastry

Filling: sour cherry from sour cherry in syrup drained (about 2 cans), 3 spoons sugar, 3 spoons flour

Divide the pastry in 2. If you use fillo pastry, butter it well and follow the instructions. If you use puff pastry, roll it and spread it.

Filling: Mix sour cherries (if you have found the real thing - take out the seeds!) with sugar and flour. Let it sit for 20 min. Spread the sour cherries and roll it in pastry. Repeat so, that you will have 2 pies. Bake at 375° F for 40 min.

CARAMEL CHOCOLATE CAKE
(tort Doboş)

Cake layers: 125 g sugar, 5 eggs, 125 g flour, ¼ tsp vanilla extract,

Cake cream: 4 eggs, 125 g sugar, 2 generous spoons cocoa, 300 g whipped butter.

Top: 8 hazelnuts, 1/3 cup sugar

Beat the yolks with sugar until sugar is completely incorporated (approx. 15 min). Add gradually the flour and the vanilla extract. Separately beat the egg white and add it to the mixture.

Butter them and flour round baking pans and set oven at 375ºF. The mixture will be enough for 5-6 layers of cake. You will have to bake them separately. Spread a very thin layer of mixture (if you want you can divide in advance the mixture in 5) and bake it for 7 - 10 min. You may need to bake it in 2 or 3 series. Cool the layers and start on the cream.

Beat the eggs with sugar and cocoa at bain-marie or in a double boiler pan over low heat. You have to keep on beating this mixture until you get the mixture to the consistency of a cream. Do not overcook - you don't want an omelet! Set it aside to cool and keep on beating until cold. Separately beat the butter and add the cocoa mixture 1 tablespoon at a time.

Alternate the layers with the cream and the last layer set on the side.

Warm 1/3 cup of sugar to caramelize it and pour over the last layer. With a knife mark down the slices - it will be easier to cut it. Set the last layer on top of the cake. Drop hazelnuts in the caramel and decorate the cake.

ROMANIAN APPLE CAKE
(prăjitură cu mere)
Sent by Ligia Lazar, Davis, CA

5 apples, peeled and cored, 3 eggs, 1 ½ cups sugar, ¾ cup oil, 1 tsp baking soda, 1 tsp cinnamon, 1 tbsp vanilla, 2 cups flour, ¾ cup walnuts

Cut apples into 1 inch wedges. Set aside. In a large bowl whisk together the eggs and sugar until blended. Mix in baking soda, oil, cinnamon and vanilla. Stir in flour, just until moistened. Fold in apples and walnuts. Pour batter into 9x13 inch pan. Bake at 350°F for about 55 minutes.

CREPES
(clătite)
Sent by Ramona Vilceanu, Marysville, CA

3 large eggs, 1¼ cups milk, pinch of salt, 1 ¼ cup all-purpose flour, 6 tbsp unsalted butter, melted, ¼ cup strawberry preserves, 1 cup frozen raspberries, ½ cups plain yogurt, 3 tbsp light brown sugar, 1 tsp pure vanilla extract

In a medium bowl, whisk the eggs with ¼ cup of the milk and the salt until blended. Whisk in the flour until the batter is smooth, then whisk in the remaining 1 cup of milk and 1 tbsp of the melted butter. Let the crepe batter stand at room temperature for about 20 minutes.

In a small saucepan, combine the strawberry preserves with the raspberries and lemon juice and cook over moderate heat until thicken, for about 5 minutes. Cover and keep warm.

In a bowl mix the yogurt with the brown sugar and vanilla.

Heat a 10-inch crepe pan or nonstick skillet over moderate heat. Brush the pan with some of the melted butter. Pour in a scant 1/3 cup of the crepe batter and immediately rotate the pan to evenly coat the bottom. Cook the crepe until lightly browned on the bottom, about 45 seconds. Flip the crepe and cook until brown dots appear on the other side, about 15 seconds longer. Transfer the crepe to a large baking plate covered with parchment paper. Continue making crepes with the remaining batter, brushing the pan with the remaining melted butter as needed. Spread 3 tablespoons of the yogurt onto each crepe and roll them up. Transfer to plates. Tablespoon the raspberry-apricot sauce on top and serve.

APPLE CAKE
(prăjitură cu mere)
Sent by Monica Mois, Sacramento, CA

2 cups sugar, ½ cup oil, 2 eggs, 4 cups dices apples, 2 cups flour, 1 tsp salt, 2 tsp cinnamon, 1 tsp nutmeg, 2 tsp baking soda.

Combine sugar, ½ cup oil and 2 eggs. Add dices apples. Stir together flour, salt, cinnamon, nutmeg and baking soda. Add sifted dry ingredients to apple mixture. Pour into 9" x 13" greased cake pan and bake for 1 hour in a preheated 350° oven.

APPLE PIE
(plăcintă cu mere)
Send by Gabriela Margareta Helvey, Sacramento, CA

Dough: 600 g flour (Gold Medal), 500 g unsalted butter, 3 eggs (yolks), 4 tbsp sugar, 8 tbsp white wine (or 7 tbsp water + 1 tbsp wine vinegar)

Filling: 6 pounds apples, 8-10 tbsp sugar, 3 full tbsp of cinnamon powder (more or less, depending on your taste).

Note: Quantities are for:
1) 2 round baking pans (10 inches diameter, with removal bottom), or

2) one-16 inches rectangular baking pan.

Preparation of the filling: Peel and shred the apple, then squeeze out by hand to release most of the juice. Mix the apples with sugar and cinnamon powder. The juice obtained by squeezing the apples is excellent for a fresh cold drink.

Preparation of the dough: Pour the flour in a large bowl, add the cold butter cut in small pieces, the egg yolks, the sugar and the wine. Combine all these ingredients and keep mixing until a smooth mass forms, striking the dough a couple of times with the roller. Then, gather the dough into a square piece and chill it for 24 hours (or more, until you are ready to prepare the pie).

Preparation of the pie: Remove the dough from the refrigerator and turn it onto a floured work surface. Divide it in 2 pieces and lightly dust the dough surface with additional flour. Using the roller, evenly strikes and roll the dough into the desired shape (round or rectangular). The bottom crust has to be thinner (1/4 thick) than the top crust (1/2 inch thick). Turn it occasionally to produce an even shape and dust more flour to keep it from sticking to the work surface. Work from the center toward the edges, rolling in different directions. Cut the dough, if necessary, to fit the pan. Transfer the dough to the pan or tray and fill the bottom going up around the pan about 1 ½ inches. Add the apple filling, about 1 inch high-even. Add the top crust and stick together both crusts, pinching away any excess dough. Using a fork, pierce the upper crust all the way down to the bottom crust to allow steam to escape. Apply egg wash to the top crust. Bake in a preheated oven at 350°F until the dough is golden brown and appears dry. Enjoy!

CHERRY CAKE
(prăjitură cu cireşe)
Sent by Mihaela Ardelean, Sacramento, CA

1 ½ cups cherries, 2 cups all-purpose flour, 2 eggs, 3 tsp yeast, 2 ¾ tbsp unsalted butter, 2 cups milk, ½ cup sugar, lemon zest, ½ lb walnut (shredded), 1/8 tsp salt

Preheat the oven to 350 F. In a large bowl, dissolve the yeast in two tablespoons of milk and let it rise for 3 minutes. Stir in the flour, yolks of the eggs, butter, sugar, lemon zest, salt, and milk in the same bowl. In a separate bowl whisk the egg whites at high speed. Fold egg white mixture into the dough. Cover and let rise in a warm place until double in size (about 45 minutes). Grease a baking pan with butter. Place the dough in the pan and sprinkle the cherries and walnut. Bake the cake at 350°Ffor about 30 minutes.

DOUGHNUT TWISTS
(gogoşi)
Sent by Ramona Vilceanu, Marysville, CA

3 to 3 ½ cups all-purpose flour, 1 package active dry yeast cup butter or margarine, 1 cup milk, 1/3 cup butter or margarine, 2 tbsp sugar, 1 tsp salt, 1 egg, cooking oil for deep frying, powdered sugar

In a large mixer bowl combine 1 ¾ cups of the flour and the yeast. In saucepan heat milk, butter or margarine, sugar, and salt just till warm and butter is almost melted, stir constantly. Add to flour mixture; add egg beat on low speed of electric mixer ½ minute, scraping the sides of the bowl constantly. Beat for 3 minutes on high speed. Using a tablespoon stir the remaining flour as you can. Cover. Let rise in a warm place till double (1 to 1 ½ hours).

Divide the dough in to 24 portions. Roll each portion into a rope 12 inches long. Fold each rope in half; twist tightly. Cover and let rise in a warm place till nearly double (30-40 minutes).

In a large saucepan or deep-fat fryer heat cooking oil to 375°F. Fry the dough twists, a few at a time, for 2 to 3 minutes or till golden brown. Drain on paper toweling. If desired, sprinkle powdered sugar over top.

"FRUIT TART"
(tartă de fructe)
Sent by Liana Ciontoş, Roseville CA

For the shell: 1 cup flour, 3 tsp soft margarine or butter, ¼ tsp salt, 1/3 cup sugar

For the cream: 2 cups heavy cream shimmer, ½ cup sugar, 1 packet gelatin, ½ cup of plain yogurt, 1 cup of frozen fruits of your choice, fresh fruits for decoration

Mix together the flour, the butter, salt and sugar. Put the dough in a pie pan, pinch the bottom with a fork on the bottom and bake for 10 minutes at 350ºF. Shortcut tip: buy pie shell and bake as directed. Let it cool for 10 minutes.

Melt baking chocolate on low heat and spread on the bottom of the baked and cooled shell. Refrigerate until the cream is ready.

Mix the heavy cream shimmer with sugar in a saucepan and heat it slowly. In a small bowl, mix 4 tablespoons water with the gelatin. Add the gelatin to the warm cream and stir until it is dissolved (30 seconds). Remove the saucepan from the heat and add the yogurt and the frozen fruits. Mix well and put in the shell .

Refrigerate for 2-3 hours and decorate with fruits, for the delight of your eyes, and serve.

"DIPLOMAT" ROLL
(ruladă Diplomat)
Sent by Delia Petrişor, Orangevale, CA

Sweet biscuits: 7eggs (separate the yolks from the whites), 7 tbsp sugar, 7 tbsp wheat.

Cream (original recipe): 2 (1 oz) packages of unflavored gelatin (preferred Knox gelatin), ¼ cup cold water, 1 caps of milk (unflavored Mocha milk), 3 eggs, 7 tbsp sugar, 3 tbsp of orange jam (or marmalade), whipping cream (8-oz Cool Whip),

Sweet biscuit roll: whisk the egg whites with sugar, adding the yolks one by one; incorporate the wheat. Use a large baking tray to bake the biscuit layer. Bake it at 350 °F for 20 minutes.

Cream: Combine gelatin and cold water and heat it up slowly. Whisk the eggs and sugar until they hold up and then add warm milk. Heat them up slowly until boil. Add the gelatin mixture. Then let them cool down to about 35-40 ºC. Add the orange jam and let the cream cool down completely. Incorporate the whipping cream.

Prepare a syrup to flavor the roll by mixing ½ cup of sugar with ½ cup water. Boil it until all the sugar is dissolved completely. Add rum or cherry liquor to flavor the syrup.

Place the biscuit sheet on a work surface, face down. Sprinkle the syrup all over the surface. Layer the cream and roll it longitudinally.

BIRTHDAY CAKE WITH ORANGES
(tort şarlotă cu portocale)
Sent by Emilia Popescu, Citrus Height, CA

4 eggs, 1 cup sugar, 1 cup milk, 3 tsp gelatin (dissolved in 1 tbsp warm water), 1 lb whipped cream (at room temperature), 5 oranges

Whisk the eggs and add sugar. Add milk and heat it up slowly while mixing. Continue to mix until the cream is getting thicker. Take it away from the stove and leave it to cool down. Add the gelatin and leaved to cool completely. Get the zest from two oranges, and then peel all of them. Cut the oranges into ¼ -inch thick slices. In a round saucepan, wet the walls with water and then line them up with orange slices. Fill in with alternative 3 layers of creams and 2 layers of sweet biscuits called "Champaign" biscuits), starting with cream. Leave over the night in the refrigerator.

YAM WAFFLES
(napolitane)
Anitta Zat Palla, Sacramento, CA

¾ cup whole wheat flour, ¾ cup all purpose flour, ½ cup rolled oats, ¼ cup sugar, 1 tsp salt, 1 tbsp baking powder, 4 ounces tofu, soft/silken, 1 egg, 6 ounces yam, cooked and mashed, 16 ounces yogurt, skim milk, 1/3 cup canola oil

Preheat waffle iron. Stir together the dry ingredients; set aside. In a blender or food processor, combine the remaining ingredients until thoroughly blended. Mix liquid and dry ingredients together. Bake in waffle iron until done, following guidelines of your appliance. This batter can also be used for pancakes.

BUTTER COOKIES
(prăjituri cu unt)
Sent by Ramona Vilceanu, Marysville, CA

1 cup of butter, 1 cup of sugar, 1 egg, 2 ½ cups all purpose flour, 2 tbsp orange juice, 1 tbsp vanilla, 1 tsp baking powder,

Frosting: 3 cups powdered sugar, 1/3 cup of butter softened, 1 tsp vanilla, 2 to 3 tbsp milk

Combine butter, sugar and egg in large bowl. Beat at medium speed until creamy. Reduce speed to low; add flour, orange juice, vanilla and baking powder. Beat until well mixed. Divide dough into three parts; wrap each part in plastic food wrap. Refrigerate until firm.

Heat the oven to 400 °F. Roll out dough on lightly floured surface, one third at a time to 1/8 to 1/4 inch thickness. Cut with 3 inch cookie cutters. Place them 1 inch apart onto ungreased cookie sheets. Bake them for 6 to 10 minutes or until edges are lightly browned. Cool completely.

Combine powdered sugar, 1/3 cup butter and 1 teaspoon vanilla in small bowl. Beat at low speed, gradually adding milk for desired spreading consistency. Frost and decorate cooled cookies as desired.

FANCY CAKES
(prăjitura-fursecuri)
Sent by Olga Iancu, Sacramento, CA

200 g wheat, 200 g sweet butter, 50 g sugar (for cookies), 200 g sugar (for meringue), 1 tsp vanilla sugar, 2 eggs, a pinch of salt.

Preheat oven to 200°F and oil a baking sheet. Beat the whites in a large bowl with an electric mixer. Gradually beat in sugar, vanilla sugar and lemon juice (from ½ lemon) and beat until meringue just holds stiff, glossy peaks. Transfer meringue to a pastry bag fitted with a ½ -inch plain tip and pipe evenly on the baking sheet. Bake meringue in middle of oven 45 minutes, or until crisp and firm. Cool meringue completely on baking sheet in turned-off oven and carefully peel them off.

Mix the wheat, butter, sugar, and the yolks to make dough. Roll the dough on the table to make a sheet. Cut the dough sheet with a small glass in the shape of circles. Bake the cookies at 275 F.

After cookies and meringue cooled down, use peach jam to bond together one cookie to one meringue. Fancy cookies may be kept, layered between sheets of parchment paper, in an airtight container in a cool, dry place 1 week.

SARATELE
(sărăţele)
Sent by Olga Iancu, Sacramento, CA

200 g salted butter, 240 g flour, 200 g parmesan cheese (powder or grated), 2 tbsp sour cream.

Mix well the butter, the flour and the sour cream. Leave it in the refrigerator for ½ hour. Take the dough out and roll it into a thick sheet. Put an egg wash over the dough sheet and sprinkle the parmesan cheese. Cut the sheet into 1"x6" ribbons. Bake it at 350 °F until turns golden (about 20 minutes).

ORANGE CAKE
(tort de portocale)
Sent by Sonia Radu, Sacramento, CA

6 eggs, 0.5 lb crushed walnuts, 0.5 lb sugar, 2 tbsp cacao, 3 oranges (medium size), 150 ml water, 2-3 tbsp flour

Cream: 3 eggs, 300 g sugar, 4 tbsp cacao, 500 g butter

Mix well the yolks with sugar. Add the walnuts, the cocoa, the water, the oranges (add the zest, too), and the flour. At the end, fold in stiffly beaten egg whites. Pour into well greased pan. Bake in preheated oven at 350°F for about 1 hour. Cut it longitudinally. Don't syrup it.

Cream: Boil in a pan the eggs, the sugar and the cocoa. When cooled at room temperature, add the butter and mix well.

Lay the cream in between the two halves and on top of the cake.

AMANDINA
(prăjitură Amandină)
Sent by Nicolae Dic, Fair Oaks, CA

Caramel cake: 7 eggs, 190 g sugar, 300 g flour, 1 tsp backing powder

Cocoa cream: 250 g sugar, 350 g butter, 50 g cocoa, rum and vanilla essence

Chocolate for icing: 100 g chocolate

Sirop: 250 ml water, 100 g sugar, lemon zest, rum essence

Whisk well the egg whites with sugar until the sugar is dissolved. Then, add gradually the yolks and the flour. Pour into well greased and bake in preheated oven at 375°F for about 35 minutes. Leave the cake to cool down to room temperature.

Prepare the syrup by boiling the sugar in water. Add the lemon zest and the rum essence and leave it to cool down.

Cut the cake into 3 equal layers with a very sharp long knife. Sprinkle syrup on each layer.

Prepare the cocoa cream by mixing well all the ingredients. Fill with the cream and glaze with the chocolate icing. You can sprinkle crushed almonds or walnuts on top of the cake.

LEMON LOAF CAKE
(prăjitură cu lămâie)
Sent by Doina Brownell, West Sacramento, CA

¼ lb very soft butter, 5 eggs, separated, 2/3 cup sugar, 1 cup sifted flour, plus 3 tbs, zest and juice of 1 lemon, 2 tbsp chopped nuts

Cream the soft butter. Add yolks and sugar beating until very fluffy. Lightly fold in sifted flour, lemon juice and rind. Fold in stiffly beaten egg whites. Pour into well greased loaf pans 3 x 6 inches. Sprinkle on top with chopped nuts. Bake in pre-heated oven at 350°F for about 1 hour.

PRALINE
(praline)
Sent by Doina Brownell, West Sacramento, CA

butter, 1/3 cup granulated sugar, 2 tbsp water, 1 cup chopped toasted hazelnuts or pecans, 1 cup butter, softened, 1 cup packed brown sugar, 1/2 cup granulated sugar, 1/2 tsp baking soda, 2 eggs, 1 tsp vanilla, 2-1/2 cups all-purpose flour, 2 ounces semisweet or bittersweet chocolate, melted and cooled

Grease a large baking sheet with butter; set aside. Stir together the 1/3 cup granulated sugar and water in a heavy medium saucepan. Cook and stir over medium-high heat until boiling. Cook for 2 1/2 to 3 1/2 minutes more or until syrup is a deep golden brown. Remove from heat. Stir in nuts. Immediately pour onto the prepared baking sheet. Cool completely on a wire rack until firm. Transfer the firm praline to a heavy plastic bag. Using a rolling pin, crush the praline into small pieces; set aside. For cookies, beat the 1 cup butter in a large mixing bowl with an electric mixer on medium to high speed for 30 seconds. Add brown sugar, the 1/2 cup granulated sugar, and baking soda; beat until combined, scraping sides of bowl occasionally. Beat in eggs and vanilla until combined. Beat in as much of the flour as you can. Stir in remaining flour and crushed praline. Drop dough by rounded tablespoon 2 inches apart onto an ungreased cookie sheet. Bake in a 350°F oven for 13 to 15 minutes or until edges are lightly browned. Cool on cookie sheet for 1 minute. Transfer to wire racks and cool completely. Drizzle melted chocolate over cookies. Makes about 48 cookies.

Make-Ahead Tip: Cool cookies completely. In an airtight or freezer container, arrange cookies in a single layer; cover with a sheet of waxed paper. Repeat layers, leaving enough air space to close container easily. Freeze up to 1 month.

APPLE CAKE
(prăjitură cu mere)
Sent by Sonia Radu, Sacramento, CA

Filling: 4 lb apples, 1 cup sugar, 1 tsp cinnamon, 1.5 oz butter

Dough: 6 egg, 5 tbsp sugar, 6 tbsp flour, 1 l milk

Peel off the apples and cut them into very thin slices. Put them in a saucepan that was greased with butter. Add sugar, cinnamon and butter. Bake them for about 30 min at 350°F until the apple slices become soft.

Mix the egg yolks with sugar and flour, and pour over the boiling milk. Leave to boil for another 2-3 minutes. Then, pour the mixture over the apples, and put back the saucepan in the oven at 350°Ffor another 30 minutes. In the mean while, prepare the meringue. Whisk the egg whites with 250 g sugar. Take the saucepan out of the oven and put meringue on top of the mixture. Bake it for another 15 minutes at 300 F. When the cake cooled down completely, put it in the refrigerator over the night to absorb the apple aroma and juice. Cut the cake just before serving.

RUM BABA
(savarină)
Sent by Lucia Tudosa, Austin, TX

5 lb flour, 1 lb sugar, 300 ml oil, 9 eggs, 1 lemon (zest), salt, dry yeast (dissolved in milk)

<u>Note:</u> ingredients are for 100 cakes.

Mix well all the ingredients. Cover the pan with a plastic foil and leave it to rise for about 2 hours. Then, knead the dough again and then leave it to rise. Repeat this process one more time (3 times total). This process will result in foamy dough, specific to this cake. Make small dough balls (about 100) and put them in a baking pan and bake them at 350°F for about 35 minutes or until the color is light brown.

<u>Syrup</u>: Mix 1 lb sugar with ½ l water and heat it up. Add rum or cherry liquor to taste. Flavor each cake with this aromatized syrup. Cut each individual cake in half, horizontally, and insert whipping cream in between the two halves.

CAKE WITH QUARTERED APPLES
(prăjitură cu mere sferturi)

12 medium peeled and quartered apples, 1 ½ cups sour cream, 5 tbsp sugar, 6 eggs, 3 heaping tbsp flour, 1 tsp vanilla, vanilla flavored confectioner's sugar, butter and flour to grease and dust the pan

Mix the yolks with the sugar and vanilla, add the sour cream and then gradually (like a rain) add the flour and mix well. Finally, add the whipped egg whites and quartered apples. Mix gently. Butter a pan, dust well with flour and pour the mixture in. Bake at medium heat until done. Serve warm sprinkled with vanilla flavored confectioner's sugar.

CAKE WITH WHOLE APPLES
(prăjitură cu mere întregi)

12 medium peeled and quartered apples, 1 ½ cups sour cream, 5 tbsp sugar, 6 eggs, 3 heaping tbsp flour, 1 tsp vanilla, vanilla flavored confectioner's sugar, butter and flour to grease and dust the pan

Prepare the same way as for cake with quartered apples. Do not quarter the apples. Peel, hollow them remove seeds and replace them with sour cherries from preserves. Arrange these apples in the pan and pour the mixture over them; bake and serve warm.

"POALE-N BRIU" PIE
(plăcintă "poale-n brâu")

2 lbs flour, 1 oz yeast, 1 cup milk, 3 eggs, 2 tbsp oil, 1 tbsp lard, 1 tsp sugar, salt, cottage cheese (to taste), egg for washing the dough, flour for the pan

In a larger bowl, mix the yeast with the sugar until liquefied. Add 2 tablespoons of tepid milk, a little flour and mix well. Cover and let sit in a warm place. When it has risen a little, add the eggs beaten with the milk, oil and lard, all of them warmish. Add salt and knead with flour until the dough comes off your hands and bowl easily. Cover and let rise in a warm place. When the dough has risen, roll into a ½ inch sheet. Cut into medium sized squares and arrange the filling, prepared like in Cottage cheese pie in the middle. Bring the corners over the Cheese envelope style. Stick well so that the filling may not come out. Sprinkle flour on the baking sheet and arrange the envelopes 1-2 inches apart. Let rise on the baking sheet for 15-20 minutes, wash with egg and bake.

ANISE BISCUITS
(pesmeți cu anason)

2 lbs flour, 7 oz sugar, 2 cups milk, 1 tsp vanilla, 3 yolks and 2 whole eggs, 5 oz butter, 1 ½ oz yeast, 1 tsp ground anise mixed with 2-3 tbsp confectioner's sugar, ½ tsp salt

Mix the yeast with a teaspoon of sugar, add ½ cup tepid milk and a little flour, so that the starter is soft. Let it rise. Then it has doubled, add the rest of the tepid milk, salt, eggs beaten with sugar, vanilla and melted butter (tepid). Knead well until it bubbles. Divide the dough into two parts and place in bread pans. Cover and let them rise in a warm place until the pans are almost full. Wash with beaten egg and bake at medium heat. Remove from pans and the second or third day, cut into finger thick slices. Arrange these slices next to one another in a baking sheet and place in a warm oven to dry out. When the slices are dry, increase the heat and bake until golden-brown. Remove from the oven and sprinkle each slice with confectioner's sugar mixed with anise. These biscuits keep well for a long time.

ACACIA FLOWER SHERBET
(şerbet de flori de salcâm)

1 ¾ lbs acacia flowers, 2 lbs sugar, 1 qt water, juice from ½ lemon

Clean the acacia flowers and set to boil with 1 qt of water. After a couple of minutes of boiling, remove from heat, cover, let cool off, then strain through Cheese cloth. Set the strained liquid to boil with the sugar (preferably lump sugar), at low heat to start with and after removing all foam, at medium heat. Wipe the inner walls of the pot with a clean, wet cloth and let boil until thickened. When tepid, beat the mixture, adding the lemon juice gradually, at the end.

ALMOND LAYERED CAKE
(tort de migdale)

8 eggs, 14 oz confectioner's sugar, 7 oz blanched and ground (not too fine) almonds,

2 tbsp potato flour, butter, filling and icing

Cream the sugar with the yolks until foamy. Add the almonds and potato flour and mix well. Add the whipped egg whites, mix gently and then pour the mixture into the pan which was covered with buttered parchment paper. Bake at medium heat. When it is completely cold, halve crosswise with a very sharp long knife. Fill with a butter cream and glaze with an chocolate icing.

LAYERED CAKE WITH VERY FINE ALMOND
(tort de migdale foarte fin)

12 eggs, 7 oz confectioner's sugar, 9 oz blanched and finely chopped almonds, 2 ½ oz flour, grated lemon peel, butter, vanilla cream II or butter cream with chocolate

Cream 6 whole eggs and 6 yolks until foamy. Add the almonds, lemon peel, flour and 6 whipped egg whites. Mix gently and pour into the buttered pan. Bake at medium heat. Fill with vanilla cream or butter cream with chocolate.

APPLE COMPOTE
(compot de mere)

5-6 tart apples, 10 oz sugar, 3 cups water, a little cinnamon, 2-3 cloves

Peel, seed and quarter the apples. Let sit in cold water. Set the water with the sugar, cinnamon and cloves to boil. When it starts boiling, add the apples, cover and simmer until the apples are soft. Serve cold

APPLE PIE ROMANIAN STYLE
(plăcintă cu mere în stil românesc)

ştrudel dough, butter to grease the pan, confectioner's sugar with vanilla flavor;

Filling: 2 lbs apples, 2-3 tbsp water, ½ cup sugar, 1 tsp ground cinnamon, 2 tbsp butter for greasing the dough

Peel the apples, grate on the vegetable grater or slice very thinly and set to boil with 2-3 tablespoons of water, stirring continuously. When the apples have softened, add the sugar and let boil until they become like a paste. Remove from heat and let cool. When cold, add the cinnamon. Continue as for cottage cheese pie, replacing the cottage cheese filling with apple filling. When the pie is done, cut into squares and sprinkle with confectioner's sugar.

APPLE PUDDING
(budincă de mere)

5-6 tart apples, 2 French baguettes (2-3 days old), 3 cups milk, 3 eggs, 2 oz raisins or sour cherries from preserves, ½ cup sugar, 4 oz butter, 1 tsp vanilla, salt, butter and bread crumbs for the mold

Peel, halve, remove seeds and cut apples in finger thick slices. Cut the baguettes in finger thick slices too. Dunk each bread slice in a mixture of beaten eggs, milk, vanilla and salt. Grease a round mold or pan with butter and arrange soaked bread slices on the bottom and sides. On top of the bread slices, arrange apple slices. Then sprinkle with sugar and raisins or sour cherries from preserves. Then arrange another layer of soaked bread slices, then a layer of apple slices. Sprinkle with sugar and Raisins or sour cherries from preserves. Continue until all apples are used up. The last layer must be bread slices. Pour the remaining egg-milk mixture on top. Dot it with little pieces of butter. Bake until golden. Serve hot.

APPLE STRUDEL
(ştrudel cu mere)

Ştrudel dough

Filling: 2 lbs apples, 1 cup sugar,1 tsp ground cinnamon, 3 tbsp melted butter or lard, shortening for greasing the pan and the dough, confectioner's sugar

Peel the apples, grate on the vegetable grater or slice very thinly. On the table there is the Strudel dough ready to be used. Moisten with melted butter or lard. Arrange the apples at one end (long end), sprinkle with sugar and cinnamon, cover with the edge of the dough and roll like a jelly roll using the table cloth as an aid. You get a long roll which you can cut in 2 or 3, depending on the size of your baking pan. Arrange in the greased pan, roll next to roll, with a little distance among them. Grease the tops with melted butter or lard. Bake until golden brown. Cut into serving size portions while still in the pan. Sprinkle with confectioner's sugar

APPLE WHIP
(spumă de mere)

1 lb apples, 2 ½ cups water, ¾ cup sugar, ½ oz gelatin

Wash and quarter the apples, remove seeds and boil until soft. Drain the liquid in another pot and sieve the apples. To the strained apple liquid, add gelatin, dissolve it, and add sugar and return to heat for another boil. After it has cooled down, pour the apple liquid in a tall bowl, add the apple puree and whip until foamy. Pour in cups or glasses and serve. You can use other fruits to prepare this.

APRICOT COMPOTE
(compot de caise)

2 lbs firm apricots, 10 oz sugar, 3 cups water, juice from ½ lemon

Set the water with sugar to boil. Peel the apricots and let sit in cold water. When the sugar has dissolved, add the apricots and lemon juice. Let simmer for a while, removing the foam as it forms. Serve cold.

APRICOT ICE-CREAM
(înghețată de caise)

8 yolks, 7 oz sugar, 1 qt milk, 1 cup whipped cream, ½ lb apricots

Beat the sugar with yolks until creamy, add the boiled milk and then cooled off and simmer, stirring continuously, until thickened (it should not come to a boil). When the ice-cream is almost done, add ripe, clean, crushed apricots. Mix well and freeze.

BABA ROMANIAN STYLE
(baba în stil românesc)

1 lb flour, 1 cup milk, 4 eggs, 5 oz butter or margarine, ¾ cup sugar, ¼ tsp salt, 4 oz raisins, 1 tsp vanilla, 1 ½ oz yeast, shortening to grease the dish;

Syrup: ¼ cup sugar, ¾ cup water, 4 tbsp wine, ½ tsp rum essence

Mix the yeast with ½ cup tepid milk, add some flour and knead well to make stiff dough. Gather into a ball and make 3-4 indentations with a knife. Place the dough in a pot with 3 qts tepid water. Cover and keep in a warm place. After 40-50 minutes when the dough rises above and doubles in volume, remove with a slotted tablespoon and place in a large bowl. Add tepid melted butter or margarine, salt, yolks beaten with sugar and vanilla and whipped egg whites. Knead well, adding the remaining flour and milk. The resulting dough should not be too stiff. Cover and leave in a warm place to rise. After it doubles again, add the Raisins, mix and then place in a greased pan. Cover and leave in a warm place until the dough fills 3/4 of the pan. Bake at slow heat for 30-40 minutes. Test with a wooden pick. Carefully remove from the pan so that it does not break. Place on a large plate and let cool without disturbing. In the meantime, prepare the syrup. Boil the water with the sugar, add the wine and rum. Pour this syrup (hot) over the cake, turning it so that the syrup gets everywhere.

BREAD WITH MILK
(pâine cu lapte)

2 lbs flour, 1 tbsp sugar, 2 tbsp oil, ½ tsp salt, 14-16 oz milk, 2 oz yeast, oil to grease the pan

Mix the sugar with the yeast in a small bowl. When it reaches the consistency of sour cream, add 2-3 tablespoons of warm milk, a little flour, mix well and cover with a cloth, leaving it until it rises. Take a larger bowl and place the warm milk, salt and dough starter (after it rises). Add flour and knead, adding oil as you do it. Knead until bubbly. Cover and leave in a warm place to rise. After it has doubled in bulk, place in the baking pan that was previously greased. Place again in a warm place for 15-20 minutes. First bake at low temperature until the dough rises, then increase the heat.

BISCUIT LAYERED CAKE
(tort de biscuiți)

3 eggs, 1 cup confectioner's sugar, 8 oz butter, 10 oz biscuits, 2 oz cacao or grated chocolate, ¼ cup rum, 10 oz whipped cream

Cream the butter with the sugar, adding the eggs one at a time and the rum, then the cacao or chocolate. Place broken biscuits (little pieces) into the resulting cream. Mix well. Place the mixture on a round platter, using a knife to pat it in place. Refrigerate. Before serving, cover with whipped cream.

BISCUITS ROMANIAN STYLE
(pesmeciori)

5 oz butter, 5 oz confectioner's sugar, 3 yolks, 1 egg white, 1 tsp vanilla, 2 tbsp ground walnuts, 1 tbsp granulated sugar, flour as needed

Cream the butter with the sugar; add the 3 yolks one by one, vanilla, ground walnuts and flour as needed, kneading quickly, to make a soft dough. Make patties about half an inch thick and 2 inches diameter. Place on a baking sheet, wash with beaten egg white and sprinkle with walnuts mixed with granulated sugar. Bake at medium heat.

BISCUITS WITH BAKER'S AMMONIA (HARTSHORN)
(pesmeți cu amoniac)

2 eggs, 1 tsp ammonia powder, ½ cup sugar, ½ cup oil, 1 tsp vanilla, flour as needed

Cream the sugar with the yolks, add the oil, mix, then add the ammonia powder and mix again. At the end add the vanilla. Knead well with flour to obtain soft dough. Cover with a cloth and let sit for 1 hour. Then roll a sheet about ½ inches thick and cut into various shapes with cookie cutters. Bake until golden. They are better after a day or two.

BISCUITS WITH LEMON
(pesmeți cu lămâie)

7 oz butter, 5 oz confectioner's sugar, 10 oz flour, 1 tsp vanilla or a little lemon peel, juice from 1 lemon, 1 egg white, 2-3 tbsp ground walnuts

Beat the butter with the sugar until creamy. Add juice from 1 lemon, vanilla and flour. Knead quickly and let rest only 2-3 minutes. Roll a medium thick sheet and cut into circles. Cut these circles with a smaller cutter so that you get a hole in the middle. Place on the baking sheet, wash with beaten egg white and sprinkle with walnuts. When they are baked, you may spread marmalade or Chocolate cream over them and then stick them together two by two.

BISCUITS WITH SOUR CREAM
(pesmeți cu smântână)

¾ cup sugar, 3 yolks, 2 whole eggs, ½ tsp baking soda, 1 cup sour cream, ½ cup butter or lard, vanilla, flour as needed

Beat the sugar with the yolks and whole eggs, add vanilla and sour cream, baking soda and butter and mix well. Add flour and knead a rather soft dough. Let rest for 10-15 minutes. Then roll into a ½ thick sheet. Cut into shapes using cookie cutters, place on the baking sheet and bake at medium heat until golden. These biscuits are tendered after 2-3 days.

DRY BISCUITS I
(uscăţele sau sărăţele)

3 eggs, 2 tbsp sugar, 2 tbsp vodka, rum or brandy, 1 tsp salt, 5 tbsp oil, vanilla or grated lemon peel, flour as needed

Beat the egg whites, adding a little sugar at a time. Add the yolks one by one, mixing continuously, then the oil, 1 tablespoon at a time and keep stirring. Add the salt, vodka, vanilla or lemon peel, flour and knead with the tablespoon a soft dough. Place the dough on a well floured pastry board and make it into a 4-5 fingers thick roll. Cut this roll into finger thick slices and flatten them into oval patties. Grease each patty with oil, sprinkle with granulated sugar and bake at high temperature.

BISCUITS, DRY II
(uscăţele)

4 oz confectioner's sugar, 7 oz butter, 10 oz flour, 24 sour cherries from preserves, vanilla

Cream the butter with the sugar and vanilla. Mix well with flour. Make the dough into a roll and cut it into 24 equal pieces. Make a ball out of each piece. With your finger, make an indentation into the ball and place a dry bean in it. Place these balls onto the floured baking sheet, about 2 inches apart and bake at medium heat. When they are cold, remove the Beans and replace with a sour cherry.

BISCUITS, NEST STYLE
(pesmeciori cuiburi)

¾ cup sugar, 5 oz butter or margarine, 2 eggs, ½ tsp baking soda, 1 tsp lemon juice (or vinegar), 1 tsp vanilla, flour as needed, 1 tbsp vanilla flavored confectioner's sugar, oil

Cream the eggs with the sugar. Add the vanilla, softened butter (margarine) and the baking soda dissolved in the lemon juice or vinegar. Knead very stiff dough and then grind it through the meat grinder. Arrange the little sticks that come out of the grinding machine in small piles, nest fashion. Place on the previously oiled baking sheet and bake at medium heat. When still hot, sprinkle with vanilla flavored confectioner's sugar.

ROUND BISCUITS
(pesmeciori perişoare)

1 cup melted butter, 1 cup water, 2 cups flour, 8 eggs, vanilla or a little grated lemon peel

Set the water to boil with the butter. When it starts bubbling, immediately remove from heat and quickly add the flour, then the 8 eggs one by one and vanilla, all without stopping the stirring. Let cool and then either with your hands or a teaspoon, shape into balls and place them on a baking sheet leaving lots of distance among them. Bake for 15-20 minutes.

WHITE BISCUITS WITH ALMONDS (OR WALNUTS)
(pesmeţi albi cu migdale (sau nuci))

1 cup confectioner's sugar, 1/2 cup melted and cooled butter, 4 sieved hard-boiled eggs, 2 whole eggs, vanilla, flour as needed, 3 tbsp sliced almonds (walnuts)

Cream the sugar, butter and the 2 raw eggs. Add vanilla and sieved hard-boiled eggs, mix well, and then knead well with flour to make medium soft dough. Let rest for ½ hour, then shape into small patties. Sprinkle them with sliced almonds or walnuts. Bake at medium heat.

CAKE WITH APRICOT MARMELADE
(prăjitură cu marmeladă de caise)

4 yolks, 1 cup sugar, 1 cup sour cream, 1 cup melted butter (tepid), ½ tsp baking soda, 1 tsp vanilla, flour as needed, marmalade, vanilla flavored confectioner's sugar

Mix the yolks with the sugar, add the sour cream, vanilla and baking soda, then tepid melted butter and mix well. Add flour and knead medium soft dough. Divide into 3 equal parts and roll each one into sheets the size of the baking sheet. Place a sheet in, spread a layer of marmalade, cover with the second sheet, spread another layer of marmalade and then cover with the third sheet. Bake, first at low temperature, and then increase it.

After it has cooled off, cut into rectangles and sprinkle with vanilla flavored confectioner's sugar. This cake is even tastier after a day or two.

BRIOCHES OR MADELEINES
(brioşe sau madlene)

2 eggs, ½ cup sugar, ½ cup butter or oil, ¾ cup flour, vanilla or lemon peel, oil to grease the dish

Mix the eggs with the sugar and vanilla, add oil and mix until the cream starts to thicken. Add flour and mix very well. Have ready brioche or tart pans. Oil them. Fill each pan about 3/4 full. Bake at medium heat. When done, remove immediately from the pans.

CAKE WITH BAKER'S AMMONIA (HARTSHORN)
(prăjitură cu amoniac)

1 tsp ammonia powder, 7 yolks, ¾ cup confectioner's sugar, ½ cup melted butter

flour as needed, a few sliced walnuts or almonds

Cream the butter with the sugar, adding the yolks one by one. Add the ground ammonia and mix until the mixture lightens in color. Add flour and knead rapidly to obtain soft dough. Roll a finger thick sheet and lay on the baking sheet. Wash with a little egg. Sprinkle sliced walnuts or almonds on top. Bake, first at low temperature, and then increase it. After it is completely cold, cut into desired shapes.

BUTTER CREAM
(cremă de unt)

8 oz confectioner's sugar, 8 oz butter, vanilla

Cream the butter with the confectioner's sugar and add vanilla.

CAKE FOR SPRING
(chec de primăvară)

4 oz butter, 5 eggs, 8 oz sugar, 8 oz flour, vanilla or lemon peel, 1 tsp baking powder, butter and flour to grease and dust the pan

Cream the butter with the sugar and the 4 yolks added one by one, add 1 whole egg, vanilla and baking powder. Add ½ cup cold milk, ¼ cup rum, and grated peel from 1 lemon. After everything is mixed well, gradually add the flour, then the 4 whipped egg whites. Mix gently. Divide the mixture into 2 parts. Pour the first part (slightly more than half), in a bread pan. To the second part, add food coloring (red or green). Bake at medium heat for about a half hour. Test with a wooden pick.

CAKE WITH CACAO
(chec cu cacao)

7 oz butter, 10 oz confectioner's sugar, 14 oz flour, 5 eggs, 1 tsp vanilla, 1 tbsp cacao, butter and flour to grease and dust the pan

Cream the butter with the sugar and vanilla, add the yolks one by one. Mix with flour and then with whipped egg whites. Take 4-5 tablespoons of this mixture and put in a bowl where you mix this with 1 tablespoon cacao. Place half of the plain (without cacao) mixture in the buttered and dusted bread pan, then pour the cacao mixture down the middle over the plain mixture (to obtain a brown strip in the middle, from one end to the other). Then pour the remaining plain mixture. Bake, first at low temperature, then somewhat higher. When done, remove onto a wooden cutting board and cover with a cloth.

CAKE WITH MARMELADE
(prăjitură cu marmeladă)

1 lb flour, 7 oz butter, 2 whole eggs, 3 tbsp sugar, 3/4 oz yeast, salt, 1 tsp vanilla or grated lemon peel, shortening for the pan, vanilla flavored confectioner's sugar

Filling: ½ lb ground walnuts, 4 oz granulated sugar, marmalade

Mix the butter with the yeast and sugar, add the eggs, salt, vanilla, flour and knead to obtain soft dough. Let rest for half an hour. Divide the dough into 4 equal parts. Roll each into a sheet. Place a sheet into the buttered pan. Spread a 1/4 inch layer of marmalade over it. Sprinkle 1/3 of the ground walnuts and sugar. Then place another dough sheet. Repeat the procedure with the marmalade and walnut/sugar mixture for this 2nd and 3rd sheets. Finally, cover with the 4th sheet and bake at medium heat. When golden brown, remove from the oven, sprinkle with vanilla flavored confectioner's sugar and cut into squares or rectangles. It is desirable to use 3 different kinds of marmalade.

CAKE WITH COTTAGE CHEESE AND WALNUTS
(prăjitura din brânză de vacă şi nuci)

14 oz cottage cheese, 4 eggs, ¾ cup sugar, 7 oz ground walnuts, 4 oz raisins, 5 oz butter, vanilla or rum, shortening and flour to grease and dust the pan

Grind the cottage cheese. Mix the sugar with the butter, adding the eggs one by one, then the cheese, walnuts, raisins, vanilla or rum. Mix everything well and pour into a buttered and dusted bread pan. Bake at medium heat and remove from the pan when cold.

CAKE WITH EGG WHITES
(chec din albuşuri)

7-8 egg whites, 10 oz sugar, 5 oz butter or margarine, 5 oz flour, 1 lemon yest, 4 oz sliced walnuts, butter and flour to grease and dust the pan

Whip the egg whites with the sugar. Gradually add the melted and still warm butter (margarine), stirring continuously. Then add the lemon peel and flour. Place half of the walnuts on the bottom of a buttered and dusted bread pan. Then pour the batter and the remaining walnuts on top. Bake, first at low heat and then increase it.

CAKE WITH GRATED APPLES
(prăjitură cu mere rase)

6 medium apples grated on the vegetable grater, 6 eggs, 6 tbsp sugar, 3 tbsp bread crumbs, 2 tbsp flour, 1/4 cup rum, syrup from 2-3 tbsp sugar and a little rum, butter and bread crumbs to grease and dust the pan

Beat the yolks with the sugar, gradually add the flour, then rum and bread crumbs. After everything has been mixed well, add the peeled and grated apples, mix some more and then add the whipped egg whites. Pour the mixture into a buttered and dusted (with bread crumbs) pan and bake at medium heat. When done, put on a platter and pour some syrup over it while still hot.

CAKE WITH PLUMS
(prăjitură cu prune)

2 tbsp sour cream, 10 oz flour, 5 oz butter or margarine, 14 oz confectioner's sugar, 5 yolks, 2 egg whites, 2 lbs peeled and pitted plums, 1 tsp ground cinnamon, shortening for the pan

Peel and pit 2 lbs of plums, sprinkle with some sugar and cinnamon and let rest. Make dough out of 10 oz sugar, 5 oz butter, 3 yolks and 10 oz flour. Knead well, roll into a finger thick sheet. Place this sheet into the greased pan and put the well drained plums over it. Pour the following mixture on top of the plums. 2 tablespoons sour cream mixed with 2 yolks, 4 oz sugar and 2 whipped egg whites. Bake at medium heat. Serve cut into squares or rectangles.

CAKE WITH POTATO FLOUR AND BITTER ALMONDS
(chec cu faină de cartofi şi migdale amare)

8 oz butter, 8 oz confectioner's sugar, 5 eggs, 8 oz potato flour, 4 oz blanched, peeled and ground bitter almonds, 1 tsp vanilla, butter and flour to grease and dust the pan

Cream the butter and sugar, then add the yolks one by one, vanilla and almonds, mixing well. Then gradually add the flour (like a rain) without stopping the mixing. At the end, add the whipped egg whites. Bake in a previously greased and dusted bread pan at medium heat. Test with a wooden pick. When cold, cut into thin slices.

CAKE WITH RASPBERRIES
(prăjitură cu zmeură)

8 oz cottage cheese, 2 hard-boiled yolks, 3 raw yolks, 2 oz butter, salt, sugar to taste, 1 lb raspberries, shortening for the pan

Sieve the cottage cheese, mix with the two hard-boiled yolks, also sieved and with 3 raw yolks. Add 2 oz butter, salt and sugar to taste. Mix everything well, to get a creamy mixture. Add 3 whipped egg whites.

Grease a pan and pour the batter in a uniform layer. Arrange raspberries on top. Bake at medium heat. Cut according to taste.

CAKE WITH SOUR CHERRIES
(prăjitură cu vişine)

7 oz confectioner's sugar, 7 oz butter, 2 eggs, 2-3 tbsp sour cream, ½ tsp baking soda, vanilla, 4 lbs sour cherries, flour as needed, vanilla flavored, confectioner's sugar

After you mix the sugar with the eggs and vanilla, add sour cream and butter, mixing well, then add the baking soda. Knead everything with flour so that you get a medium stiff dough. Roll into a finger thick sheet and lay into a pan. Bake only until the dough lightens in color. Remove from the oven and quickly arrange the pitted and well drained sour cherries on top of the dough. Let it bake. When it is done, cut into medium squares, while still hot in the pan. Arrange the squares on a plate and sprinkle with confectioner's sugar. When they are cold, sprinkle some more vanilla flavored confectioner's sugar on them. Strawberries or apricots may be used instead of sour cherries.

CAKE WITH VARIOUS FRUITS
(prăjitură cu diferite fructe)

14 oz flour, 14 oz sugar, 14 oz butter, 4 eggs, assorted fruits

Cream the butter with the sugar, adding the eggs one by one, then the flour. Mix well. Bake in a round pan, at medium heat. When the batter in the pan rises a little and lightens in color, remove from the oven and arrange various fruits (not unripe) all over the cake. grapes may be added too, as long as they do not have seeds. Fresh fruits may be replaced with fruits from preserves. Place in the oven again. When done, remove from the oven and slice like a layer cake.

CAKE WITH WALNUTS AND CHOCOLATE
(prăjitură cu nuci şi ciocolată)

1 lb butter, 1 lb confectioner's sugar, 100 walnuts, shelled and ground, juice from 1 lemon and a little lemon peel, 1 egg, 10 oz grated chocolate or 50 g cacao, butter and bread crumbs to grease and dust the pan

Cream the butter with the sugar, add beaten yolks, lemon juice, lemon peel, chocolate (grated or melted with 1 tablespoon hot water). In the end, add whipped egg whites and walnuts, mixing gently. The baking pan must be well buttered and sprinkled with fine bread crumbs. Bake at medium heat for 20-25 minutes. As soon as it is done, remove from the oven and cut into squares, rectangles or diamonds.

"SNOW STORM" CAKE
(prăjitura Viscol)

½ cup melted butter, 1 cup water, 1 cup flour, 5 eggs, shortening for the pan, granulated sugar

Boil the butter with the water. Remove from heat, gradually add flour and keep stirring. Boil like a mămăligă, then set aside to cool. When only slightly warm, add the eggs one by one, mixing well. Grease a pan and pour the mixture in a layer the width of a matchstick. Sprinkle with some granulated sugar and bake. When done, cut into pieces to taste.

ENGLISH CAKE
(chec englezesc)

14 oz butter, 1 cup sour cream, 6 eggs, 1 tsp ammonia powder, 7 oz chopped walnuts, 7 oz golden raisins, 4 oz ground almonds, 1 cup flour, ½ cup chopped fruits from preserves, 14 oz confectioner's sugar, juice from ½ lemon, vanilla, shortening and flour for greasing and dusting the pan

Cream the butter with the sugar, adding the yolks one by one, then the sour cream and ammonia; mix well then add the walnuts, almonds, raisins, fruits, vanilla and lemon juice. In the end, add flour and whipped egg whites. Mix gently. Pour the batter into the buttered and dusted bread pan. Bake for 40-45 minutes at medium heat. Test with a wooden pick and cut only when cold.

CAKE WITH WALNUTS AND MARMALADE
(prăjitură cu nuci şi marmeladă)

1 cup sour cream, 1 cup lard or butter, 1 cup confectioner's sugar, 4 yolks, ½ tsp baking soda, 1 tsp vanilla, flour as needed, 2 oz ground walnuts, 6 whipped egg whites, 1 cup sugar, marmalade

Cream 1 cup of sugar with the butter or lard and 4 yolks, add sour cream, baking soda and vanilla, mix well, add flour and knead a medium soft dough. Roll a sheet the size of the baking pan, place in the pan and spread marmalade on it. Whip 6 egg whites, gradually add 1 cup sugar, and then add the ground walnuts. Mix gently. Place this mixture on top of the dough with marmalade, smooth into a uniform layer and bake at medium heat to start with and then at higher heat. When done, cut into squares or rectangles.

STRASBOURG STYLE CAKE
(prăjitura Strasburg)

8 oz flour, 8 oz butter, 2 lbs apples, 1 cup granulated sugar, 1 tsp confectioner's sugar, 1 tbsp water, 2 yolks, salt, cinnamon, shortening for greasing the pan, egg mixed with sweetened water

Put the flour in a mound on the pastry board. Put 1 tablespoon water, yolks, butter, salt and 1 teaspoon confectioner's sugar in the middle of the flour. Knead well. Let the resulting dough rest, covered with an inverted bowl, for two hours. In the meantime, peels the apples, cut into thin slices and sprinkle with cinnamon. Then divide the dough into 2 equal parts. Roll each of them into a 1/4 inch thick sheet. Lay the first sheet in the greased pan, the apples sprinkled with 1 cup granulated sugar on top of the first sheet. Cover with the second sheet and wash with a little egg mixed with 1 tablespoon sweetened water. Bake at medium heat and when done, cut into medium squares.

TURKISH CAKE
(prăjitură turcească (Tis-pis-tiri))

1 egg, 1 ½ cups oil, 1 cup water, 1 tbsp confectioner's sugar, grated peel from 1 lemon, salt, flour as needed, shortening and flour to grease and dust the pan, Syrup:1 lb sugar, 1 ¼ cups water, vanilla, juice from 1 lemon

Beat the sugar with the egg, mix with oil, salt, lemon peel, sugar and water. Add flour and knead soft dough. Let it rest for 10 minutes and then roll into a finger thick sheet. Cut into squares (not too big) and arrange on the greased and dusted baking sheet, at a distance one from the other. While they bake, prepare the syrup.

Set to boil the sugar with 1 1/4 cup water and vanilla; after a few minutes, add lemon juice and remove from heat. When the squares are nicely golden-brown, scald with this syrup and bake a little longer so that the syrup gets well into the dough.

BROWN CAKE
(chec maron)

4 oz butter, 5 eggs, 8 oz sugar, 8 oz flour, vanilla or lemon peel, 1 tsp baking powder, butter and flour to grease and dust the pan, 4 tbsp chocolate, 2 tbsp milk

Cream the butter with the sugar and the 4 yolks added one by one, add 1 whole egg, vanilla and baking powder. Add 4 tablespoons chocolate melted in 2 tablespoons hot milk. After everything is mixed well, gradually add the flour, then the 4 whipped egg whites. Mix gently. Pour into the buttered and dusted bread pan. Bake at medium heat for about a half hour. Test with a wooden pick.

DELICIOUS CAKE WITH WALNUTS
(prăjitură delicioasă cu nuci)

1 lb confectioner's sugar, 1 lb ground walnuts, 8 oz butter, 5 eggs, 1 tsp baking powder, grated peel from 1 lemon, butter for the pan

Cream the butter with the sugar and the gradually added yolks. Add lemon peel, baking powder and walnuts, mixing well. Then add the 5 whipped egg whites. Cover the bottom and sides of the pan with buttered paper, pour the batter in and bake at medium heat for 20-25 minutes. Cut in the pan, while still hot, into small squares or rectangles.

ROLLED CAKE
(prăjitură rulată)

8 oz flour, 2 yolks, 4 oz butter, 1 tbsp sugar, vanilla, ¾ cup milk, ½ oz yeast, salt

Filling: ¼ cup milk, 7 oz sugar, 7 oz walnuts, ¼ cup rum, vanilla

Mix the yeast with ½ teaspoon sugar, salt, tepid milk and 1 tablespoon flour. Cover and leave in a warm space to rise. When the starter has risen, add sugar, tepid butter, yolks, vanilla and flour (a little at a time). Knead for 15 minutes. Place in a warm place to rise again.

In the meantime, prepare the filling. Set the sugar to boil with the milk and vanilla. When the sugar has melted and the syrup starts to boil, add the ground walnuts. After a few minutes of boiling, remove from heat, add rum and let cool. When the dough has risen, roll into a sheet slightly thinner than a pencil. Spread filling over ¾ of the sheet. Roll the dough so that the part which is not spread with filling comes on top. Place into a long pan, cover and leave in a warm place to rise. When it has risen a little, wash with slightly sweetened water, sprinkle some granulated sugar on top and bake at slow heat to start with. When the cake has risen nicely, increase the heat. Cut when cold, just before serving, into finger thick slices.

CAKE "ECONOMIC"
(chec economic)

4 oz butter, 5 eggs, 8 oz sugar, 8 oz flour, vanilla or lemon peel, 1 tsp baking powder, butter and flour to grease and dust the pan

Cream the butter with the sugar and the 4 yolks added one by one, add 1 whole egg, vanilla and baking powder. After everything is mixed well, gradually add the flour, then the 4 whipped egg whites. Mix gently. Pour into the buttered and dusted bread pan. Bake at medium heat for about a half hour. Test with a wooden pick.

CAKE WITH SOUR CHERRIES
(chec cu vişine)

2 cups pitted and drained sour cherries, 1 cup sugar, 4 eggs, 3 tbsp oil, 1 ½ cups flour, 1 tsp vanilla

Mix the eggs with the sugar about a half hour. Add oil and vanilla and mix well, then add flour. Place 1/3 of this mixture into the bread pan, put 1 cup of sour cherries over it, cover with 1/3 of the mixture, add another cup of sour cherries over this and finally, place the last 1/3 of the mixture on top. Bake at medium heat.

WHITE CAKE
(chec alb)

12 egg whites, 2 cups sugar, 1 lemon (juice and grated peel), 2 cups flour, 10-12 chopped walnuts, 5-6 pieces variously colored rahat-lokum (cubed), 1 tbsp raisins, butter to grease the pan

Whip the egg whites; add the sugar little by little. When the sugar has completely dissolved, add juice and peel from 1 lemon, flour (gradually), and the walnuts, rahat-lokum, add raisins at the end. Grease a bread pan and cover the bottom and sides with well greased paper. Pour the batter in and bake at medium heat, testing with a wooden pick.

WHITE CAKE WITH OIL
(chec alb cu ulei)

2 eggs, 13 oz flour, 1 cup sugar, 1 cup oil (or melted margarine), ¾ cup milk, a pinch of baking soda, 5 oz sliced walnuts, 5 oz colored rahat-lokum cut in strips, 2 oz Raisins, butter to grease the pan

Beat the eggs with the sugar, add the milk, then oil and mix well. Add the baking soda and the flour (gradually). Dredge the walnuts, rahat-lokum and Raisins through flour, shake and add to the mixture. Grease a bread pan, cover the bottom and sides with paper and slowly pour the batter in. Bake at low heat to start with, then at higher heat. Test with a wooden pick. The cake is tastier after 2-3 days.

CANOLI WITH CREAM OR WHIPPED CREAM
(cornet cu frişcă sau cremă)

4 oz butter, 4 oz confectioner's sugar, 1 egg, ½ cup wine, 2 tbsp oil, 2 tbsp rum, flour as needed;

Filling: 0.5 qt milk, 2 tbsp flour, 3 eggs, 4 oz butter, 8 oz sugar, 1 tsp vanilla, egg for washing

Cream the butter with the sugar and egg, then add wine, rum, oil and the flour at the end. Knead a medium soft dough and let it rest for 10-15 minutes. Then roll into a ¼ inch thick sheet, cut into strips and wind these strips around the special canoli molds. Wash with egg and bake. When the canoli are done, remove and let cool. When cold, fill with whipped cream or other fillings. For filling, set the milk to boil, and then gradually add the eggs previously beaten with sugar and flour. Stir continuously until the filling thickens. When cooled, add vanilla and creamed butter.

CARAMEL LAYERED CAKE
(tort caramel)

1 cup sour cream, 4 oz butter, vanilla, flour (as needed to make a dough)

Filling: 5 oz caramelized sugar, 1 cup milk, 5 oz confectioner's sugar, vanilla or ¼ cup rum, 5 oz butter

Make a dough out of sour cream, butter, vanilla and flour. Knead a medium soft dough. Let rest for a half hour, then divide into 9 equal parts. Roll each part into round sheets the size of the baking pan. Bake the sheets one by one, after pricking them with a fork. In the meantime, caramel 5 oz/150 g sugar in a small pan. In another pan, place the milk, 5 oz/150 g sugar, vanilla (or rum) and the butter. Add the caramelized sugar, mix and let come to a boil. Spread this mixture on 8 of the sheets. Break the 9th sheet into little pieces and sprinkle on the last sheet with cream on it. Serve this cake the following day after preparation.

CARAMELIZED SUGAR CREAM
(cremă de zahăr ars)

6 eggs, 6 tbsp sugar, 3 cups milk, 3 tbsp of sugar for caramelizing, vanilla (stick), salt

Boil the milk with vanilla at slow heat. After the first boil, cover and keep aside. Beat the eggs with the sugar and the latter dissolves. Heat the milk again, add a little salt, and pour, a little at a time, into the egg and sugar mixture, constantly stirring, until it is almost cool. Take a 3 qt pan and put 3 tablespoons of sugar in it. Heat until the sugar melts and becomes yellowish. Remove from heat and tilt the pan in such a way, that the melted sugar spreads all over the interior walls of the pan.

Stir the cream a little and then pour into the pan. Cover and set this pan into a larger pan filled with boiling water. The boiling water must be ¾ of the height of the pan with the cream. Keep on medium heat for 25-30 minutes. The cream is ready when it comes off the pan walls quite easily. Remove from the water and keep in a cool place. After it has cooled completely, refrigerate. Before serving, take a large round plate and cover the pan with it. Then turn the pan upside down.

CHERRY COMPOTE
(compot de cireşe)

2 lbs cherries, 3 tbsp sugar, water to cover, a little vanilla stick

Wash the cherries and place in a pot. Add the sugar, vanilla and water to cover. Let boil for a little while. Serve cold.

CHESTNUT CHARLOTTE
(şarlotă de castane)

4 lbs boiled, peeled, crushed, strained chestnuts, 80 sugar cubes made into a thick syrup, 1 cup rum, 2 oz butter, ½ vanilla stick, 7 oz whipped cream

Mix the chestnut cream with the sugar syrup to which you added 1 cup of rum and vanilla. The syrup must be warm. Add the butter and mix to homogenize. Place the mixture on a plate moistened with rum. Garnish with whipped cream and refrigerate.

CHOCOLATE FANCY CAKES
(fursecuri cu ciocolată)

4 oz butter, 7 oz confectioner's sugar, 1 egg white, 8 oz roasted and ground hazelnuts, 4 tbsp flour, vanilla, butter and flour to grease and dust the pan

Cream: 3 oz chocolate or 2 tbsp cacao, 1 tbsp sugar, 2 tbsp water, 1 tsp rum

Mix the sugar with the butter, add the egg white and cream everything well. Add vanilla, hazelnuts and flour, mix well and pour the batter into a buttered and dusted pan. Bake at medium heat. When cold, spread hot cream over the cake. Cut into small squares. For cream, boil the chocolate with sugar and water, add rum and mix.

CHESTNUT LAYERED CAKE
(tort de castane)

12 eggs, 9 oz confectioner's sugar, 3 heaping tbsp fine bread crumbs, 1 tsp ground cinnamon, 9 oz boiled and crushed chestnuts (puree), butter, filling and icing

Beat the sugar with 12 yolks, add the bread crumbs and cinnamon and mix gently. Add the chestnut puree and 6 whipped egg whites at the end. Pour the mixture in the buttered cake pan and bake at slow heat for 45 minutes. Fill and glaze as desired.

CHOCOLATE CREAM
(cremă de ciocolată)

8 oz butter, 8 oz sugar, 5 yolks, 2 oz milk, vanilla (stick), 2 tbsp grated chocolate or cacao

Beat the yolks with the sugar until creamy. Add the vanilla, milk and cocoa and set on heat, stirring continuously until it starts to thicken. Remove from heat, let cool a little, then gradually add the butter, processing until the cream starts to lighten in color. Refrigerate.

CHOCOLATE ICE-CREAM
(înghețată de ciocolată)

10 yolks, 10 oz, 1 qt milk, 4 oz chocolate or 2 oz cacao, vanilla

Boil the milk with the vanilla stick, cover and remove from heat. Separately, beat the yolks with the sugar, add the chocolate melted with a tablespoon of warm water and beat again. Then add a little milk at a time. Without quitting stirring, set to boil. As soon as it comes to a boil remove from heat and refrigerate. When it is completely cold, remove the vanilla stick, mix well and freeze.

CHOCOLATE ICING
(glazură de ciocolată)

6 oz sugar, 1/2 pint water, 3-4 tbsp grated chocolate or cacao

Set the water to boil with the sugar. Remove foam. Test the syrup as for sherbets. When it is sufficiently thick, remove from heat and mix with 3-4 tablespoons grated chocolate or cacao. When still soft, spread over the cake.

CHOCOLATE JELLO PUDDING
(jeleu de ciocolată)

10 oz chocolate, 10 tbsp milk, ½ qt sour cream, 5 oz confectioner's sugar, vanilla, 8 envelopes gelatin, oil

Put the warmed milk, vanilla and chocolate in a pot. When the chocolate has melted; pour everything over the sugar beaten with the sour cream and mix well. Then add the dissolved and strained gelatin. Grease a mold with oil, fill it with the mixture and refrigerate. Before serving, briefly place the mold in hot water and turn onto a plate.

CHOUX A LA CREME
(choux a la crème)

7 oz water, 2 ½ oz butter, 2 tsp sugar, 4 oz flour, 3 eggs, salt, shortening for greasing the pan, Vanilla cream I, whipped cream

Set the water to boil with the butter, salt and sugar. When it starts boiling, gradually add the flour (like a rain), stirring continuously until the dough starts to come off the sides of the pan. Remove from heat. When the mixture is still warm, gradually add 3 eggs, mixing continuously. Then let cool. Grease a baking sheet and place spoonfuls of the batter in piles on the sheet. Leave considerable distance among them. When done, let cool, then with a very sharp knife, cut a thin top slice, leaving the lid attached on one side. Fill the little balls with vanilla cream. Top with some whipped cream.

COFFEE CHARLOTTE
(şarlotă de cafea)

2 lbs whipped cream, 11 tbsp gelatin, 4 cups cold black coffee, sugar to taste, 1 cup milk, sour cherry preserves (optional)

Set the black coffee and milk to boil. Add the gelatin and mix well until dissolved. Strain through a dense sieve and let cool. When only tepid, pour into the whipped cream with confectioner's sugar to taste. Mix well. Pour in cups or glasses and refrigerate. When serving, you can garnish with whipped cream or sour cherry preserves.

COFFEE ICE-CREAM
(înghețată de cafea)

1 qt milk, 14 oz sugar, 1.5 cups concentrated and strained coffee, 10 oz whipped cream, vanilla, 4 yolks (optional)

Boil the milk with a little vanilla stick. Remove from heat and mix with sugar and coffee. After it has cooled off, add the whipped cream, mix well and freeze. Serve with a little whipped cream.

If using egg yolks, follow the Vanilla ice-cream procedure.

COFFEE ICING
(glazură de cafea)

7 oz sugar, 2-3 tbsp coffee

Mix the confectioner's sugar with 2-3 tablespoons of very concentrated and very hot coffee. Stir for ½ hour until creamy and then immediately spread over the cake.

COFFEE JELLY PUDDING
(jeleu de cafea)

5 yolks, ½ qt milk, vanilla (1/4 stick), 4 tbsp confectioner's sugar, 8 envelopes gelatin, ½ cup very strong strained black coffee, oil

Set the milk to boil with the vanilla. After it comes to a boil, remove from heat and cover. Beat the yolks with the sugar and pour, gradually, in the warm milk, stirring continuously in the same direction. Return to heat and stir until thickened. After it has cooled off a little, add the coffee and the gelatin that was dissolved in a few tablespoons of warm water. Mix and pour in a mold greased with oil. Refrigerate. Before serving, briefly place the mold in a pan with hot water and turn onto a plate.

ASSORTED COMPOTE FOR WINTER
(compot asortat pentru iarnă)

4 lbs sugar, 8 cups water, 2 lbs cherries, 2 lbs sour cherries, 2 lbs apricots, 4 lbs peaches, 2 lbs plums, 2 lbsg pears, 4 lbs fragrant grapes, 3 cups rum or vodka

Set the water to boil with the sugar. Remove foam. After 4-5 boils, add the cherries. Let come to another boil and remove from heat. Remove the cherries with a slotted tablespoon and place on the bottom of a 10 qt glass jar. Add a cup of rum or vodka to the cherry liquid, mix and pour over the cherries in the jar. Tie the jar mouth with a clean cloth and then cellophane. Let it sit in a cool and dry place, keeping it until the sour cherries come on the market.

Choose ripe sour cherries and wash them. Untie the jar, drain the liquid in a pan and set to boil. When it starts to boil, add the sour cherries and let come to a single boil. Remove from heat, take out the sour cherries with the slotted tablespoon and place them in the jar, on top of the cherries.

Pour the hot liquid in the jar over the fruits. Tie the jar mouth as before and keep until apricot time. Do this with all fruits. The apricots, plums and peaches are used whole. The Pears are peeled, seeded, quartered and each quarter cut in half. The Pears must be firm. The grapes are the last to be added. Remove each grape from the cluster and wash well. Untie the jar, remove all liquid and set it to boil. After the first boil, add the grapes and let come to another boil. Remove from heat, take out the grapes with the slotted tablespoon and place in the jar on top of the other fruits. To the hot liquid, add two cups of rum or vodka and pour in the jar. Tie the jar and keep cool until you use it. During the winter, the compote is taken out by ladle and served as needed. Retie the jar each time. It keeps quite well all winter.

COOKIES I
(pricomigdale I)

4 oz sugar, 4 oz flour, 4 oz ground walnuts, 1 egg, 3 oz lard, a few drops rum essence, shortening for greasing the baking sheet

Cream the sugar with the egg and lard, add walnuts, rum essence and flour. Knead well. Make little balls (walnut sized) and arrange on the previously greased baking sheet, leaving a lot of space among them. Bake at medium heat.

COOKIES II
(pricomigdale) II

4 cups walnuts, 1 cup confectioner's sugar, 1 egg, 1 yolk, 1 tsp flour, 1 tsp vanilla, oil

Beat the sugar with the whole egg and yolk until foamy. Add the ground walnuts, vanilla and flour and mix well. With you wet hands, shape little balls, flatten them slightly and arrange on the oiled baking sheet. Leave space between them because they increase their size during baking.

COTTAGE CHEESE PASTE
(pasta de brânză de vacă)

14 oz cottage cheese, 7 oz butter, ½ cup sour cream, 2 eggs, ¼ cup milk, 4 oz raisins, 2 oz ground walnuts, salt, 1 cup confectioner's sugar, vanilla

Sieve or grind the cheese. Beat the eggs with the sugar, add milk, salt, vanilla and set on the range, stirring until it starts to thicken. Remove from heat, add butter, mix well. When the mixture is almost cold, add cheese, sour cream, raisins and walnuts. Put this mixture into a cloth, tie tightly and weigh down with something heavy for 5-6 hours. Keep refrigerated. Then remove from the cloth and cut like a layer cake.

COTTAGE CHEESE PIE
(plăcintă cu brânză de vacă)

ştrudel dough, butter to grease the pan

Filling: 14 oz cottage cheese, 3 eggs, 3 tbsp melted butter, salt

Mix the Cheese with the eggs and salt. Cut the strudel dough into pieces the size of the baking pan. Arrange 6-7 strudel leaves into the greased pan. Grease each and every leaf. Then put the cottage cheese in a uniform layer. Place another 6-7 individually greased strudel leaves on top.

Bake until golden brown. Cut into squares while still in the pan.

COTTAGE CHEESE STRUDEL
(ştrudel cu brânză de vacă)

ştrudel dough, confectioner's sugar with vanilla flavor;

Filling: 1 ¾ lbs cottage cheese, 2 eggs, 2 tbsp sugar (optional), salt, 3 tbsp melted butter or lard

Mix the cheese with the eggs, salt and sugar. Knead with your hands. Arrange the cheese mixture at one end of the greased strudel dough. Cover with the edge of the dough and roll like a jelly roll. Continue as for apple strudel. When it is done, cut and sprinkle with vanilla flavored sugar.

CREAM OF WHEAT CAKE
(prăjitură cu griş)

3 eggs, 3 tbsp confectioner's sugar, 1 cup cream of Wheat, vanilla, syrup from 2 tbsp sugar with 0.5 qt milk, salt, vanilla, shortening for greasing the pan

Mix the yolks with the sugar and vanilla; add cream of wheat, then the whipped egg whites. Pour into a greased pan and bake. In the meantime, prepare the syrup. Set the milk to boil with the sugar, vanilla and some salt. When the cake is baked, pour the hot syrup over it. Let the syrup soak into the cake, then cut and arrange on a plate. This may be served plain, with whipped cream or a fruit syrup.

CREAM OF WHEAT LAYERED CAKE
(tort de griş)

6 leveled tbsp of cream of wheat, 7 oz confectioner's sugar, 6 eggs, 4 oz walnuts, 1 lemon, 20 lumps sugar, 1 tbsp milk, 4 tbsp marmalade, butter, syrup

Cream the sugar with the yolks, add the grated lemon peel, finely ground walnuts, then, gradually, the cream of wheat, alternating with the whipped egg whites. Butter the cake pan, pour the mixture in and bake at low heat. When done, halve crosswise and pour a little syrup (boiled water with sugar) on it. Fill with marmalade and glaze with the following icing: Cover 20 lumps of sugar with water and let boil as for sherbets. Mix the warm syrup, adding the lemon juice and 1 tablespoon milk. When it turns white, spread on the cake with a moistened knife.

CREAM OF WHEAT WITH FRUIT
(griş cu fructe în formă de şarlotă)

25 oz water, 1 lb fruit (sour cherries or raspberries, strawberries, wild strawberries, gooseberries), 3-4 tbsp sugar, 5 oz cream of wheat, vanilla

Boil the fruits. After coming to a few boils, remove from heat, let cool, and then sift fruits and liquid. oil, adding sugar, vanilla and cream of wheat, adding this last a little at a time, like a rain, stirring continuously until it thickens like a cream. Remove from heat and beat until foamy. Then pour into a charlotte or pudding mold which was previously moistened with cold water. Refrigerate for 2-3 hours. Before serving, turn onto a plate and garnish with some raw fruit.

DATE LAYER CAKE WITH WHIPPED CREAM
(tort de curmale cu frişcă)

8 oz confectioner's sugar, 10 oz chopped dates, 10 oz ground hazelnuts, 1 tbsp fine bread crumbs, 10 egg whites, 1 lb whipped cream, vanilla

Beat the egg whites with the sugar until foamy. Add the dates cut lengthwise, hazelnuts, bread crumbs and vanilla. Pour the mixture in the cake pan and bake at medium heat. Let cool, then halve crosswise and fill with whipped cream. Cover all the cake with whipped cream and garnish with cut dates.

DELICIOUS "LIES"
(minciunele delicioase)

3 yolks, 1 whole egg, 1 tsp confectioner's sugar, 2 tbsp sour cream, 2 tbsp plain seltzer, vanilla or rum to flavor, flour as needed, salt, shortening for frying, vanilla flavored confectioner's sugar

Place the sifted flour in a pile on the pastry board. Make an indentation in the middle and place the eggs, sugar, sour cream, seltzer, vanilla and salt in it. Knead a rather stiff dough. Divide it into 2 parts and let it rest for 1 hour. Then roll into a very thin sheet. Cut it into 1 ½ inches wide strips. Each strip should be 4 inches long. Cut a notch in the middle of each strip and bring one of the ends through that notch (so that the strips look knotted). Do this for all strips. Fry in a pan with hot oil or lard or golden brown. Remove with the slotted tablespoon and sprinkle vanilla flavored confectioner's sugar over them.

DESSERT WITH EVERYTHING
(desert "Băcănie")

6 eggs, 1 cup confectioner's sugar, 7 oz butter, 6 tbsp flour, 4 oz peanuts, 4 oz walnuts, 4 oz almonds, 4 oz Raisins, 4 oz rahat-lokum, 4 oz figs, 4 oz orange peel from preserves, 1 tsp vanilla, 1 tsp baking powder, oil

Slightly roast the peanuts, walnuts and almonds, and then chop roughly. The raisins, rahat-lokum and figs are also chopped roughly. Cream the butter with the sugar, add the yolks one by one, then the baking powder, vanilla and flour. Mix well. Then add all the fruits and nuts. In the end, add the whipped egg whites, gently fold them in and pour the whole thing in an oiled pan, covered with oiled paper. Bake at medium heat and let cool in the pan. Cut into rectangles.

DOBOSH TORTE
(tort Doboş)

10 eggs, 7 oz confectioner's sugar, 4 oz fine flour, grated peel and juice from 1 lemon, butter

Filling: 6 eggs, 7 oz sugar, 7 oz butter, 6 tbsp grated chocolate, 4 tbsp water

Beat the yolks with the sugar, peel and juice from 1 lemon until creamy. Gradually add the whipped egg whites and flour, gently mixing. Make 10 very thin (like a knife's edge) sheets from the resulting batter. Bake in a buttered rectangular baking pan. When all the sheets are baked and cold, spread cream on them, lay one on top of the other and glaze with caramelized sugar or the same cream as the one used for filling. For the filling, in a pan placed in a larger pan with boiling water set on heat, beat the whole eggs with the sugar until thickened. Remove from heat and add the chocolate melted with 4 tablespoons of water and the butter. Beat everything well until cold.

DOUGH FOR VARIOUS USES
(aluat pentru diferite prăjituri)

1 cup cream, 1 cup flour, 1 tsp butter, salt

Knead dough from the cream, flour, butter and salt. Roll into a sheet and cut according to your need:

- you can make small crescents filled with rahat-lokum, marmalade or preserves; so, replace the salt with a little sugar;
- you can make biscuits, spread with marmalade or stuck two by two; in this case, replace the salt with a little sugar;
- you can make small tartlets to be filled with peas, carrots, spinach sautes, Beef salad, etc.

FRENCH DOUGH I
(aluat franțuzesc) I

Butter dough: 4 oz flour, 8 oz butter or margarine;

Water dough: 7 oz flour, 1 yolk, 1 tsp lemon juice or vinegar, salt, water as needed, flour to dust the pastry board

Knead a medium stiff dough out of 7 oz/200 g flour, 1 yolk, lemon juice, salt and water. Gather it into a ball and cover.

In the meantime, mix 8 oz/250 g butter or margarine with 4 oz/100 g flour, knead quickly and set aside. Roll the dough with water into a pencil thin sheet. Lay the flattened, square butter dough in the middle of the water dough.

The butter dough should be three times smaller than the water dough. Cover the small square with the larger one, envelope style, and place the dough on a plate. Refrigerate for 45 minutes.

Sprinkle the pastry board with flour and then roll the dough into a square sheet. Fold three times lengthwise and three times crosswise. Refrigerate for 20-30 minutes. Repeat this procedure four times. Finally, roll into a square, cut into 4 finger thick strips and then cut each strip into squares. Place the desired filling (cheese, meat, etc.) in one corner and cover with the opposite corner. Bake at high heat.

DOUGHNUTS ROMANIAN STYLE
(gogoşi în stil românesc)

Sweet bread dough, 0.5 qt oil, confectioner's sugar with vanilla flavor

Sprinkle flour on the work surface and then roll a one finger thick sheet of sweet bread dough. Cut rounds of dough with the doughnut cutter and place them on a cloth. Cover and let them double their bulk. Heat oil in a pot and fry the doughnuts, turning them on all sides. Keep the heat low. When they are ready, remove with the slotted tablespoon and sprinkle with vanilla flavored confectioner's sugar. You can make doughnuts filled with marmalade or preserves. In this case, place the filling in the middle of one doughnut, cover with another one and stick the edges together. Then fry. Anyway, Romanian doughnuts are round with no hole and delicious!

FRENCH DOUGH II
(aluat franţuzesc) II

1 lb flour, 14 oz butter or margarine, 1 cup water, juice from ½ lemon, ½ tsp salt, flour for dusting

Make dough out of 8 oz/250 g flour and the cubed butter. Knead quickly with a wooden tablespoon and roll into a slightly less than 1 inch thick square. Place on a floured plate and refrigerate. Prepare dough from the remaining 8 oz/250 g flour, water, lemon juice and salt, kneading well with your hands. Gather into a ball, cover and let rest for 20-30 minutes. Then roll this second dough into a sheet that is twice as wide and slightly longer than the sheet made from the butter dough. Place the butter dough sheet in the middle of the water dough sheet. Then cover the butter sheet with the corners of the water sheet, envelope style. Press down on the edges. Sprinkle flour on the pastry board, roll the dough into a 1/2 inch thick sheet, fold four fold and refrigerate for 30-40 minutes. #Repeat this folding-refrigerating procedure three times. Then roll into a 1/2 inch thick sheet and cut either into circles or squares. Put the desired filling

(Cheese, meat, etc.) in the middle of the dough pieces, wash with egg and bake for 10-15 minutes.

BUTTER DOUGH
(aluat de unt)

For the first dough: 10 oz flour, 3 yolks, 3 tbsp white wine, 3 tbsp sour cream, a little salt;

For the second dough: 10 oz butter, 4 oz flour

Mix the yolks with the sour cream, wine and salt, add flour and knead well until the dough starts to bubble. Let it rest until you prepare the second dough. Knead the butter with the flour and leave aside until you roll the first dough into a pencil thin square. Then roll the second dough into another slightly smaller, but equally thin square. Lay the small square over the big square and then fold three times lengthwise and then three times crosswise. Roll the dough into a pencil thin square and fold again, the way explained above. Refrigerate for 10-15 minutes. Again, roll the dough into a square and fold again the same way. Again, refrigerate for 10-15 minutes. Repeat this for the third time, then roll into a finger thick sheet and use according to your need.

DOUGH, TENDER, FOR VARIOUS USES
(aluat fraged pentru diferite întrebuinţări)

1 lb flour, 2 tbsp butter or lard, 2 yolks, 2 tbsp sour cream, 2 tbsp sugar, a little salt, 1 tsp vanilla, 2 tbsp white wine

Knead the butter or lard with as much flour as necessary to make into soft dough. Add the yolks, sour cream, sugar, vanilla, wine and salt. Add the remaining flour, knead well, cover and let it rest for a half hour. Divide the dough into 2 parts and roll each one into a pencil thick sheet. Lay one sheet on the bottom of the baking pan, prick with the fork and bake. When the dough has risen a little and has lightened in color, quickly spread the desired filling (cottage cheese, grated apples or other fruits, marmalade or preserves, etc.). Cover with the second sheet, prick this one with a fork too, wash with egg white and bake at medium heat until golden-brown.

When ready, cut into squares and sprinkle confectioner's sugar on top. This may also be filled with meat or liver; in this case, reduced the sugar to 1 level teaspoon and omit vanilla.

EASTER CAKE WITH CHOCOLATE
(pască cu ciocolată)

Sweet bread dough

Filling: 5 eggs, 5 oz confectioner's sugar, a little vanilla, 3 tbsp grated chocolate melted in a tbsp of warm milk

Beat the yolks with the sugar; add the vanilla and the melted chocolate. Mix well and add the whipped egg whites at the end. Then continue as for Easter cake with cottage cheese.

EASTER CAKE WITH COTTAGE CHEESE
(pască cu brânză de vacă)

Sweet bread dough

Filling: 1 lb cottage cheese, 4 oz raisins, 3-4 eggs, 1 tbsp butter, sugar to taste, and a little grated lemon peel, salt

Mix the ingredients for filling to obtain a homogeneous paste. Roll a pencil thick sheet out of the sweet bread dough. Place in a baking pan. From another piece of dough form a long, finger thick roll and arrange it around the sheet, sticking to the walls of the pan. Place the filling within, without covering the roll on the edges. Make two more such dough rolls and place them over the filling in an X shape. After the cake has risen a bit in a warm place, use a little egg wash over the dough rolls. Set in the oven to bake. Remove from the pan when it is cold.

QUICK DOUGHNUTS
(gogoşi pripite (fără drojdie))

4 eggs, 1 cup water (milk), 1 ½ tbsp butter, 2 cups flour, 2-3 tbsp sugar (to taste), juice from ½ lemon, salt, oil for frying

Set the water (milk) to boil with butter and salt; when it starts boiling, remove from heat, add the flour and at the same time, start stirring with a spoon. Return to slow heat and keep stirring until the mixture starts to come off the sides of the pan. Let cool; add lemon juice and 4 eggs previously mixed with sugar. Mix everything well. With a well greased teaspoon, take spoonfuls of the mixture and drop into hot oil to fry. The paste should not be too runny or too firm. It should keep its shape where it is dropped. Fry until golden-brown and then sprinkle with vanilla flavored confectioner's sugar.

EASTER CAKE WITH RICE
(pască cu orez)

Sweet bread dough

Filling: 1 cup rice, 4 cups milk, sugar to taste, 4 eggs, 1 tbsp melted butter, 6 oz raisins, a little vanilla, salt

Boil the rice with the milk and vanilla (as for rice with milk). Add salt. When done, let cool, then add sugar, yolks, butter, raisins and mix well. Add the whipped egg whites at the end. Then continue as for Easter cake with cottage cheese.

EASTER CAKE WITH SOUR CREAM
(pască cu smântână)

Sweet bread dough

Filling: 2 lbs sour cream, 3 tbsp flour, 6 yolks, 3 egg whites, a little vanilla, sugar to taste, salt

Mix the yolks with the sugar, add salt, vanilla, sour cream and mix well, adding the flour gradually. Add the whipped egg whites. Then continue as for Easter cake with cottage cheese.

EGG ICING
(glazură de ou)

8 oză sugar, 2 egg whites, juice from 1 lemon

Mix the confectioner's sugar with the egg whites and the juice from 1 lemon or 1 orange. Stir for almost 1 hour until thick. Cover the cake with this paste.

EGG WHITE BISCUITS
(pesmeciori din albuş)

1/2 oz (2 tbsp) melted butter, 5 oz confectioner's sugar, 1 tsp vanilla, 7 whipped egg whites, 3-4 tbsp vanilla flavored sugar, 5 oz flour, and butter for greasing the pan

Cream the butter with the sugar, add vanilla and flour, mixing well, then add the whipped egg whites, gently folding them in. Pour the mixture into a bread pan covered with buttered paper and bake at medium heat. Test with a wooden pick. Remove from the pan and leave until the next day when you cut into very thin slices. Cut each slice into 4-5 pieces. After that, put all the pieces into a large baking sheet and bake until crisp. When done, roll into vanilla flavored confectioner's sugar.

ENGLISH BISCUITS
(pesmeţi englezeşti)

3 eggs, ½ stick vanilla, 8 oz confectioner's sugar, ½ cup milk or sour cream, ½ oz ammonia powder, flour as needed

Mix the sugar with the eggs, add the vanilla ground with a little sugar, sour cream and ammonia. Mix well and knead with flour to make medium stiff dough. Gather into a ball, cover with a cloth and let rest for 4-5 hours. Divide into 2 parts and roll each one into a 1/5 inch thick sheet. Cut with cookie cutters. Put onto an ungreased, warm baking sheet. Bake at medium heat. These biscuits may be kept for a long time.

FIGARO
(prăjitură Figaro)

5 oz butter, 3 tbsp confectioner's sugar, 4 eggs, 8 oz flour, peel and juice from ½ lemon, 1 tsp vanilla, ¼ tsp baking soda, 5 oz sugar, 5 oz ground walnuts, 10 oz marmalade or preserves without syrup

Mix the butter with 3 tablespoons confectioner's sugar, add the yolks one by one. Mix well. Add juice and grated lemon peel, baking soda and vanilla and knead with the flour. Roll into a finger thick sheet and place in a pan. Bake at low heat until the sheet starts to rise and gets a crust. Then remove from the oven and quickly spread a layer of marmalade or preserves, topping with the whipped egg whites which have been mixed with 5 oz/150 g sugar and ground walnuts. Put in the oven again and bake. When done, let it cool in the pan. Then cut into squares or rectangles.

FRIED LITTLE PIES
(plăcinţele prăjite)

3 tbsp oil, 1 cup water, 1 lb flour, 2 tbsp lard, salt

Filling: may be meat, the same as for meat pie, cottage or sheep's cheese, the same as for, cottage cheese pie, liver, mushrooms or marmalade

Make dough from oil, water, salt and flour. Knead well. It should be on the soft rather than hard side. Cover and let sit for 10-15 minutes.

Then roll into a sheet a little thinner than a pencil, grease with a little melted lard and fold three-way across. Grease again with lard and fold again three-way, this time lengthwise. Refrigerate for 10 minutes. Repeat the folding procedure, this time starting lengthwise and then across. After being refrigerated for 10 minutes, roll into a sheet a little thinner than a pencil and cut into 3 inch squares. Put a teaspoon of the desired filling on. Cover one corner with the opposite corner to obtain a triangle. These pies can be fried or baked. They may be served with soup.

FRUIT CAKE II
(prăjitură cu fructe) II

Mixture I: 10 oz flour, 4 oz confectioner's sugar, 4 oz butter, peel from 1 lemon, 2 eggs

Mixture II: 3 eggs, 3 tbsp sugar, 3 tbsp flour, 3 tbsp sour cream, fruits sprinkled with sugar

Cream the butter with the sugar, lemon peel and eggs, and then add the flour. Refrigerate the dough for 1 hour. Then roll into a finger thick sheet, place in the baking pan and prick with a fork. Arrange a layer of fruit (pitted and sprinkled with 2-3 tablespoons of sugar) over it. Over the fruit, pour the following mixture: mix 3 eggs with 3 tablespoons sugar, 3 tbsp flour and 3 tbsp sour cream. Place this on the range and when it starts to thicken, pour it over the fruit in the pan. Bake at medium heat and when done, cut into squares.

FRUIT CHARLOTTE
(şarlotă de fructe)

2 cups fresh, strained fruit juice, 7 oz sugar, 1 lb whipped cream, 9 tbsp gelatin

Warm the fruit juice (any of apricot, strawberry, gooseberry, and wild strawberry, peach, raspberry), add Sugar and keep on heat until the sugar dissolves. Do not boil. Remove from heat and add the gelatin dissolved in a few tablespoons of warm water. Mix well and let cool. When still a little warm, add the whipped cream, mix and pour into a charlotte mold. Refrigerate for a few hours.

Before serving, place the mold into a bowl with hot water (for a second) and turn upside down onto a plate.

GOOSEBERRY JELLO PUDDING
(jeleu de coacăze)

1 lb gooseberries, 18 oz sugar, 1 cup water

Wash and clean the gooseberries. Set 14 oz gooseberries to boil with the sugar and water.

Boil until the berries are soft, then strain and crush them. Strain again through cheese cloth and set to boil until the mixture starts to gel. (Test by placing a few drops onto a cold plate. If ready, in a few minutes they gel.) On the bottom of a deeper dish, arrange a few whole gooseberries, slowly pour a thin layer of jelly and refrigerate.

Keep the rest of the jello in a warm place. After the poured layer has gelled, arrange a few more gooseberries on top of it and then pour another thin layer of jello. Repeat this procedure until you use all gooseberries and all jello. Before serving, turn onto a plate and garnish with a few sprigs of gooseberries.

FRUIT BASKET
(coşuleţ cu fructe)

8 oz butter, 1 lb flour, 4 tbsp slightly sweetened cold water, a little salt, 1 lb whipped cream, sugar, rum,

Cream: 8 yolks, 2 cups milk, 8 tbsp sugar, vanilla, 3 tsp potato flour, 4 oz butter

Seasonal fruits: 2 lbs strawberries or wild strawberries, sour cherries, apricots, grapes

Mix the water, flour and salt; roll a sheet the width of a pencil. Then spread the butter over it in a uniform layer. Fold envelope style and refrigerate for 20-30 minutes. Repeat the rolling and folding of the dough 3 times, refrigerating it each time for 20-30 minutes. Roll into a large circle and place this in a layer cake pan (with removable bottom) with the edges hanging outside. Bake at medium heat until golden. Remove from the oven and with a sharp knife, cut the dough that overhangs the rim of the layer cake pan. Then release the bottom and take out the baked basket.

For the cream, boil the milk with the vanilla and sugar. After coming to a boil, cover and remove from heat. In a bowl, beat the yolks, gradually adding the milk mixture and stirring continuously until all the milk is used up. Then add the potato flour which was previously mixed with a little of the yolk and milk mixture. Pour everything into a double boiler and stir until it starts to resemble a soft paste. Remove from heat, add butter, mix well and refrigerate 15-20 minutes before serving, spread the cream on the bottom of the basket and top with the washed and drained fruits, sprinkled with sugar and rum. On top of the fruits, put some whipped cream and garnish with a few fruits. The basket may be prepared 1-2 days in advance but the filling is placed just before serving.

GRATED QUINCE PRESERVES
(dulceață de gutui rase)

2 lbs sugar, ¾ qt water, 2 large quinces

Peel and grate the quinces. Place immediately in the sugar syrup. Simmer until well thickened. Remove the pan from heat and cover with a wet and squeezed cloth. Place in jars when cold.

GREEN WALNUTS PRESERVES

(dulceață de nuci verzi)

2 lbs sugar, 3 cups water, 22 oz peeled green walnuts, ½ cup honey, ½ vanilla stick, juice from ½ lemon

Remove the green peel from the walnuts and as you peel, place in a bowl with cold water lest they darken. Then place the walnuts in a pot with boiling water and leave for 15 minutes. Drain and place in a pot with cold water, also for 15 minutes. Repeat this procedure (hot water to cold water) three times. In the meantime, make the syrup, remove foam, and add honey and vanilla. When the syrup starts to thicken, add the walnuts and lemon juice, letting simmer until the preserves are done. Remove from heat, cover with a wet cloth and place in jars when cold. \

ALCAZAR LAYERED CAKE
(tort Alcazar)

6 egg whites, 6 tbsp sugar, 8 oz ground walnuts, vanilla, oil;

cream: 6 yolks, 6 tbsp sugar, 8 oz butter, ½ cup milk, ¼ cup coffee, 1 tbsp cacao, ¼ cup rum

Whip the egg whites with the sugar and vanilla, add the walnuts and mix gently. Pour the mixture into a rectangular baking pan, (previously covered with parchment paper and lightly greased with oil), using a knife to spread it into a uniform layer. Bake at medium heat and when ready, invert onto a cutting board, moisten the paper and peel it off the cake. Cut lengthwise in two or three equal parts and spread the following cream on each of them. Mix the yolks with the sugar, add the milk, coffee, set on heat and keep stirring until the mixture starts to thicken. Do not let boil.

Remove from heat, mix with cacao and let cool. Beat the butter until creamy, add the rum and mix with the boiled mixture; mix well and spread the cream on the sheets. Cover the cake with the same cream and garnish with ground walnuts. Serve cut in triangular pieces.

HAZELNUT CHARLOTTE
(șarlotă de alune)

10 oz whipped cream, 1 qt milk, 6 eggs, 6 tbsp gelatin, 7 oz toasted and ground hazelnuts, 12 oz sugar, 1 cup rum, some grated lemon peel

Mix the yolks with the sugar. Add the milk, mix well, and set to heat, mixing continuously until very hot and thickened. Remove from heat; add the beaten whites and ground hazelnuts, then the rum, lemon peel and gelatin dissolved in 2-3 tablespoons of hot water. Pour the mixture into a mold and refrigerate. Serve garnished with whipped cream.

HAZELNUT LAYERED CAKE
(tort de alune)

3 oz roasted and ground hazelnuts, 3 oz roasted and ground almonds or walnuts, 5 egg whites, 7 oz confectioner's sugar, butter;

Filling: 7 oz butter, 5 oz confectioner's sugar, 5 oz roasted hazelnuts, 2 tbsp grated chocolate or cacao, 2 tbsp sour cream

Mix the whipped egg whites with the sugar, hazelnuts and almonds (or walnuts). Divide this mixture in two and bake each part in a round pan covered with buttered parchment paper. When the sheets are done and cold, fill with the following cream: Mix the butter with the confectioner's sugar, roasted and finely ground hazelnuts, grated chocolate and sour cream. Spread the cream on the two sheets, place one on top of the other and garnish with the same cream, with a few whole hazelnuts and a few chopped almonds or walnuts.

LADYFINGER CHARLOTTE
(şarlotă de pişcoturi)

5 egg yolks, 1 cup milk, 1 cup sugar, 8 tbsp gelatin, ½ lb ladyfingers, ½ lb whipped cream, 5 oz Praline walnut or hazelnut cream, peanuts or walnuts, vanilla, rum

Set the milk to heat, adding the yolks beated with the sugar, vanilla and rum, mixing continuously until it starts to thicken. Remove from heat and add the gelatin dissolved in 2-3 tablespoons of hot water. Mix well and let cool a little. During this time, set the ladyfingers that have been previously soaked in a thin sugar and rum syrup in the special charlotte mold. Arrange them both on the bottom and the sides of the mold. After the mixture has cooled a little, add the hazelnuts, whipped cream and rum and mix well. Pour into the mold with ladyfingers. Refrigerate for 3-4 hours. When serving, turn onto a plate.

JOFFRE LAYERED CAKE
(tort Joffre)

7 egg whites, 10 oz confectioner's sugar;

Filling: 10 oz chocolate, ½ cup milk, 10 oz butter, 7 yolks, 5 oz confectioner's sugar, 1 tbsp rum

Whip the egg whites with the sugar in a bowl placed in a larger one with boiling water. From this mixture, bake 5 sheets in the cake pan which was previously lightly waxed. Spread cream on the cold sheets, place one on top of the other and glaze with the same cream. For the cream, melt the chocolate in milk, let bubble for a minute or two, then refrigerate. In the meantime, beat the butter with the sugar, add the yolks, one by one, then gradually add the melted chocolate, mixing well, and the rum.

MICADO LAYERED CAKE
(tort Micado)

14 oz butter, 14 oz sour cream, ¼ tsp baking soda, flour as needed to make dough, glacee fruits (preserves);

Filling: 1 cup milk, 1 ½ cup sugar, a pinch baking soda, 1 tsp butter

Beat the butter, add the sour cream and baking soda, the flour and knead medium soft dough, which you then divide into 4 equal parts. Roll each part into a round, finger thick sheet. Bake each of them separately and let cool. Then spread with the following cream:

Caramelize 1/2 cup sugar, add milk, and add another cup of sugar, baking soda and butter. Boil all this until you get thick syrup as for sherbets. Remove from heat and beat (the same way as for sherbets). When it is almost cold, spread on the sheets. This must be done very fast. Place the sheets one on top of the other and glaze with the same cream. Garnish with glacee fruits or preserves

MOCHA LAYERED CAKE
(tort Mocha)

8 eggs, 8 oz confectioner's sugar, 8 oz ground walnuts or almonds, 2 tbsp fine white bread crumbs

Filling: 8 oz butter, 8 oz confectioner's sugar, 5 yolks, ½ vanilla stick, 1 small cup coffee essence, 4 oz blanched almonds

Cream the yolks with the sugar, add the walnuts or almonds, bread crumbs and the whipped egg whites at the end. Pour the mixture into the cake baking pan, bake and after it has cooled, cut in two layers. Fill and glaze with the following cream. Beat the sugar with the butter, then add the yolks one by one and the ground vanilla until you get a cream. Gradually add the coffee essence and mix well. After the cake is filled and covered with cream, garnish with sliced almonds.

NAPOLEON LAYERED CAKE
(tort Napoleon)

Filling: 5 yolks, ½ cup sugar, 2 tbsp flour, 1 ¼ cup milk, vanilla (stick)

4 oz butter, 4 oz sour cream, ¼ tsp baking soda, flour as needed, vanilla, flavored confectioner's sugar

Mix the melted butter with the sour cream, add baking soda and mix well. Add flour and knead until you get medium soft dough. Divide it into 3 equal parts and roll each into 1/2 inch thick round sheets. Prick with a fork and bake individually at medium heat. When they are cold, spread the following cream. Beat the eggs with the sugar until foamy. Add flour and mix. Pour hot milk with vanilla over the egg-sugar mixture, mixing quickly. Set on heat and keep mixing until the cream starts to thicken. Let cool completely and then spread over the sheets. Sprinkle the last layer with vanilla flavored confectioner's sugar.

OTHELLO LAYERED CAKE
(tort Othello)

9 eggs, 9 tbsp sugar, 2 tbsp coffee essence, 2 oz cacao, 2 oz flour, 2 oz chopped walnuts, hazelnuts or almonds, oil, flour to dust pan, fruits from preserves;

Filling: 5 tbsp water, 2 ½ oz cacao, 7 ½ oz sugar, 7 ½ oz butter, ¼ cup rum

Whip the egg whites, gradually adding the 9 tablespoons of sugar. Then gradually add the 9 yolks, stirring continuously. Add cacao, flour, ground walnuts, coffee essence (strained and cooled) and mix well. Pour into a rectangular pan which was previously greased with oil and dusted with flour and bake at medium heat. When done, turn onto a cutting board. After it is completely cold, cut lengthwise in 3 equal parts. Spread the following cream on each sheet. Mix the sugar with the cacao, add water and set to boil to thicken like sour cream. Let cool, then mix with beaten butter and rum. Mix well. Divide the cream into 2 equal parts. Use one of these parts to spread on the sheets and lay them one on top of the other. Use the other half of the cream to cover the cake. Garnish with fruits from preserves and serve the following day, cut in triangles.

LAYERED CAKE, RICHARD
(tort Richard)

8 oz ground almonds or walnuts, 8 oz confectioner's sugar, 10 egg whites, butter, chocolate cream, chocolate icing

Whip the egg whites; mix with the sugar and almonds (walnuts). Divide the resulting paste in 3-4 equal parts and bake 3-4 sheets in the cake pan that was covered with buttered parchment paper. When the sheets are baked and cooled, spread chocolate cream on each of them, arrange one on top of the other and glaze with chocolate icing.

BROWN LAYERED CAKE
(tort maroniu)

7 oz ground almonds, 4 oz confectioner's sugar, 7 oz grated chocolate, 5 level tbsp fine flour, 12 eggs, butter, butter cream, whipped cream

Beat the yolks with the sugar until foamy, add the chocolate, almonds and flour, mix well, and then add the 12 whipped egg whites at the end. Fold in gently. Pour the mixture into the buttered baking pan and bake at medium heat. Fill with butter cream and cover with whipped cream.

INEXPENSIVE LAYERED CAKE I
(tort ieftin) I

5 eggs, 4 oz butter, ¾ cup confectioner's sugar, 1 cup cold milk, 1 tbsp baking powder, vanilla, flour as needed, butter to grease the pan, filling

Cream the sugar with the butter and yolks, add vanilla, cold milk and baking powder, mixing everything well. Add the whipped egg whites and then at the end, as much flour as necessary to make a thick but still liquid paste. Pour in the baking pan that was previously buttered and dusted with flour and bake at medium heat. Test with a straw to see if it is done. Then let cool, cut into two layers and fill with the desired filling, with preserves or marmalade.

INEXPENSIVE LAYERED CAKE II
(tort ieftin) II

2 eggs, 3 tbsp sugar, 1 tbsp vinegar, ½ tsp baking soda dissolved in lemon juice, 3 tbsp oil, zest from 1 lemon, vanilla, flour, oil, filling and icing

Beat the eggs with the sugar; add a tablespoon of vinegar and the baking soda dissolved in a little lemon juice, vanilla and lemon peel, 3 tablespoon of oil and mix everything well. Then knead with flour to make medium soft dough and let rest for 5-10 minutes. From this dough, make a roll which you divide into 6-7 equal parts. Roll each part into a round sheet, the size of a large pan. Grease the pan with a little oil, set one sheet in and cook on both sides on top of the range, at low temperature. When all sheets are done, spread with the desired filling and glaze like you normally would.

FAIRYTALE LAYERED CAKE
(tort poveste)

1 oz ground walnuts, 5 eggs, 5 tbsp confectioner's sugar, 1 tbsp cacao, 1 tsp vanilla, oil, flour, fruits from preserves;

II. 3 egg whites, 3 tbsp sugar, vanilla;

Filling: 3 yolks, 3 tbsp confectioner's sugar, 2 tbsp cacao, 8 oz butter, 5 oz whipped cream

Whip 5 egg whites with 5 tablespoons of sugar and vanilla. Add the slightly beaten yolks, mix, add a tablespoon of cacao and the ground walnuts. Pour this mixture into a baking pan which was lightly greased with oil and dusted with flour. Bake at medium heat.

In the meantime, whip 3 egg whites with 3 tablespoons of sugar and vanilla. When the batter in the oven is done, remove, spread the whipped egg whites on top, in a uniform layer and place it back into the oven so that the egg whites layer gets baked. Then remove from the pan, set on a plate and let cool. For the cream, beat the butter with 3 tablespoons confectioner's sugar and cacao. Add the yolks one by one, mixing well. Use this cream to cover the cake, laying a thicker layer on top. Garnish with 5 oz/150 g whipped cream and various fruits from preserves.

LAYERED PUNCH CAKE
(tort Punch)

8 eggs, 7 oz confectioner's sugar, 5 oz flour, juice from 1 lemon and 1 orange, ¼ cup rum, 1 ½ oz chocolate, 2-3 tbsp apricot marmalade, butter and flour for the pan, chocolate icing

Beat the yolks with the confectioner's sugar. Add the sugar gradually and keep mixing. Then add the whipped egg whites, then the flour at the end. Mix gently. Pour this mixture into a rectangular pan which was previously greased with butter and dusted with flour. Use an appropriate size pan so that the batter is not thicker than 1/2 inch. Bake the batter until golden brown. When ready, use a round cutting board or plate to cut 2 round sheets out of the rectangle.

The remainder is cubed and divided into 3 equal parts. Soak one third of the cubes with orange and lemon juice. Soak another third with red colored (use food coloring) rum. Add the last third to the chocolate melted with 4 tablespoons of water. Then mix all the different cubes together. Spread apricot marmalade on the first sheet. Place the mixed cubes over the marmalade, pressing with a knife so that there are no empty spaces between cubes. Place the second sheet on top, pressing it slightly. Glaze with chocolate icing.

LAYERED PYRAMID CAKE
(tort piramida)

12 eggs, flour, butter, sugar (the quantity for each of these last 3 ingredients to be the same as the weight of the 12 eggs in their shells), butter for the pan, various fillings and preserves

Beat the butter adding sugar a little at a time and the eggs one by one. When the mixture is creamy-like, gradually add the flour, mixing continuously. Have ready 6-8 rounds of white paper. The largest round must be the size of a dinner plate, the next smaller 1 inch smaller, the next smaller, 1 inch smaller and so on, down to the last one. Grease the paper circles with butter and spread the mixture on them, about one finger thick. Bake 2-3 circles at a time, at medium heat, in a large baking sheet. When all 6-8 circles are baked, spread various creams and preserves (one with chocolate cream, another with preserves and another with vanilla cream, etc.) on each of them. Arrange the rounds one top of the other with the largest one forming the base and the smallest one the top of a pyramid. On top of the last circle, arrange fruits from preserves.

SIMPLE LAYERED CAKE
(tort simplu)

6 eggs, 1 cup confectioner's sugar, 1 cup flour, grated peel from 1 lemon, marmalade

Beat the yolks with the sugar in a heat resistant bowl. Set this bowl inside a larger pan with boiling water in it and set this on heat. Beat the cream until hot. Remove the bowl with the cream from heat and keep beating until cooled off. When it is completely cold, add the whipped egg whites, folding gently, and then the flour and lemon peel. Divide this mixture into 3-4 equal parts (depending on the size of the baking pan). Bake 3 sheets, individually, and as soon as they are out of the oven, cover with a cloth. Keep them like this for 1-2 hours. Spread marmalade on each of them and arrange one on top of the other. The cake may be filled with any desired cream and glazed with any icing.

LAYERED CAKE, SPECIAL, WITH CACAO

(tort special cu cacao)

8 oz sugar, 8 oz walnuts, 5 egg whites, rum, 10 oz whipped cream, oil;

Filling: 8 yolks, 8 oz confectioner's sugar, 8 oz butter, 2 tbsp cacao, 2 tbsp sugar, ½ cup water

Caramelize 8 oz/250 g sugar. When it starts to turn yellow, add the walnuts, letting them roast a little. Remove from heat and spread on a cutting board, previously oiled. When cold, finely crush with a mortar and pestle. Whip the egg whites and mix with the roasted and crushed walnuts.

Divide this mixture into 3 equal parts and bake, individually, in baking pans greased with oil and covered with parchment paper. Bake at medium heat until golden. Spread cream on the cooled sheets that were previously sprinkled with rum. Spread cream on the last layer as well. Then cover the whole cake with whipped cream. To get the cream, beat the yolks with the confectioner's sugar until creamy. Mix with the butter, previously creamed separately, then add the following, also previously prepared separately. 2 tablespoons cacao with 2 tablespoons sugar and 1/2 cup water are boiled until thickened. Mix everything very well.

LEMON CREAM
(cremă de lamiie)

2 lbs whipped cream, 11 tbsp gelatin, zest and juice of ½ big lemon, sugar to taste, 5 cup milk, sour cherry preserves (optional)

Set the milk to boil. Add the gelatin and mix well until dissolved. Strain through a dense sieve and let cool. When only tepid, pour into the whipped cream with confectioner's sugar to taste. Mix well. Pour in cups or glasses and refrigerate. When serving, you can garnish with whipped cream or sour cherry preserves.

LEMON ICE-CREAM
(înghețată de lămâie)

9 oz sugar, 1 cup water, 3 lemons, grated peel from ½ lemon

Boil the sugar with the water for a few minutes, then add the peel from the half lemon and juice from 3 lemons. Cover and let cool off. Then strain it and freeze.

LITTLE SHIPS
(corăbioare)

¾ cup lard, 1 tbsp confectioner's sugar, ½ cup sour cream or milk, 2 oz yeast, 1 tsp vanilla, salt, flour as needed, vanilla flavored confectioner's sugar

Beat the lard with the sugar and vanilla, then add sour cream, yeast dissolved in a little milk and salt. Knead with flour medium stiff dough. Cover and leave in a warm place to rise. When raised, place on the pastry board and divide into 3 equal parts. From each part, make a roll with your hands. Cut each roll into finger wide pieces. Place these pieces at considerable distance one from the other on the baking sheet. Let them rise. Then bake. When ready, roll each piece in vanilla flavored confectioner's sugar.

LEMON ICING
(glazură de lămâie)

7 oz sugar, juice from 2 lemons

Put the juice from the lemons in a small bowl. Add the sifted confectioner's sugar. Mix very well until you get white foam. Use this mixture to cover the cake.

LITTLE SQUARES
(pătrăţele)

2 cups flour, 1 ½ cups sour cream, 1 cup sugar, 6 eggs, vanilla, shortening for greasing the pan, vanilla flavored confectioner's sugar

Beat the yolks with the sugar until they lighten up. Add vanilla (stick ground with a little sugar) and sour cream mix well and then gradually add the flour. At the end, gently fold in the whipped egg whites. Pour the batter into a greased pan and bake, at low heat, for 25-30 minutes. When done, invert onto a wooden cutting board, laid with a cloth, sprinkle, while still hot, with vanilla flavored confectioner's sugar and when completely cold, cut into small squares and arrange on a plate.

MARMELADE ROLLS
(rulouri cu marmeladă)

5 oz well drained cottage cheese, 5 oz butter, 5 oz flour, 2 tbsp confectioner's sugar, salt, ¼ tsp baking soda, marmalade, egg for washing, granulated sugar

Mix together the cheese, sugar, salt and baking soda. Then add flour and knead well. Roll into a sheet the thickness as for noodles. Cut into medium sized rectangles, spread marmalade on them and shape each rectangle into a roll. Wash with egg, sprinkle a little granulated sugar and bake. They may also be filled with cottage cheese mixed with 1 egg and a little sugar.

YEASTED MAZURKA
(mazurca dospită în apă)

13 yolks, ½ cup warm melted butter, ½ cup tepid milk, 1 cup confectioner's sugar, 1 oz yeast, salt, 1 tsp vanilla, flour as needed

Mix the yeast with 1 teaspoon sugar, pour the tepid milk and a little flour to obtain a dough starter. Let it rise a little. Then add yolks beaten with sugar and tepid butter, salt and vanilla. Knead with flour the same way as for sweet breads. Put this dough into a cloth or fabric sack, tie tightly (but leave room for the dough to rise) and submerge into a large pot or bucket with cold water. Leave it this way from morning till evening (or from the preceding evening to the next day). When the dough has risen enough, bring it to the surface of the water. Remove from the cloth, place on the pastry board and shape into little pretzels, small figure eight or snails.

Place on the baking sheet, leave ½ hour in a warm place, wash with egg (they may be sprinkled with ground walnuts or ground blanched almonds). Bake at medium heat.

MAZURKA I

(Mazurka) I

8 eggs, 14 oz confectioner's sugar, 14 oz flour, 2 cups sliced walnuts, 1 cup raisins, butter

Beat the sugar with the yolks added one by one, add flour, walnuts and raisins and the whipped egg whites at the end. Mix gently and pour everything in a rectangular pan covered with buttered paper. Bake at medium heat. When done, invert onto a wooden cutting board, cover with a cloth and let cool. After that, cut into squares or diamonds.

MAZURKA II
(Mazurka) II

10 eggs, 1 cup sugar, 1 cup flour, 1 cup golden raisins, 1 cup dark raisins, 1 cup chopped figs, finely chopped peel from 1 orange, 1 tsp vanilla, 1 cup sliced almonds, butter

Beat the sugar with the yolks, add flour, mix well, then add the fruits and sliced almonds, vanilla and orange peel; at the end add the whipped egg whites. Fold them in gently and pour everything in a buttered rectangular pan covered with paper. Bake at medium heat. When becomes cold, cut into the desired shape.

MAZURKA SALAMI STYLE
(Mazurca salam)

14 oz honey, 14 oz grated chocolate, 1 ½ cups walnuts, cacao

Set the honey to boil with the grated chocolate; when it starts boiling, add walnuts, stirring continuously. Let them boil for another 5 minutes. Remove from heat and let cool a little. When you can touch it without discomfort, put the mixture on a cacao dusted board. With your hands, shape into a thick Sausage. Roll it into the cacao powder and let cool. When it is cold, cut slices with a very sharp knife. Arrange on a platter.

MAZURKA WITH ALMONDS
(mazurca cu migdale)

14 oz butter, 7 oz confectioner's sugar, 6 eggs, ½ cup ground almonds, 7 oz flour, 1 tsp vanilla, butter to grease the pan

Cream the butter with sugar and add the yolks one by one. Mix very well. To the resulting cream, add almonds and vanilla, mix well, and then add flour and at the end the whipped egg whites.

Bake in a greased and papered pan, at medium heat. When done, cut in the shapes desired.

MAZURKA WITH CHOCOLATE
(mazurca cu ciocolată)

7 oz sugar, 8 yolks, 2 whipped egg whites, 4 tbsp minced almonds, 4 tbsp grated chocolate, 5 tbsp flour, butter

Beat the sugar with the yolks, add almonds and chocolate and mix well. Gradually add the flour and at the end the 2 whipped egg whites. Fold in gently. Bake at low heat in a pan covered with greased paper. When becomes cold, cut into squares.

MAZURKA WITH CHOCOLATE AND WHIPPED CREAM
(Mazurca cu ciocolată şi frişcă)

7 oz sugar, 8 yolks, 2 whipped egg whites, 4 tbsp minced almonds, 4 tbsp grated chocolate, 5 tbsp flour, 14 oz whipped cream, butter to grease the pan

Prepare the same way as mazurka with chocolate. When baked, turn onto a board and cut into 2 layers (parallel to the bottom, as for layer cakes). Spread a 2 finger thick layer of whipped cream onto the first sheet and cover with the second sheet. Cut into squares or diamonds.

DELICIOUS MAZURKA
(Mazurca delicioasă)

14 oz confectioner's sugar, 14 oz butter, 2 cups blanched, peeled and finely chopped almonds, 1 ½ cups flour, 12 eggs, vanilla, butter to grease the pan

Cream the butter, add the almonds and mix again. Add flour, then yolks, one by one, vanilla and sugar, little by little; mix very well. At the end, gradually add the whipped egg whites. Fold them in gently. Pour the batter into a baking pan covered with buttered paper and bake at medium heat. When becomes cold, cut into medium sized squares.

MAZURKA, DIAMOND SHAPED
(Mazurca în formă de romb)

7 oz butter, 7 oz confectioner's sugar, 3 eggs, 1 cup flour, a few ground cloves, 1 tsp ground cinnamon, vanilla flavored sugar, 1 lemon (zest + juice), 4 lbs baked and sieved (crushed) apples, 2 tbsp sugar

Cream the butter with sugar and add the eggs one by one. Then gradually add the flour (like a rain), lemon juice and peel, ground cinnamon and cloves. Have ready to use 8 paper diamonds (4 inch sides). Butter these paper diamonds and lay them onto a baking sheet. Cover the paper diamonds with the prepared mixture in a 1/2 inch layer. When the diamonds are baked, spread each of them with the apple paste to which you added 2 tablespoons sugar and cinnamon. Place the diamonds on top of one another. Sprinkle vanilla flavored confectioner's sugar on top.

MERENGUE LAYERED CAKE
(tort bezea)

7 egg whites, 7 tbsp sugar, vanilla, oil;

Filling: 1 cup granulated sugar, 7 oz walnuts, 8 oz butter, 3 tbsp confectioner's sugar, 1 tsp vanilla or ¼ cup rum

Place the egg whites, sugar and vanilla in a heat resistant bowl. And place this bowl into a larger one, full of boiling water and set on heat. Beat the whites until thick. Bake 3 sheets out of this mixture. The procedure is as follows: cut 3 equal rounds of white paper, the size of a round layer cake. Grease each paper round with oil and place it on the inverted bottom of a baking pan. Place a uniform layer of egg whites (1/3 of the mixture) on the greased circle and bake at very low heat. When done, place the rounds face down on the work surface, moisten the paper with water and pull it off. Fill these rounds with cream. To get the cream, caramelize a cup of granulated sugar; when it starts to turn yellow, add the slightly roasted walnuts and let them roast a little with the sugar, mixing continuously. After the mixture turns a deeper gold, remove from heat and turn onto an oil greased plate to cool. In the meantime, beat the butter with 3 tablespoons of confectioner's sugar and vanilla or rum, adding the finely crushed walnuts. Put 1 tablespoon of crushed walnuts aside for garnish. Spread this cream over the sheets, place one on top of the other and cover with the same cream. Sprinkle with the 1 tablespoon of crushed walnuts.

MOLDAVIAN 8 SHAPES
(mucenici moldoveneşti)

2 lbs flour, ¾ oz yeast, ½ qt water (or half water, half milk), a little salt, egg wash from 2 eggs, 1 cup sugar, 1 cup water, ½ lb ground walnuts

Make dough from the flour, yeast and water (or water/milk combination). The dough should be rather soft. When the dough has risen, make 8 shapes. Place in a baking sheet dusted with flour and let the shapes rise again. Then spread the egg wash on the shapes. Bake at medium temperature until golden brown. Meanwhile, prepare syrup from the 1 cup sugar and 1 cup water. When the 8 shapes are cool, dip them briefly, one by one, in hot water. Drain well. Place them on a platter, pour the syrup on top and sprinkle ground walnuts on them.

MILK CREAM WITH CHOCOLATE
(cremă de lapte cu ciocolată)

6 eggs, 6 tbsp sugar, 3 cups milk, 3 tbsp of sugar for caramelizing, 3 tbsp grated chocolate or cacao, vanilla (stick), salt

Boil the milk with vanilla at slow heat. After the first boil, cover and keep aside. Beat the eggs with the sugar and the latter dissolves. Heat the milk again, add a little salt, the chocolate that was previously dissolved in two tablespoons of warm water and pour, a little at a time, into the egg and sugar mixture, constantly stirring, until it is almost cool. Take a 3 qt pan and put 3 tablespoons of sugar in it. Heat until the sugar melts and becomes yellowish. Remove from heat and tilt the pan in such a way, that the melted sugar spreads all over the interior walls of the pan.

Stir the cream a little and then pour into the pan. Cover and set this pan into a larger pan filled with boiling water. The boiling water must be 3/4 of the height of the pan with the cream. Keep on medium heat for 25-30 minutes. The cream is ready when it comes off the pan walls quite easily.

Remove from the water and keep in a cool place. After it has cooled completely, refrigerate. Before serving, take a large round plate and cover the pan with it. Then turn the pan upside down.

NOUGAT ROMANIAN STYLE
(nuga în stil românesc)

7 egg whites, 1 lb confectioner's sugar, 8 oz walnuts, 8 oz honey, juice from ½ lemon

Whip the egg whites with the sugar in a double boiler on the range. Gradually add hot honey. Beat until the mixture starts to come off the egg-beater. At this moment, remove from heat, set aside and add walnuts and lemon juice. On a wooden cutting board, lay 2 wafer sheets (one on top of the other), spread with the prepared mixture in a uniform layer and cover with the other 2 wafer sheets. When it's cold, cut into pieces of the desired shape.

PEAR COMPOTE
(compot de pere)

2 lbs pears, 3 cups water, 10 oz sugar, juice from 1 lemon, a little cinnamon, 2-3 cloves

Peel, seed and quarter the pears. Dip each quarter into lemon juice. Set the water and sugar to boil. Add pears, cinnamon and cloves. Cover and let simmer until the pears are soft. Serve cold.

PLUM COMPOTE
(compot de prune)

2 lbs plums, ½ qt water, 10 oz sugar, juice from one lemon, a little piece of vanilla stick

Set the water and sugar to boil. Peel the plums and dip in lemon juice. Place the plums in the syrup; add vanilla and a little lemon juice. Let boil for 5-6 minutes from the moment that the syrup comes to a boil, removing the foam as it forms. Serve cold.

ORANGE MARMELADE
(marmeladă de portocale)

4 large oranges, 1 lemon, as much sugar as the weight of oranges, lemon and the water in which they boiled, three times as much water, by weight, as the weight of the oranges and lemon, juice from 1 lemon

Wash the oranges and lemon. Slice each fruit in 16 sections lengthwise and then halve each section. You will now have 32 pieces of each fruit. Weigh the fruit and add three times as much as the water. Leave them like this for 24 hours. Then set to boil and keep on heat for 1 hour since the moment it starts boiling. Remove from heat and add the lemon juice, refrigerating for another 24 hours. Weigh the oranges again together with the water they boiled in and add as much sugar. The sugar should be added after the oranges and water have been heated. Boil for 40-50 minutes. Pour in warmed jars while still warm. Tie the jars with cellophane after the marmalade is cold.

POTATO DOUGHNUTS II
(gogoși de cartofi) II

7 oz potatoes, 7 oz flour, a little warm water, pinch of salt, ½ oz yeast, confectioner's sugar

Boil the potatoes, peel them, pass them through a Potato ricer and then mix with the flour. Mix in enough warm water to make a soft dough. Add a little salt and the yeast which was previously moistened with 2 tablespoons warm water. Knead well, cover and let it rise in a warm place. Then roll a sheet of dough the width of a finger. Cut rounds with a cookie cutter. Brown them in hot oil. Remove with a slotted tablespoon with they are nicely puffed up and brown. Sprinkle confectioner's sugar on them.

POTATO DOUGHNUTS II
(gogoși de cartofi) II

7 oz potatoes, 7 oz flour, a little warm water, pinch of salt, ½ oz yeast, confectioner's sugar

Boil the potatoes, peel them, pass them through a Potato ricer and then mix with the flour. Mix in enough warm water to make a soft dough. Add a little salt and the yeast which was previously moistened with 2 tablespoons warm water. Knead well, cover and let it rise in a warm place. Then roll a sheet of dough the width of a finger. Cut rounds with a cookie cutter. Brown them in hot oil. Remove with a slotted tablespoon with they are nicely puffed up and brown. Sprinkle confectioner's sugar on them.

PRALINE WALNUT OR HAZELNUT CREAM
(cremă de nuci sau alune pralinate)

8 oz butter, 7 oz confectioner's sugar, 5 oz granulated sugar, 5 oz walnuts or hazelnuts

Cream the butter with the confectioner's sugar. Separately, heat the granulated sugar. When it starts to melt and turn yellow, add the hazelnuts or walnuts and mix quickly until the sugar is completely melted. Turn onto a wet wooden cutting board, spread on its entire surface and let cool. Then grind very finely and gradually add to the previously prepared butter-sugar mixture.

QUICK CHARLOTTE
(şarlotă la iuţeală)

7 oz ladyfingers or butter biscuits, ½ lb whipped cream, 7 oz ground walnuts or hazelnuts, ½ lb milk sweetened with 6 tsp of sugar, 2 cups rum, some fruits from preserves

Mix the milk with the sugar and rum. Soak the ladyfingers in it. Arrange the ladyfingers side by side on a platter, spread walnuts on top, then a layer of whipped cream, then another layer of ladyfingers, walnuts and whipped cream. Garnish with fruit from preserves.

QUINCE COMPOTE
(compot de gutui)

2 lbs quinces, 1 lb sugar, 3 cups water, a little cinnamon

Peel, seed and slice the quinces one inch thick. Place in cold water. At this time, boil the water with sugar and cinnamon. When the syrup is half done, add the quinces, cover and let simmer until softened. Serve cold.

PUMPKIN STRUDEL
(ştrudel cu dovleac)

Ştrudel dough, confectioner's sugar;

Filling: 1 large plateful of grated pumpkin, 3-4 tbsp oil, 3-4 tbsp sugar, 1 tsp ground cinnamon, salt

Peel a piece of pumpkin and grate on the vegetable grater. A large plateful of pumpkin is enough for one strudel leaf. Roll the leaf, let it rest for a few minutes, then sprinkle with oil. Place the pumpkin at one end of the dough, sprinkle with sugar, ground cinnamon and a little salt. Roll and place in the baking sheet greased with oil. Grease the top with a little oil. Bake at medium heat until golden brown. Cut into pieces while still on the sheet and sprinkle with confectioner's sugar.

LAYERED QUINCE CAKE
(tort de gutui)

14 oz quince paste (obtained from approx. 20 oz quinces), 14 oz confectioner's sugar, 10 whipped egg whites, 3-4 tbsp quince marmalade, oil, fruits from preserves

Boil and sieve the quinces. When the quince paste is cold, mix it with 14 oz/400 g sugar, added gradually, by tablespoon. Add the whipped egg whites and mix gently. Divide the mixture into 4 equal parts. Bake each part individually, for 5-10 minutes each, in the baking pan that was covered with oiled paper. As they are done, immediately moisten the paper with water and remove it. Let all sheets cool off then spread quince marmalade on each of them. Garnish the cake with fruits from preserves.

SWEET BREAD
(cozonaci obişnuiţi)

2 lbs flour, 10 oz sugar, 1 ½ cups milk, 6 eggs, 2 oz yeast, 7 oz butter, 2 tbsp oil, vanilla stick, salt, egg for washing the dough, grease for the pans

Make a starter from yeast and a teaspoon of sugar. Mix until the consistency of sour cream, add 2-3 tablespoons tepid milk, a little flour and mix well; sprinkle some flour on top, cover and let sit in a warm place to rise. Boil the milk with the vanilla stick (cut in very small pieces) and leave it on the side of the range, covered, to keep warm. Mix the yolks with the sugar and salt, and then slowly pour the tepid milk, stirring continuously. Place the risen starter in a large bowl and pour, stirring continuously, the yolk-milk mixture and some flour, a little at a time. Then add 3 whipped egg whites. When you finish this step, start kneading. Knead, adding melted butter combined with oil, a little at a time, until the dough starts to easily come off your palms. Cover with a cloth and then something thicker (like a blanket). Leave in a warm place to triple in bulk. If during kneading the dough seems too hard, you may add a little milk. If, on the contrary, the dough seems too soft, you may add a little flour. When the dough has risen well, take a piece of it, place on the floured work surface, give it the desired shape (round, oval, braided, etc.) and place in the baking pan previously greased with butter. Let rise some more in the pan in a warm place. Wash with egg and bake at medium heat. Take out of the pan as soon as it is done, place on a cloth and let cool.

RICE WITH MILK I
(orez cu lapte) I

1 cup rice, 3 cups milk, 1 cup water, 1 piece vanilla stick, sugar (to taste), salt, preserves (syrup, whipped cream)

Set to boil the milk with the water and vanilla. When it comes to a boil, add the washed rice. Let boil, at slow heat, stirring now and then. It is ready when the rice grain can be easily crushed between your fingers. Remove the vanilla, place the rice on a plate and serve warm or cold, with preserves, glacee fruits, syrup or whipped cream.

RICE WITH MILK II
(orez cu lapte) II

1 cup rice, 3 cups milk, 1 cup water, 1 piece vanilla stick, sugar (to taste), salt, 1/2 cup rum, 2 yolks, 1 tbsp butter, whipped cream (preserves)

Prepare as Rice with milk I. When ready, remove from heat, add salt, rum, egg yolks, butter and mix well. Arrange on the serving plate and garnish with whipped cream and fruits from preserves.

ROLLED CAKE WITH MARMELADE OR PRESERVES
(ruladă cu marmeladă sau dulceaţă)

6 eggs, 6 tbsp sugar, 5 tbsp flour, vanilla or grated lemon peel, marmalade or preserves, butter and flour to grease and dust the pan, confectioner's sugar

Beat the yolks with the sugar and vanilla, add the whipped egg whites, gently fold them in, gradually add the flour (like a rain). Pour the mixture uniformly into a greased and dusted rectangular pan and bake at medium heat. Test with the wooden pick to see when it is done.

When ready, turn onto a wooden cutting board covered with a soaked and squeezed cloth. Quickly spread marmalade or preserves on the dough, roll tightly and leave it wrapped in the wet cloth for several minutes. Then wrap the roll in a dry cloth and leave it for 2-3 hours. Then remove the wrap, place the cake onto a long platter, sprinkle it with confectioner's sugar and cut into finger thick slices.

ROLLED CAKE WITH WHIPPED CREAM
(ruladă cu frişcă)

6 eggs, 6 tbsp whipped cream, 1 heaping tbsp flour, 3 tsp cacao, 12 oz whipped cream for filling, oil and flour to grease and dust the pan

Beat the yolks with the sugar until foamy. Add flour and cacao, mix well, and then add the whipped egg whites. Pour the mixture into an oiled and dusted rectangular pan and bake at medium heat. When done, invert onto a wooden cutting board previously covered with a soaked and squeezed cloth. Wrap dough with the wet cloth and let it cool completely. Then spread the whipped cream uniformly and roll with the help of the cloth. Place on a platter and garnish with whipped cream.

ROSE PRESERVES
(dulceaţă de trandafiri)

2 lbs sugar, ¾ qt water, ½ lb rose petals with white parts removed, juice from 1 lemon

Set the sugar and water to boil with the lemon juice until well thickened. During boiling, keep removing the foam until the syrup is clear. While the syrup is boiling, sprinkle some lemon juice onto the rose petals and rub with your hands. When the syrup is thickened, add the rose petals and simmer. Place into jars when cold.

ROLLED CAKE WITH WALNUTS
(ruladă cu nuci)

6 eggs, 6 tbsp sugar, 5 tbsp flour, vanilla or grated lemon peel, butter and flour to grease and dust the pan, confectioner's sugar

Filling: 8 oz ground walnuts, 1 cup milk, 3 tbsp sugar, 1 tsp vanilla or a little rum

Beat the yolks with the sugar and vanilla, add the whipped egg whites, gently fold them in, and gradually add the flour (like a rain). Pour the mixture uniformly into a greased and dusted rectangular pan and bake at medium heat. Test with the wooden pick to see when it is done. When ready, turn onto a wooden cutting board covered with a soaked and squeezed cloth.

Boil the milk with the sugar and walnuts at low heat, mixing continuously until you get a soft paste. Add vanilla or rum. Use this paste to quickly spread on the dough, roll tightly and leave it wrapped in the wet cloth for several minutes. Then wrap the roll in a dry cloth and leave it for 2-3 hours. Then remove the wrap, place the cake onto a long platter, sprinkle it with confectioner's sugar and cut into finger thick slices.

RUM ICING
(glazură de rom)

15 oz sugar, ½ cup water, 2 tbsp rum, juice from ½ lemon

Set the water to boil with the sugar; when thickened as for sherbets, add rum and lemon juice. Remove from heat, stir well and when it lightens in color, quickly cover the cake with it.

RUSSIAN SWEET BREAD
(cozonaci ruseşti)

For 2 lbs flour: 22 yolks, ½ lb melted butter, 1 tbsp oil, 1 tbsp honey, 1 cup milk, 10 oz confectioner's sugar, grated peel from ½

lemon and ½ orange, ¼ ground vanilla stick, 3 oz yeast, salt, butter and bread crumbs for the pan, egg for washing the dough

Over the yeast mixed with 1 teaspoon of sugar, pour 2-3 tablespoons tepid milk and add 2-3 tablespoons of flour. Mix everything very well. Cover and leave in a warm spot. In the meantime, in a large bowl, pour the scalded milk over 3-4 tablespoons of flour, mixing very well.

Cover with a cloth and let cool off. When it is only a little warm, add the previously made starter, which has risen. Mix well, sprinkle some flour on top, cover and leave again in a warm spot until well risen. In the meantime, beat the yolks with the sugar in a bowl sitting in a bowl with hot water. When the sugar is melted and the mixture warm, pour, a little at a time, over the starter, also adding a little flour, salt, vanilla, lemon and orange peel. Mix everything very well to make a homogeneous paste. Sprinkle some flour on top, cover and let rise again in a warm place. Now you start kneading, adding tepid melted butter, tepid oil and tepid honey. Keep kneading until the dough starts to easily come off your hands. Cover and let rise until it triples in bulk. Then take a piece of dough and place in the pan, greased and sprinkled with bread crumbs. Fill only 1/3 of the pan with dough. Cover and leave in a warm spot until it almost fill the whole pan. Wash the surface of the dough with an egg-water mixture and set into the oven, first at slow heat until it rises some more, then increase the heat to medium. On the average, it should be baked for 1 hour. Test with a cake tester. When it is done, remove from the pan and onto a cloth and let cool off.

ROSES
(trandafiri)

Sweet bread dough. Filling: 6 oz butter, 6 oz confectioner's sugar, vanilla

Beat the butter with the sugar and vanilla until creamy. Refrigerate. Roll a rectangular sheet from the dough. Then spread, all over the sheet, the butter mixed with the sugar. Roll like a jelly roll. Then cut 3 inch long pieces out of the roll. Place these pieces in a round baking pan. The baking pan is previously greased with butter and parchment paper, also greased, is placed in the pan. The dough pieces are placed so that the cut part is on the bottom and at the surface of the pan (like cinnamon rolls).

Let rise for a little while and bake at slow heat until well risen. Then increase the heat. Remove from the pan after they are cold.

RUSSIAN TRIANGULAR DUMPLINGS
(cornuleţe ruseşti)

1 cup lard or butter, 1 cup sour cream, a little salt, 1 tsp vanilla, flour as needed, marmalade, sour cherries from preserves or rahat-lokum, ¾ cup vanilla flavored confectioner's sugar

Mix the lard or butter with salt, vanilla and sour cream. Add flour to obtain soft dough; let rest for 20 minutes. Then roll into a very thin sheet and cut into triangles. At the wide side of the triangle, put a sour cherry from preserves, a little marmalade or a small piece of rahat-lokum. Roll into a crescent and place on a baking sheet, leaving some distance among them. After baking, roll the crescents in vanilla flavored confectioner's sugar.

SAVARIN ROMANIAN STYLE
(Savarină)

5 tbsp sugar, 5 eggs, 5 tbsp fine bread crumbs, grated peel from 1 lemon, juice from 1/2 lemon, whipped cream.

Syrup: 5 oz sugar, 1 cup water, 1 tbsp rum

Cream the sugar with the yolks, add, mixing continuously, lemon peel and juice, bread crumbs and finally whipped egg whites. Pour the mixture into savarin molds (little Bundt pans, with hole in the middle). Bake at medium heat. Then pour syrup made from sugar, water and rum all over them. When they are cold, fill the middle hole with whipped cream. You may garnish with sour cherries or other fruits from preserves, on top of the whipped cream.

SAVOY BREAD
(pâine de Savoia)

4 oz confectioner's sugar, 4 eggs, 2 oz potato flour, 2 oz wheat flour, 1 tsp baking powder, salt, 1 tsp vanilla, shortening for greasing the pan

Beat the sugar with vanilla and yolks; add the two flours, salt and baking powder, mixing well. Then add the whipped egg whites. Bake into a greased bread pan and serve with tea, cut into thin slices.

SESAME BISCUITS I
(pesmeți cu susan) I

1 cup oil, 1 cup confectioner's sugar, ¾ cup water, 8 oz sesame seeds, 1 tsp vanilla, a little baking soda, flour as needed

Mix the sugar with the oil, water, baking soda, vanilla and sesame seeds. Add flour to get medium soft dough. Knead and roll into a ½ inch thick sheet. Cut into circles or 3 inch long and 2 inch wide strips. Or you may cut into squares, diamonds or other shapes. Bake until golden-brown at medium heat.

SESAME BISCUITS II
(pesmeți cu susan) II

8 oz butter, 1 egg, 4 tbsp sugar, 2 oz sesame seeds, 2 ½ cups flour, 1 tsp vanilla

Cream the butter with the sugar, yolk and vanilla, add flour and knead. Then shape the dough into a roll. Cut this into small pieces. Shape each piece into a little ball which you roll into egg white and then into sesame seeds. Place on a baking sheet at considerable distance one from the other and bake at medium heat.

SIMPLE "LIES"
("Minciunele")

2 yolks, 1 whole egg, 1 tsp confectioner's sugar, salt, vanilla, flour

Make medium stiff dough, let it rest awhile. Divide it into 2 parts and let it rest for 1 hour. Then roll into a very thin sheet. Cut it into 1 ½ inches wide strips. Each strip should be 4 inches long. Cut a notch in the middle of each strip and bring one of the ends through that notch (so that the strips look knotted). Do this for all strips. Fry in a pan with hot oil or lard or golden brown. Remove with the slotted tablespoon and sprinkle vanilla flavored confectioner's sugar over them.

SOUR CHERRY PIE
(plăcintă cu vişine)

Strudel dough, butter for the pan, confectioner's sugar with vanilla flavor;

Filling: 2 lbs pitted sour cherries, 1 lb sugar, 2 tbsp butter for greasing the dough

Prepare the same way as cottage cheese pie, replacing the cottage cheese filling with pitted sour cherries that have been sprinkled with sugar. After the pie is done, cut into squares and sprinkle with vanilla flavored confectioner's sugar.

SOUR CREAM JELLO PUDDING
(jeleu din smântână)

1 qt sour cream, 7 envelopes gelatin, 1 envelope gelatin colored red, ½ cup water, ¼ vanilla stick, 12 oz sugar, ½ lb whipped cream

Set the vanilla to boil with the half a cup of water, until it comes to a few boils, then remove from heat and add the gelatin so that it dissolves. Then strain. Separately, beat the sour cream with the sugar until foamy. Add the dissolved gelatin and 1/2 lb whipped cream.

Place into a mold and refrigerate. Remove from the mold the same way as for the chocolate jello pudding.

STRAWBERRIES WITH CREAM
(căpşuni cu frişcă)

2 lbs strawberries, 1 cup rum, ½ cup sugar, whipped cream to taste

Wash and hull the strawberries. Take a trifle bowl and arrange a layer of strawberries, some sugar, some rum. Repeat until you use up all strawberries. Refrigerate. When serving, add a layer of whipped cream and garnish with a few strawberries on top.

STRAWBERRY/RASPBERRY ICE-CREAM
(îngheţată de fragi sau zmeură)

½ qt strawberry/raspberry juice, 12 oz sugar, 1 ½ cups water, juice from 1 lemon, 1 cup whipped cream

Prepare the same way as sour cherry ice-cream. When the mixture is almost frozen, add a cup of whipped cream. Mix well and freeze.

STUFFED CANTALOUPE
(pepene galben umplut)

1 large cantaloupe, 2 large pear, 1 large apple, 2-3 peaches, 2-3 plums, 1 cup mixed white and red grapes, 1 cup wine, 1 cup rum, ½ cup sugar, 3 tbsp gelatin, 1 tbsp vanilla

Peel, seed and cube the apple and pear. Do the same for the plums and peaches. Wash the grapes well. Put all these fruits in a bowl and mix with a tablespoon of sugar. Cut a slice off the top of the cantaloupe and remove all seeds. Then fill with the other fruits, shaking the cantaloupe well for the fruits to settle and mix. Heat the wine and sugar to a boil, add the gelatin and mix with a tablespoon so that it dissolves well. Strain through a sieve and add the rum and vanilla. When the mixture is almost cold, pour into the cantaloupe to cover the fruits and then refrigerate. When serving, halve lengthwise and then each half in slices.

SUGAR ICING
(glazură de zahăr)

15 oz sugar, 1 cup water, a few drops lemon juice

Boil the sugar with 1 cup of water until the syrup thickens and sticks to the spoon. Add a few drops of lemon juice. When the mixture is warm, beat it as for sherbets, without letting it harden. When still soft, cover the cake with it. You can color this icing with food coloring.

SQUARES WITH CREAM
(pătrate cu cremă)

10 oz flour, 1 egg, 2 oz butter, 2/3 oz ammonia powder, 3 tbsp sugar, 1 tsp vanilla, ¼ cup milk, oil;

Cream: ½ cup milk, 7 oz sugar, 3 oz flour, 7 oz butter, almond essence

Make dough from the ingredients given, let rest for 1/2 hour. Then divide the dough into 3 equal parts. Roll each into a sheet and bake separately into a greased and dusted pan. For the cream, mix the milk with the sugar and flour, on the range, until the mixture starts to thicken.

Remove from heat and add butter and almond essence, mixing well. Spread this cream over all three sheets and place one on top of the other. Serve cut into squares.

SWEET BISCUITS WITH CARAWAY AND WALNUTS
(pişcoturi cu chimen şi nuci)

8 oz flour, 2 eggs, 4 oz sugar, 1 tsp lard, 1 tsp baking soda, 20 ground walnuts, 1 tsp caraway, butter to grease the pan

Beat the eggs with the sugar, then add lard, walnuts, baking soda, caraway and finally the flour. Knead well. Roll into 2 one inch thick sheets. Grease a baking pan and lay the two sheets next to each other and bake at medium heat. Cut while hot into long, finger thick strips.

SWEET BREAD SNAIL SHAPED
(melci)

Sweet bread dough, 2-3 tbsp ground walnuts, mixed with a little sugar,

Syrup: 3 tbsp sugar, 1 cup water, vanilla

Take pieces of dough the size of an egg and make finger thick ropes. Roll in the shape of a snail, set on a greased pan and let rise a little. Bake the snails, remove from the pan and quickly dunk into the hot syrup. Arrange on a plate and sprinkle with ground walnuts mixed with sugar.

TARTS
(tartă)

1 lb flour, 8 oz butter, 4 oz confectioner's sugar, 1 egg, 1 tsp vanilla

Cream the butter with the sugar, egg and vanilla, add flour and knead into dough. Cut into smallish pieces and roll each one into a 1/2 inch thick circle. Place each circle into a special tart mold. Make sure the bottom and sides of the molds are uniformly covered with dough. Prick the bottom of the dough with a fork a few times. Bake. When done, gently remove the tarts from their molds and let cool. They may be filled with:

- Vanilla cream I and garnished with whipped cream or a few fresh fruits;
- Gooseberry jello pudding, prepared from fruit juice (refrigerated);
- Fruits, over which you pour jello (for 1 cup sweetened fruit juice, 3 tablespoons gelatin). Refrigerate.

TENDER LAYERED CAKE WITH MARMALADE
(tort fraged cu marmeladă)

7 yolks, ¾ cup confectioner's sugar, ¾ oz ammonia powder, ½ cup melted butter, vanilla, flour as needed to make dough, marmalade to taste, a few chopped walnuts or almonds, 1 whole egg

Beat the sugar with the butter until foamy. Add the yolks, one by one, ammonia powder, vanilla and flour at the end. Knead soft dough and let rest for 20 minutes. Divide the dough in 3-4 equal parts and roll sheets about 1/2 inch thick. Place one sheet in the baking pan, spread a layer of marmalade on top, place a second sheet over the marmalade and spread this one with marmalade too. Do this with all sheets. Do not top the last sheet with marmalade. Instead, wash with a beaten egg and sprinkle with sliced walnuts or almonds. Bake for 30 minutes at medium heat.

TEA BISCUITS
(pesmeciori pentru ceai)

4.5 oz butter, 4.5 oz confectioner's sugar, 4 oz flour, 2 eggs, 4 oz small dark raisins, 2 tbsp rum, butter and flour for greasing and dusting the pan

Beat the eggs with the sugar, add creamed butter, mix well, then add flour, rum and Raisins and mix again. Butter a baking sheet, dust with flour and keep handy. With a wet teaspoon, take a half- teaspoon of the prepared mixture and place on the baking sheet. Repeat this procedure until you have all little piles of the batter on the baking sheet. Bake at medium heat. Do not over bake. When removing from the baking sheet, use a spatula.

TRIANGULAR DUMPLINGS

(cornuleţe)

8 oz lard or butter, ¾ cup confectioner's sugar, 3 yolks, 1 whole egg, 1 beaten egg white, 2-3 tbsp ground walnuts, flour as needed, 4 tbsp water, 1 tsp baking powder, vanilla

Melt the butter or lard. When it is slightly warm, add sugar and cream together. Then add the yolks one by one, then the whole egg, water, vanilla, baking powder. Mix well and then add flour, knead to make medium soft dough. Cut little pieces of dough and shape into triangular dumplings. Place the dumplings on the baking sheet leaving considerable distance between them as they increase in size. Cook at 350°F for 13-15 minutes. Wash each of them with whipped egg white and sprinkle each with ground walnuts. When you take them out of the oven, roll each one into confectioner's sugar.

TRUFFLES
(trufe)

4 hard boiled, sieved yolks, 1 raw yolk, 8 oz blanched and finely ground almonds, 1 cup confectioner's sugar, 7 oz grated chocolate, 2 oz butter, ¼ cup rum

Cream the sugar, butter and raw yolk. Add rum, hard-boiled yolks, mixing continuously, then add almonds. Keep refrigerated for 1/2 hour. Then with wet hands, shape into balls which you then roll in grated chocolate and place in paper molds. Keep refrigerated.

TENDER LAYERED CAKE I
(tort fraged) I

20 oz flour, 14 oz butter, 2 yolks, 1 whole egg, 3 tbsp sour cream, vanilla, fruits from preserves

Beat the butter with 2 yolks; add 1 whole egg, sour cream, vanilla and flour. Knead well and divide the resulting dough in 3 equal parts. Roll three rounds and bake them. After cooling, fill with finely chopped fruits from preserves.

TENDER LAYERED CAKE II
(tort fraged) II

10 oz butter, 10 oz confectioner's sugar, 10 oz flour, 8 eggs, ¼ cup rum, juice from 1 lemon, filling

Melt the butter and beat with the sugar, adding the 8 yolks one by one, until the mixture is foamy. Add flour, lemon juice and rum; mix well, then add the whipped egg whites, folding in gently. Pour the mixture into the buttered baking pan and bake at medium heat. Fill with the desired cream.

COFFE TRUFFLES I
(trufe de cafea) I

1 tbsp cold coffee essence, 1 raw yolk, 8 oz sugar, 8 oz sugar, 8 oz butter, 3 hard boiled, sieved yolks, cacao

Cream the butter with the sugar and raw yolk, add a tablespoon of very concentrated and strained coffee essence, then the 3 hard-boiled yolks. Mix everything very well. Put cacao on a plate and roll each little piece (teaspoonfuls) taken from the dough into the cacao. Put the truffles into special bon-bon papers. They can also be served on a plate garnished with granulated chocolate. Keep refrigerated.

COFFE TRUFFLES II
(trufe de cafea) II

1 yolk, 8 oz confectioner's sugar, 8 oz butter, 1 tsp coffee essence, granulated chocolate or cacao

Beat the yolk with the sugar until creamy, gradually adding cold and well strained coffee essence. Separately, cream the butter, and then add the coffee cream to the butter. When everything is well creamed, take teaspoonfuls, make into little balls which you roll into granulated chocolate or cacao. Arrange in special paper molds or on a plate sprinkled with cacao or coffee. Keep refrigerated.

TURKISH BAKLAVA
(baclava turcească)

Ştrudel dough, butter for greasing the pan;

Filling: 14 oz ground walnuts, 10 oz sugar, ½ tsp ground cinnamon, 2 tbsp melted butter;

Medium thick syrup from 10 oz sugar

Mix the ground walnuts with the sugar and cinnamon. Out of the strudel dough, cut pieces the size of the baking pan. Grease the pan with butter and place three sheets one on top of the other, sprinkle with some melted butter, place three more sheets, sprinkle with butter, place three more sheets and sprinkle with butter. Place the 1/2 inch thick filling over these nine sheets. On top of the filling, place another nine sheets, greased the same way. Grease the last sheet well and then, with a very sharp knife, cut into squares. Set in the oven to bake. When almost done, pour the syrup over it and bake until golden brown. Remove each square and arrange on a platter.

VIENNESE BRAID
(colac vienez)

Sweet bread dough.

Filling: 6 oz butter, 6 oz confectioner's sugar, vanilla, 3 tbsp cubed sugared orange peel

Mix the butter with the sugar and vanilla until creamy. Refrigerate. Roll a square shaped sheet of dough, about a finger thick. Then spread the butter mixture, uniformly, over the dough. Sprinkle the orange peel on top. Then fold the dough three ways (three-fold), so that the right third comes over the left third. Cut it lengthwise in three equal strips and braid. Join the ends securely and arrange the braid in a round pan that was covered with buttered paper. Let it rise a little in the pan and then set into the oven, at low heat, until well risen, then at medium heat. Remove from the pan after is has cooled off.

VANILLA CHARLOTTE
(şarlotă de vanilie)

½ lb sugar, 6 egg yolks, 1.5 qt milk, ½ vanilla stick, 8 tbsp gelatin

Boil the milk with the vanilla. During this time, mix the yolks with the sugar. When the milk is boiled, remove from heat and pour the yolk mixture, mixing continuously until thickened. Dissolve the gelatin in 4-5 tablespoons of hot water and mix with the warm mixture. Pour in a mold and refrigerate. Before serving, place the mold in a bowl with hot water (for a second) and turn onto a plate.

VANILLA CREAM I
(cremă de vanilie) I

1 pint boiling milk, ½ vanilla stick, 6 yolks, 7 oz sugar, 2 oz flour, 1 tsp butter

Set the milk to boil with the vanilla. Then remove from heat, cover and let stand for 1 hour. In the meantime, mix the yolks with the sugar and flour and then gradually add the milk that was warmed again. Set on heat, stirring continuously, until it starts to thicken. Remove from heat, add the butter and stir until the cream starts to cool.

VANILLA CREAM II
(cremă de vanilie) II

8 oz butter, 8 oz sugar, 5 yolks, 2 oz milk, vanilla (stick)

Beat the yolks with the sugar until creamy. Add the vanilla and milk and set on heat, stirring continuously until it starts to thicken. Remove from heat, let cool a little, then gradually add the butter, processing until the cream starts to lighten in color. Refrigerate. Use this cream as filling, decoration for various cakes, tortes, etc.

VANILLA ICE-CREAM
(înghețată de vanilie)

8 yolks, 7 oz sugar, 1 qt milk, 1 cup whipped cream, 1 vanilla stick

Beat the sugar with yolks until creamy, add the milk boiled with the vanilla and then cooled off and simmer, stirring continuously, until thickened (it should not come to a boil). Let the mixture cool off and set to freeze. When almost frozen, add 1 cup whipped cream, mix well and freeze.

VANILLA JELLO PUDDING
(jeleu de vanilie)

5 yolks, ¾ qt milk, vanilla (1 stick), 4 tbsp confectioner's sugar, 8 envelopes gelatin, oil

Set the milk to boil with the vanilla. After it comes to a boil, remove from heat and cover. Beat the yolks with the sugar and pour, gradually, in the warm milk, stirring continuously in the same direction. Return to heat and stir until thickened. After it has cooled off a little, add the gelatin that was dissolved in a few tablespoon of warm water. Mix and pour in a mold greased with oil. Refrigerate. Before serving, briefly place the mold in a pan with hot water and turn onto a plate.

WALNUT LAYERED CAKE
(tort de nuci)

10 egg whites, 2 cups confectioner's sugar, 2 cups ground walnuts, butter, icing;
Filling I: 14 oz butter, 3 yolks, 1-2 tbsp cacao or chocolate, 1 cup confectioner's sugar;
Filling II: 14 oz butter, 3 yolks, 1 tsp vanilla or grated peel from 1 lemon, 3 tbsp sour cream, 1 cup confectioner's sugar

Whip the 10 egg whites, and then add the sugar, beating continuously. When the sugar has melted, add the ground walnuts and fold in gently. Pour some of the resulting mixture into the baking pan that was covered with buttered paper. The layer must be about 1 finger thick. The number of sheets depends on the size of the pan. After baking each sheet individually, let cool. Then spread with the desired cream (chocolate, butter, etc.) and arrange one on top of the other. Glaze with the desired icing. The most appropriate fillings for this cake are the following. I. cream 14 oz/400 g butter, adding 3 yolks one by one, 1-2 tablespoons cacao or grated chocolate and 1 cup confectioner's sugar.

II. cream 14 oz butter with 1 cup confectioner's sugar and then add 3 yolks one by one, 1 teaspoon vanilla or grated peel from 1 lemon (or 1/4 cup rum) and 3 tablespoons sour cream. Mix everything well until creamy.

VANILLA TRIANGULAR DUMPLINGS WITH WALNUTS
(cornuleţe de vanilie cu nuci)

5 oz butter, 2 oz ground walnuts, 2.5 oz sugar, 6 oz flour

Cream the butter with the sugar and walnuts, add flour and knead. Take pieces out of the dough and shape into finger thick rolls. Cut the roll into 1-2 inches long pieces and curve each piece to look like a crescent. Place on a buttered baking sheet and bake at low temperature.

WALNUT CREAM
(cremă de nuci)

1 cup milk, 8 oz walnuts, 5 oz sugar, ¼ cup rum

Set the milk to boil with the ground walnuts and sugar. Keep stirring until the paste is thick. Remove from heat, let cool, add rum and mix well.

WALNUT STRUDEL
(ştrudel cu nuci)

Strudel dough, oil for greasing the pan, confectioner's sugar with vanilla flavor;

Filling: 10 oz ground walnuts, 3 tbsp plain breadcrumbs, 10 oz confectioner's sugar, ½ cup tepid oil, vanilla

Mix the ground walnuts with the sugar, bread crumbs and vanilla. Grease the dough with tepid oil and sprinkle filling all over the dough. Roll like a jelly roll using the table cloth as an aid. Cut into pieces the size of the baking pan. Arrange in the greased pan. Before baking, with a very sharp oiled knife, cut them into 1 ½ inches portions. Bake. Then carefully remove each piece and sprinkle with vanilla flavored confectioner's sugar. You may use butter instead of oil.

WALNUT SWEET BREAD
(cozonac cu nucă)

Regular sweet bread dough.

Filling: 10 oz ground walnuts, 1 cup milk, ¾ cup sugar, ¼ cup rum, vanilla

Melt the sugar in the warm milk with vanilla in a pot on the range. When the sugar is melted, add the walnuts and keep stirring. After a few minutes of boiling, and after the filling has thickened, remove from heat and add rum. When the filling is cold, roll a sheet of dough about one finger thick, uniformly spread the walnut filling on top and roll like a jelly roll. Grease a bread pan, place the roll inside, let rise for a while and then set in the oven to bake at medium heat.

YEASTED FANCY CAKES
(fursecuri cu drojdie de bere)

4 yolks, 1 egg white, 5 oz butter or lard, ½ cup milk, walnut sized piece of yeast (cake), salt, 2-3 tbsp ground walnuts, 2-3 tbsp sugar, flour

Soak the yeast in milk; add yolks, butter, salt and then flour. Knead into stiff dough. Put the dough into a cloth or fabric sack; tie well but in such a way to leave room for the dough to rise.

Submerge the dough thus prepared into a large pot with cold water and leave for 4-5 hours. The dough tied in the cloth will surface above the water. Remove the dough and roll into a thin sheet.

Cut into 3 inches long and 1 inch wide strips. Roll each strip in egg white and then in ground walnuts mixed with sugar and shape into a crescent dumpling like this: hold the strip by the ends with both hands. Twist one end in one direction and the other end in the opposite direction and then bend to make a crescent. Place onto the greased baking sheet. Bake at medium heat.

WHEAT AND NUT SWEET
(colivă)

½ pound ground wheat, 1 qt water, pinch of salt, 4 oz sugar or to taste, 4 oz ground walnuts or to taste, ½ tsp cinnamon or lemon zest, fine bread crumbs, confectioner's sugar/coffee and small colored candy for topping

Boil the ground Wheat at low to medium temperature. Start with cold water. Add a little salt and sugar to taste. When it is well boiled and the liquid is almost gone, set aside from the heat to cool off. Add ground walnuts. Mix well. Add cinnamon or lemon zest. Arrange on a large platter on top of a sheet of parchment paper. Smooth the top with a wet knife. On top, sprinkle some fine bread crumbs, then either confectioner's sugar or ground coffee. Decorate with small colorful candies.

WINE JELLO PUDDING
(jeleu de vin)

1 qt red wine, 7 oz sugar, ¼ vanilla stick, 10 envelopes gelatin

Boil the wine with the sugar and vanilla; after a few minutes of boiling, remove from heat and add the gelatin that was dissolved in a few tablespoons of warm water. Strain everything, pour into the mold and refrigerate. Remove from the mold the same way as chocolate jello pudding.

Table of Contents

PUDDINGS....................35

SOUPS & BORSCHES 42

BEEF, PORK, LAMB, POULTRY AND FISH 67

DESSERT 149

Poftă bună!
Bon appetit!

CPSIA information can be obtained at www.ICGtesting.com
Printed in the USA
LVOW05s1015160315

430739LV00009B/82/P